Reconceptualising Caste, Class and Tribe

Reconceptualising Caste, Class and Tribe

K.L. SHARMA

RAWAT PUBLICATIONS
Jaipur • New Delhi • Bangalore • Guwahati • Kolkata

ISBN 978-81-7033-695-2

Reprinted, 2019

Published by
Prem Rawat for **Rawat Publications**
Satyam Apts., Sector 3, Jawahar Nagar, Jaipur 302 004 (India)
Phone: 0141 265 1748 / 7006 Fax: 0141 265 1748
E-mail: info@rawatbooks.com
Website: www.rawatbooks.com

New Delhi Office
4858/24, Ansari Road, Daryaganj, New Delhi 110 002
Phone: 011-23263290

Also at *Bangalore, Guwahati* and *Kolkata*

Typeset by Rawat Computers, Jaipur
Printed at Nice Printing Press, New Delhi

Contents

Introduction

Caste is not class or race or ethnicity. However, caste is in class to a considerable extent, and in a given sense, it is also in race and ethnicity. Since caste is present in one way or other in other systems of social stratification, taxonomic problem persists relating to the distinction of caste from other stratificatory systems. Caste is increasingly becoming a matter of interpretation rather than substantialisation. Caste refers to a purposive rationality, and at the same time, it provides a description and explanation of the pathologies of modern polity and economy. It is no more an absolutised system as it was characterised by punitive acts like ostracisation and social neglect. Caste outbursts, which occur occasionally by way of killing and torture of the violators of caste ethics, are incongruent with the dwindling of the caste system in recent times.

There is no unilinear hierarchy of caste; in fact, today, multiple hierarchies characterise the Indian society. Castes are 'discrete categories', because they are no more related to each other organically, nor are they segmentary entities. Inter-caste relations, which were the bedrock of caste system, have disappeared. *Jajmani* has become a defunct institution, and family and individual have taken over the place of caste in everyday life. Caste is thus loosing its unique cultural ambience in Indian society. Increasingly, caste is becoming a desideratum, a state of mind, a plastic and malleable institution. No more hypersymbolisation is manifest to express caste differences and typifications on a continuing basis. Though there is a process of delegitimisation of the 'essential' of caste, yet the sporadic appearance of caste-based decisions, and articulation of religious and metaphysical interpretations of caste and its divinity, pose a serious challenge to the secularised understanding of social reality.

The essays incorporated in the volume bring out clearly that caste framework has not been unchanging, and this is because the political and economic aspects have remained integral considerations throughout the Indian history. While strongly denouncing Dumont's theory of caste as homo hierarchicus, Irfan Habib observes: "The caste system, in its classic form, could therefore function with as much ease in a natural economy as in a market-oriented one. In either case it helped essentially to maintain not a fabric of imagined purity (if it did, this was incidental), but a system of class exploitation as rigorous as any other."[1] Drawing upon medieval writings, Habib states that the caste system remained an important pillar of the system of class exploitation in medieval India as well. The British colonised the caste system along with the entire country by putting one caste against other, and by issuing norms of social distance. The census of 1901, under the leadership of Sir Herbert Risley, specified commensal relations between different castes and accordingly ranked them in the census.[2] J.H. Hutton corroborated Risley's thesis by defining positive functions of the caste system for individual members and family, for a given caste as a whole, and for the entire state and society.[3] Obviously, both Risley and Hutton carried out the colonial mandate given to them by their masters.

1. Habib, Irfan, 1995, *Essays in Indian History: Towards a Marxist Perception*, New Delhi, Tulika, pp. 161–179.
2. Risley, H.H., 1969, *The People of India* (2nd ed.), Delhi, Orient Books. It was published for the first time in 1908 from London.
3. Hutton, J.H., 1963, *Caste in India* (4th ed.), Oxford, OUP.

However, most of the western scholars have viewed caste as a unique cultural institution, a complete contrast to their system of social stratification.[4] 'Culturology' as an explanation sounds quite strong in their writings. Lately, an ethnosociology of Indian society has been in vogue.[5] Emphasis on indigenous concepts and categories[6] could provide a new paradigm to rectify the misunderstandings caused by the western academic sophistry and the superimposed frameworks. A fresh debate implying to what extent caste is a structural phenomenon and to what extent it is a cultural aspect needs to be initiated to locate caste in economic, political and cultural domains and vice versa.[7]

The politico-economic and colonial interpretations of caste also find substantiation in Suvira Jaiswal's recent book, *Caste: Origin, Function and Dimensions of Change*.[8] Jaiswal observes that caste ideology has gained strength and not the structural reality of the caste in everyday life. Ramifications of class can be seen in a given caste, and a caste can be observed in different classes. Hence, caste-class polarity/divide would not allow us to peep into the presence of one into other. A pattern of nexus as well as divide characterises the caste-class formation.[9] A peasant movement is basically a mobilisation of those who are engaged in agriculture and suffer from

4. Dumont, Louis, 1970, *Homo Hierarchicus: The Caste System and its Implications*, London, Weidenfeld and Nicholson.
5. Marriott, McKim (ed.), 1989, *India Through Hindu Categories*, New Delhi, Sage Publications. See also McKim Marriott and Ronald B. Inden, 1977, "Toward an Ethno-Sociology of South Asian Caste Systems", in Kenneth A. David (ed.), *The New Wind: Changing Identities in Sough Asia*, The Hague, Mouton.
6. Ostor, Akos, 1984, *Culture and Power: Legend, Ritual, Bazaar and Religion in a Bengali Society*, New Delhi, Sage Publications.
7. See, for example, Anthony de Reuck and Julie Knight (ed.), 1967, *Caste and Race: Comparative Approaches*, London, J & A, Churchil Ltd.
8. Jaiswal, Suvira, 1998, *Caste: Origin, Function and Dimensions of Change*, Delhi, Manohar.
9. Sharma, K.L., 1994, *Social Stratification and Mobility*, Jaipur, Rawat Publications, Chapter 4, pp. 79–101.

exploitation and indignities. It may involve all those castes and families which share the sufferings in common. In the Shekhawati region of Rajasthan in the 1930s, it so happened that only Jats were involved in the peasant movement which was launched against the jagirdars.[10] A Vaishya Sabha, for example, is apparently a caste association, but in effect, it also functions as an interest group, as an organisation of traders and entrepreneurs. Most of the caste associations are today effective political and economic organisations.[11]

Ursula Sharma suggests that caste should be studied with comparative interest in inequities and social justice with more emphasis on process rather than structure of caste.[12] Hence, no monolithic ideology and pattern of caste can be found wherever it is found, namely, India, Sri Lanka, Pakistan, etc. Caste needs to be seen in the context of its setting and surroundings. In a recent exciting book, *Interrogating Caste: Underlying Hierarchy and Difference in Indian Society*,[13] Dipankar Gupta argues quite emphatically in favour of an intersubjective sociology/anthropology against typification to study the caste system. Castes need to be viewed as discrete entities being all abiding and durable identities. Gupta rightly ventures to search 'individual' in caste. He observes that individuals interrogate their own social existence, reflect on it, and maximise their options.[14] Locating such an individual in caste would demythologise the rigid and closed hyper-symbolisations, typifications and binary oppositions of Louis Dumont and his tribe. Individual was always present in caste, but its sensuousness has increased considerably, which has enabled

10. Sharma, K.L., 1998, *Caste, Feudalism and Peasantry: The Social Formation of Shekhawati*, New Delhi, Manohar.
11. Ibid.
12. Sharma, Ursula, 1999, *Caste*, Buckingham, Open University Press.
13. Gupta, Dipankar, 2000, *Interrogating Caste: Underlying Hierarchy and Difference in Indian Society*, New Delhi, Penguin Books, Chapter 9, pp. 224–264.
14. Ibid.

him to decide for himself rather than being guided by the received knowledge and socio-cultural recipes.[15]

The main purpose is to know about the encounters which caste, class and tribe come across in the recent uncertain times in Indian society and then to reconceptualise them based on the experiential inputs. Caste refers to inequality, difference, discrimination, in both theory and practice. Theoretically, caste is more a state of mind of an individual rather than an ideology dictating collective actions. However, in practice, individual members of a caste may appropriate their caste identities in their own favour or against the interests of others. However, a pre-given ideology is not taken as seriously as the contingent use of caste identity and mobilisation. Mobilisation is generally for extracting gains from the state and the society by a select few who can mesmerise members of their castes. However, the manipulation of caste is short-lived, because it has no bearing on inter-caste relations, which were in the past the basis of caste functioning in everyday life. Therefore, caste-class nexus approach, as an alternative to caste-class dichotomy, explains caste historically and contextually taking into account structure, process, history and dialectics.

Caste is not reducible to class and vice versa. It is also not an explosive class. More important is to understand the caste-class nexus, it continuity and change. Class functions within the context of caste. Caste conflicts are also class conflicts. By appropriating the caste-class nexus, a new power elite has emerged in the countryside. New forms of power blocs, alignments and strategies are being created for capturing political power, and by appropriating it, access to jobs and positions of high status and prestige it also made possible. A shift in the discourse on caste and social change is evident because, today, more than the question of social inequalities and development of the village community, the emphasis,

15. Ibid.

which is being laid on status and honour (*izzat*) of the backward, the poor, deprived and the womenfolk, has become the key to the new discourse. The new classification, particularly vocalised in Bihar, which comprises categories such as 'forwards', 'upper backwards', 'lower backwards', 'minorities', 'SCs', 'STs', 'dalits', 'Bahujan Samaj', etc., has replaced the conventional hierarchisation.[16] Such a classification not only denounces the conventional one, but also indicates a paradigm shift and conveys a message of challenge to the entrenched sections. Caste clusters or alliances are becoming a common feature to extract political gains.

Approximating to the Bihar model of social stratification is the process of change relating to the 'untouchables' of India. Gandhi's 'Harijan' became the 'Scheduled Caste' after Independence, and the same turned into 'dalit' as a consequence of the struggle of the SCs to gain more respectability and an identity of their own.[17] 'Dalit' implies 'knowledge' and 'power', hence a new social language, conveying new meanings, strategies, situations and status parameters. Incorporation of class and status in caste is the main message of dalitism. The peasant movement in Shekhawati region of Rajasthan in the 1930s, as referred earlier, also reflected that caste alone could not do good to the Jat peasants. Besides seeking concessions and reliefs from the landlords, the Jat peasants strove to gain political power, though not quite successfully. However, the economic betterment proved to be an asset for gaining political power after independence. Networking by the peasants within the region and outside it was felt as a great injection to keep the movement alive against the oppressive rulers.

The remaining articles in this volume were written before the formation of the State of Jharkhand on November

16. Blair, Harry, 1980, "Ruling Kulaks and Backward Classes in Bihar: Social Change in the Late 1970's", *EPW*, Vol. 5, No. 2, pp. 64–74.
17. Sharma, K.L., 1997, *Social Stratification in India: Issues & Themes*, New Delhi, Sage Publications, Chapter 5, pp. 107–132.

15, 2000. Since this volume is being published nearly after one year of the creation of the new state, some observations and statements may not be in tune with this new development. However, I have taken care to make necessary amendments, wherever required, in the text. Struggle for more than six decades, preceded by many revolts, rebellions, insurrections and movements, ultimately brought about the formation of the new state. The question of Jharkhandi identity occupied the centre-stage during these long years of protracted and chequered history of the Jharkhand movement.[18] Who is a Jharkhandi? Besides the tribals, there are Sadans, Marwaris, Punjabis, Bengalis, and the North Bihari *dikus* (exploiters). A conjunction between ethnicity (tribe), class and power characterises the Jharkhand State even today as it did before its coming into existence. The long time taken in realisation of the formation of the state was due to the interests of the entrenched North Biharis in administration and politics. Since the Marwari businessmen and Punjabi entrepreneurs also felt the pinch of the Bihari mandarins, they extended a supporting hand to the *adivasi* leadership of the Jharkhand movement. Such a matrix of tribe, class and power, along with inter- and intra-tribal distinctions, complicated the Jharkhand movement and also created frictions and cleavages from time to time.[19] In such a situation 'sons of the soil' versus outside exploiters was a natural corollary.[20] Even after the formation of the state, this riddle continues to haunt the new power elite.

Two main objectives set out for the new state were: (i) to destroy the institutions and mechanisms by which the

18. Sharma, K.L., 1993, 'The questions of identity and sub-nationality: A case of Jharkhand Movement in Bihar", in Mrinal Miri (ed.), *Continuity and Change in Tribal Society*, Shimla, Indian Institute of Advanced Study, pp. 463–73.
19. Singh, K.S., 1985, *Tribal Society in India: An Anthropo-Historical Perspective*, Delhi, Manohar Publications.
20. Weiner, Myron, 1978, *Sons of the Soil: Migration and Ethnic Conflict in India*, New Jersey, Princeton University Press.

dikus had been able to dehumanise the Jharkhandis, and (ii) to empower the Jharkhandis. In a short period of less than one year, the people are disenchanted and feeling disgusted with the new leadership because of the imitation of the Bihar model of administration and management. Jharkhand is different, it is not simply a territory. It is a socio-cultural formation, and an eco-system. There is a Jharkhandi identity and consciousness. The new mandarins should act in tune with this ground reality.

While analysing social stratification among tribes in India, the complex juxtaposition of ethnicity, class and power hinges on the questions of class/caste/tribe approach, land alienation, forest takeover by government, etc. One can say that all this is in essence a class question. But, besides the class question, the question of ethnicity is equally significant.[21] In fact, a synthesis/convergence of class and ethnicity may be found more appropriate in the understanding of tribal social stratification. Colonial rule, differentiation of peasantry, exploitation by *dikus* were somewhat different in the case of tribes compared to the non-tribals. Inter-tribal and tribal-non-tribal distinctions and relations, and conversion to Christianity and Hinduisation, and lately Islamisation, are again specific to the tribal people. The pattern and process of social stratification among tribes have therefore been different compared to the non-tribal people. The new pattern is evident in the emergence of a new middle class among tribes since independence, and at the same time, detribalisation and ethnicisation are the new processes of change, which in turn are appropriated for acquiring power and dominance by the alert and articulate sections.

Lastly, I have briefly discussed uneven consequences of economic development and education among the tribes of India, especially in the case of Jharkhand. A down-to-earth

21. Badgaiyan, S.D., 1986, "Class and Ethnicity: Chhota Nagpur in the 19th Century", in K.L. Sharma (ed.), *Social Stratification in India*, Delhi, Manohar, pp. 293–308.

approach and practice, without destroying culture, ecology and everyday life of the tribal people, can bring about positive and egalitarian consequences. The mission schools and colleges have created status cleavages and divides, besides socio-cultural divisions such as the converts and the non-converts. Though education has produced cleavages and select enclaves among the people, it has raised their level of aspirations in general. Jharkhand has also witnessed development because of its mineral wealth and industrialisation. But, who have been the beneficiaries? Who are the sons of the soil? Have they been gainers? These are perennial questions, and one has to ask them in all epoches and situations.

I am quite sure that these essays, which were written over a decade, will be beneficial to the students of social sciences and other interested and concerned readers. I thank sincerely Mr. Kailash Rawat, the proprietor of Rawat Publications, for pressurising me to work on these essays in a concerted manner.

1 Conceptualisation of Caste-Class Nexus as an Alternative to Caste-Class Dichotomy

I

Both caste and class have been debated from narrow ideological standpoints. One view is that Indian society can be best studied from a 'caste model' or 'caste perspective'. According to this view caste is an overarching ideological system encompassing all aspects of social life of Hindus in particular and of other communities in general. One implication of such a view is that caste is the basic infrastructural basis of Indian society, and occupation, division of labour, rules of marriage, interpersonal relations, etc., are superstructural phenomena as reproductions of the ideology of caste. Another view is reflected in the question: In what way is caste a normative system and how is it a system of actual social-structural relations? Perhaps, the answer would be both yes and no. In certain spheres caste adheres to its normative sanctions whereas in other domains caste groups and their members have taken up activities which depart from traditional sanctions of the caste system. The crux of the matter is the very definition of the caste system. It is a very complex and complicated system. Members of a caste compete with each other, at the same time they cooperate with each other. Class-based distinctions within the caste have always been found in a pronounced form. Members of a caste in a given village can sometimes be representatives of India's class structure. While observing all the pertinent rules of marriage, members of a caste may accord premium to economic status in matrimonial alliances.

Caste refers to inequality both in theory and practice. Dumont[1] considers inequality based on the caste system to be a special type of inequality. 'Ideas and values' are considered by Dumont as basic for knowing actual and observable behaviour of people. For Dumont, therefore, the idea of the pure and the impure is basic to the understanding of caste. This idea is the basis of hierarchy in Hindu society. Dumont's main concern is with the understanding of traditional social organisation of India from the viewpoint of ideas and values. He constructs an 'ideal type' of the caste system based on ethnographic and indological descriptions. Madan[2] upholds Dumont's view which regards hierarchy as a 'universal necessity'. Society in India has remained largely static, change *in* society has occurred, but the change *of* society is yet to take place. The criticality of the nexus between caste and class can be discerned by comprehending the normative regulations as an 'externalist' aspect and the actual contextual functioning as its 'internalist' determinant. How one affects the other is the main point in the understanding of the caste-class nexus.

For understanding the caste system as an empirical reality we may have to locate caste groups as *jatis* in a specific rural/urban context. Caste is seen as an actual status group in these contexts. It is a source of placement in the given social set-up. But at a macro level, caste is also a means of identity. At this level it is not a functioning reality of informal, day-to-day relations. Caste does not become the basis of marriage between

1. Dumont, L., 1970, *Homo Hierarchicus*, London, Paladin Granada Publishing Ltd.
2. Madan, T.N. 1971, "On Understanding Caste", *Economic and Political Weekly*, Vol. VI, No. 34, pp. 1806–8.

a Tamil Brahmin and a Kanyakubja Brahmin of Uttar Pradesh. But still a Tamil Brahmin and a Brahmin from Uttar Pradesh can always have a sense of belonging to the same stock and even may cooperate for a common good in situations of crises and challenges. One may ask: Is caste an interest group? Can common interests bring together more smoothly men of different castes from various regions than those of the same caste? Caste is certainly a resource, but the nature of this resource varies from caste to caste depending upon the status of a given caste in a given area. Caste identity/membership has become a liability for members of the upper and middle castes because a certain percentage of jobs, seats in parliament and state legislatures, and admissions in institutions of higher learning have been reserved for the Other Backward Castes (OBCs), Scheduled Castes and Scheduled Tribes (SCs and STs).

Thus, the view that caste and class are polar opposites is not correct. The assumption that class can emerge as a social reality only when caste is destroyed and eliminated from Indian society—is a misapprehension and misconstrued conception of the relationship between the two. Both have been an inseparable part of India's social formation, hence the study of their nexus, continuity and change. Therefore, the view that recent processes of change have given way to a change from caste to class in Indian society is also untenable and unconvincing. Caste is a very complex system as it is not simply a system of power relations and economic activities for namesake. If it gets weakened in one aspect, it also gets strengthened in another, no doubt with certain alterations, additions and accretions. What we need is a study of the dynamics of this complexity of the system. One obvious inference is that there is a caste-basis of class, and also a class-basis of caste, hence both are inextricably interrelated. There is a class-basis of rituals, pollution-purity and other nonmaterial aspects of social life. Examples of some associations may be cited. Jat Sabha is not a simple caste association; in effect, it is a peasants' organisation. Kisan Sabha is not a simple peasants' organisation; it is very much an association of castes engaged in agriculture, particularly of Jats in northern India and of their counterparts in other states. The same logic applies to the Vaishya Sabha, Kshatriya Mahasabha, Bhooswami Sangh, etc.

To consider caste mainly as a rural phenomenon and class as a reality of towns and cities is a myth. An example of caste elections in Jaipur city may be mentioned here. The annual elections of Khandelwal Vaishya Mahasabha were held in the heart of the city of Jaipur, opposite to the Central Reserve Police Lines on the Station Road. Hundreds of cars, jeeps, auto-rickshaws and two-wheelers were deployed in the elections. About 60 stalls were installed for electioneering on both sides of the road. Traffic was diverted and police pickets were posted to watch/control the situation. It was not only a show of casteism, but also of strength of different factions within the caste. Why all this show? What elected people would get out of this show by spending thousands of rupees on these elections? One should seriously consider these questions to understand the caste-class nexus in urban India. There is no uniform pattern of caste structure in reality throughout India. The same can be said about class structure. Both caste and class bear ideological contents as conceptual schema. Both have substantive elements as existential and mundane schemes of relations. There are thousands of castes in India with different names and nomenclatures, but only five or six classes exist throughout the country. The number of castes or classes is not so important in determining the basic relations—social or economic or both. More important is that these apparently distinct bases of social division in Indian society are not realistically very different from each other. There are numerous middle classes, which are not directly related to production processes, and they are an offshoot of the modern Indian state apparatus.

In India, class struggle is also, in effect, caste struggle, and vice versa. Separation of the two seems to be superfluous and mechanistic. A nomological plea that the two are distinct as they refer to different 'social' and 'economic' realities cannot be accepted because of the lack of ample substantive support and evidence about the two as separate entities.

Caste-class nexus approach for studying India's social formation would focus on the understanding and analysis of structure, culture, history, and dialectics, both 'from above' and 'from below'. Both the dominant as well as the not-so-dominant elements of the formation become known at macro and micro levels by analysing the caste-class nexus historically and contextually.

Caste-class nexus implies observation of caste and class as mutually inherent phenomena. The caste-class nexus as a framework goes beyond micro-transactions and alternatively filters down the macro conceptualisations to the ground reality. Caste-class nexus implies going 'beyond caste' and also going 'beyond class' for a fuller comprehension of social reality. I define 'nexus' as "a set of ties in terms of connections which becomes the basis of structural and cultural changes... Nexus does not imply a correspondence or symmetry between caste and class. Interdependence, contradictions, symmetry, and hegemony of social relations are integral features of nexus as a frame of reference."[3] André Béteille notes: "The hierarchies of caste, class and power in the village overlap to some extent, but also cut across."[4] Béteille also states that many areas of social life are now becoming to some extent 'caste-free'.[5] Besides the Brahman tradition, the idea of the martial Rajput, the traditions of Indian craftsman, the Indian merchant, and the class and cultural traditions existed side by side in Indian society.[6]

3. Sharma, K.L., 1991, "Country-Town Nexus in India: A Macro-View", in K.L. Sharma and Dipankar Gupta (eds), *Country-Town Nexus*, Jaipur, Rawat Publications, p. 41.
4. Béteille, André, 1966, *Caste, Class and Power*, Bombay, Oxford University Press, p. 4.
5. Ibid., p. 3.
6. See, for example, Milton Singer (ed.), 1975, *Traditional India: Structure and Change*, (reprinted), Jaipur, Rawat Publications. See Part I: The Social Organisation of Tradition (articles on cultural traditions).

II

Admittedly, due to multidimensionality and complexity of the caste system, one encounters numerous difficulties in giving a precise definition of caste. The structural aspect of caste is explained by accepting it as a general principle of stratification.[7] Caste as a cultural system is understood in terms of prominence of the ideas of pollution-purity and notions of hierarchy, segregation and corporateness.[8] Caste is also viewed by Bailey as a 'classed system' of stratification,[9] whereas Béteille considers caste system as both 'closed' and 'open'.[10] He finds that caste is becoming increasingly 'segmentary' because of the emergence of differentiated structures in India. These analytic variations hinder a common definition of caste. However, these variations also explain the fact that caste is like all other systems of stratification in some ways while it is quite unique in some other respects. Although caste is not really a very flexible system, yet

7. Barth, F. 1960. "The System of Social Stratification in Swat, North-West-Pakistan", in E.R. Leach (ed.), *Aspects of Caste in South India, Ceylon and North-West Pakistan*, Cambridge: Cambridge University Press, pp. 113–46; and Berreman, G.D., 1967, "Stratification, Pluralism and Interaction: A Comparative Analysis of Caste", in Anthony de Reuck and J. Knight (eds), *Caste and Race: Comparative Approaches*, J and A Churchil Ltd., pp. 45–73.

   See also Llyod I. Rudolph and Susanne H. Rudolph, *The Modernity of Tradition, Political Development in India*, Delhi, Orient Longman, 1967, pp. 17–29. Rudolphs observe that caste has responded to changes in its political and economic environment by transforming itself from below and within. Hierarchy, privilege, and moral parochialism no longer exhaust its secular significance. Caste has become a means to level the old order's inequalities by helping to destroy its moral basis and social structure. Caste attaches its members to the political ideas, processes and institutions (p. 17). However, the explicit glamourisation of 'adaptive functions of caste' in Rudolphs and several other western writings of the 1960s and 1970s undermine the dysfunctional and nonequalitarian consequences of caste-based mobilisations and empowerment as well de-empowerment of different castes.

8. Dumont, L., op. cit., 1970, and Leach, E.R., 1960 "What Should We Mean By Caste", in E.R. Leach (ed.), op. cit., pp. 1–10.

9. Bailey, F.G. 1963, "Closed Social Stratification in India", *European Journal of Sociology*, Vol. IV, 1, pp. 107–24.

10. Béteille, André, 1966, "Closed and Open Social Stratification in India," *European Journal of Sociology*, Vol. VII, pp. 224–46.

a caste permits mobility in certain areas to its members. A given caste is guided by the norms of the caste system regarding inter-caste dependence; but a given caste has also its autonomy in regard to observance of its practices, rituals and rites in relation to other castes. In fact, caste has adapted itself because of encounters with innumerable diverse situations, forces and constraints. Caste has evolved simultaneously in several directions and adjusted with ideologically antagonistic systems. It has not allowed the emergence of an alternative system of stratification and social relations though it has undergone significant changes from time to time.[11] Features and functions of the caste system as listed by Risley, Ketkar, Senart, Hutton, Furnivall, Sherring and Ghurye are no more cited.[12] But, the fact remains that caste has been eulogised by these writers as a positive and functional system. Srinivas notes that even today agricultural production requires cooperation of several castes.[13] The use of the caste idiom is quite widespread. Even Marx related the Asiatic mode of production to the stability of the caste system in India.[14] Similarly, Maine considered caste as an illustration of a non-contractual 'status-society'.[15] Dumont and

11. Sharma, K.L., 1977, "New Introduction", in J. Murdoch, *Review of Caste in India*, Jaipur, Rawat Publications, p. vii.
12. Risley, H.H., 1969, *The People of India* (2nd edition), Delhi, Orient Books, p. 47; Ketkar, S.V., 1909, *The History of Caste in India*, Ithaca, New York, Cornell University Press, p. 15; Senart, E., *Caste in India: The Facts and the System*, 1930, London, Methew and Co., p. 35; Hutton, J.H., 1946, *The Caste in India*, Oxford, Oxford University Press; Furnivall, J.S. Netherlands, 1909, *India: A Study of Plural Economy*, Cambridge, Cambridge University Press; Sherring, M.A., 1974, *Hindu Castes and Tribes*, Delhi, Cosmo Publications, p. 214; and Ghurye, G.S., 1950, *Caste and Class in India*, Bombay, Popular Book Depot, p. 18.
13. Srinivas, M.N., 1979, "The Future of Indian Caste", *Economic and Political Weekly*, Vol. XIV(AN), Nos. 7 and 8, pp. 237–42.
14. Marx, K., 1951, *Articles of India*, Bombay, Asia Publishing House; and Marx, K., 1965, "Pre-Capitalist Economic Formations", translated by Jack Cohen, with an Introduction by E. Hobsbawn, New York, International Publishers.
15. Maine, H.J.S., 1890, *Village Communities in the East and the West*, London, John Murray.

Bougle thought of caste as an ideological system of a unique nature.[16] Such a view was also held earlier by Hocart.[17] Weber too considered caste as a system of status stratification.[18] None of these views and explanations offer a properly diagnosed understanding of the adaptive capacity and dynamic nature of the caste system. They explain caste basically as a cultural system implying that significant structural changes have not occurred in Indian society due to its stable character and cultural dictum.

It is argued that a 'caste model' of Indian society has emerged as a result of implicit and explicit ideas and values. Béteille blames Dumont in particular for encouraging a 'caste view' of Indian society.[19] 'Caste model' as viewed by Béteille does not provide an analysis of material interests along with the study of ideas and values. There is a dialectical relationship between the two, and Dumont and Pocock's notion of 'binary opposition' is far from the notion of 'dialectics'.[20] Béteille also suggests that economic and political conflicts occur with a certain degree of autonomy of their own, hence they could be studied independent of caste and religious beliefs and ideas. 'Caste model' would not permit such a path of understanding. To say that castes cooperate with each other is also a misconceived perception. Non-antagonism and hierarchy both are nomological constructions. In reality, defiance and conflict among castes are not uncommon. Leach's view that co-operation refers to caste and competition refers to class is

16. Dumont, Louis, 1970, op. cit.; and Bougle, C., 1971, *Essays on the Caste System*, Cambridge, Cambridge University Press.
17. Hocart, A.M., 1950, *Caste*, London: Methew and Co.
18. Weber, M., 1948, *From Max Weber: Essays in Sociology*, London, Routledge and Kegan Paul.
19. Béteille, A., 1969, "Ideas and Interests: Some Conceptual Problems in the Study of Social Stratification in India", *International Social Science Journal*, Vol. 21, No. 7, pp. 17–31.
20. Dumont, L. and Pocock. D.F., 1959, "Pure and Impure", *Contributions to Indian Sociology*, Vol. III.

naive and unconvincing.[21] Not only do families of the dominant castes compete with each other to extend patronage to the lower castes for maintaining their dominance, but the lower castes families also compete to seek favours from the families of dominant castes. Such a competition is really not a new phenomenon. Even feuds, due to conflicting claims on territory, were quite common among Kshatriyas and Brahmins for seeking power in ancient and medieval India.[22] Leach's view that caste was simply 'caste', and a 'class-like situation' emerged only when patrons started competing with each other, ignores the fact that intercaste conflicts and protests by lower castes against upper castes have always been a social reality.

Two serious but erroneous consequences of the analysis of caste as a unique, closed and corporate system of social ranking are: (a) caste and class are juxtaposed as polar opposites; and (b) 'caste view' becomes monocausal explanation. Srinivas' concept of 'dominant caste'[23] and his collection of essays on caste,[24] Mathur's work on caste and ritual,[25] Marriott's studies on caste,[26] and Kothari's works on

21. Leach, E.R., 1960, op. cit.
22. See, for example, Gail Omvedt (ed.), 1982, *Land, Caste and Politics in India*. Delhi, Authors Guild Publications; and *Economic and Political Weekly*, 1979, Vol. XIV(AN), Nos. 7 and 8, on debate on Caste and Class in India.
23. Srinivas, M.N., 1959, "The Dominant Caste in Rampura", *American Anthropologist*, Vol. LXI, No. 1.
24. Srinivas, M.N., 1962, *Caste in India and Other Essays*, Bombay, Asia Publishing House.
25. Mathur, K.S., 1964, *Caste and Ritual in a Malwa Village*, Bombay, Asia Publishing House.
26. Marriott, M., 1965, *Caste Ranking and Community Structure in Five Regions of India and Pakistan*, Poona, Deccan College, Poona; Marriott, M., 1959, "Interactional and Attributional Theories of Caste Ranking," *Man in India*, Vol. 34, No. 2; Marriott, M., 1968, "Caste Ranking and Food Transactions: A Matrix Analysis," in M. Singer and B.S. Cohn (eds), 2000, *Structure and Change in Indian Society*, Jaipur, Rawat Publications, and Marriott, M., 1968, "Multiple Reference in Indian Caste System," in J. Silverberg (ed.), *Social Mobility in the Caste System in India*, The Hague, Mouton Publishers.

role of caste in India's politics[27] are some of the notable examples of the application of the 'caste model'. Emphasis in these studies has singularly been on the hegemony or overdetermination of caste as their emphasis is on cultural/ normative criteria rather than on economic and political. However, in the late 1960s and 1970s, 'multiple criteria'[28], 'levels of caste dominance'[29] and 'levels of mobility in caste system, structural processes of change and downward mobility'[30] were discussed with a conscious intent to counter the falsity of the culturological paradigms like dominant caste, pollution-purity, sanskritisation, and westernisation. Some of these multidimensional studies also repudiate the exaggerated significance of the concepts of 'reference group' and 'relative deprivation' in the analysis of social mobility in the caste system in India.

Interaction between members of different castes was never uniformly the same. A.M. Shah[31] enlists three patterns of intracaste differentiation: (a) participation of members of several different religions and castes in a single occupation; (b) occupational diversification within a caste; and (c) existence of sub-divisions within a caste division (of the first order).

In a detailed study of rural-urban networks in Gujarat, Shah finds that there were 'orders' of castes and each order was

27. Kothari, R., 1970, *Caste in Indian Politics*, New Delhi, Orient Longman Ltd., and Kothari, R., 1970, *Politics in India*, New Delhi: Orient Longman Ltd.

28. Hazlehurst, L.W., 1968, "Multiple Status Hierarchies in Northern India", *Contributions to Indian Sociology*, New Series, No. II, pp. 38–57.

29. Dube, S.C., 1968, "Caste Dominance and Factionalism", *Contributions to Indian Sociology*, New Series, No. II, pp. 83–97.

30. See, Sharma, K.L., 1969, "Stresses in Caste Stratification", *Economic and Political Weekly*, Vol. IV, No. 3; Sharma, K.L., 1974, *The Changing Rural Stratification System*, New Delhi, Orient Longman Ltd.; Sharma K.L., 1980, *Essays on Social Stratification*, Jaipur, Rawat Publications; and Sharma, K.L., 1983, "Caste and Class: Factors Affecting Social Mobility Among the Scheduled Castes", *The Journal of Sociological Studies*, Vol. 2.

31. Shah, A.M., 1991, "Rural-Urban Networks in India." in K.L. Sharma and Dipankar Gupta, op. cit.

internally divided. There were also primarily rural, primarily urban and rural-cum-urban castes. Such divisions are based on occupational pursuits of these castes in rural and urban settings.[32] To understand fully the Hindu castes one has to take into account the non-Hindu groups too.[33] Thus, every caste was a multifaceted group, binding its members to various kinds of links.[34] Further, Shah emphatically analyses that the principle of division competed with the principle of hierarchy in castes in the past. Today, this principle has become stronger than the principle of hierarchy.[35] Feudalism subordinated the caste system in practice in the princely states of Rajputana.[36] Variability of caste-class nexus in different states is reported in several case studies.[37] Regional patterns of dominance, and caste-class nexus in the form of inter-caste alliances, such as AJGAR, forwards, backwards, caste coalitions and inter-caste *senas*, speak of the inseparability of caste, class and power as phenomena of the same social formation.[38]

Those who draw a sharp line of demarcation between caste and class observe the two systems as different forms of social stratification. They perceive that units ranked in the class system are individuals, and those ranked in the caste are groups. D'Souza[39] draws a distinction between caste and class guided

32. Ibid., pp. 19–22.
33. Ibid., p. 26.
34. Ibid., p. 28.
35. Ibid., p. 37.
36. Sharma, K.L. 1994, "Feudalism, Caste and Class in Rajasthan", in K.L. Sharma (ed.), *Caste and Class in India*, Jaipur, Rawat Publications, pp. 209–24.
37. See K.L. Sharma (ed.), ibid., for case studies of caste-class situation in various states of India.
38. For profiles of caste, class and dominance, see, for example, F.R. Frankel and M.S.A. Rao (eds.), 1989 and 1990 (two vols.), *Dominance and State Power in Modern India*, Delhi, Oxford University Press; and K. L. Sharma 1995 (ed.), *Social Inequality in India, Profiles of Caste, Class, Power and Social Mobility*, Jaipur, Rawat Publications.
39. D'Souza, V.S., 1967, "Caste and Class: A Reinterpretation," *Journal of Asian and African Studies*, Vol. 2, Nos. 3–5, pp. 192–211.

by the attributional notion of class. In other words, class for D'Souza is a result of what he calls "objective rating of positions based on certain attributes". D'Souza refers to the rigidity-fluidity dimension of social stratification implying class as a case of fluidity and caste of rigidity. Understanding caste through concepts of status rigidity, immutability, organic solidarity, functional interdependence, homo hierarchicus, and pollution-purity, and understanding class by the ideology of individualism, competition and equality, are grossly erroneous parameters. Caste as a system of social stratification represents a semblance of rigidity and fluidity, cooperation and competition, holism and individualism, organic and segmentary divisions, interdependence and autonomy, and inequality and equality. The genesis of these so-called polar characteristics lies in the falsely conceived notion of superiority of the non-caste western society. These being 'analytic' explanations of caste lack 'historic' and 'experimental' contents. No static and abstract model of caste or class would help in understanding of the composite character of caste-class nexus in the Indian society.

The falsity is that caste is thought of as antithetical to class, hence both caste and class have been guided by the experience of an alien situation. Weber's notion of 'status group' has been equated with 'caste group', and his notions of 'class', 'class situation' and 'market situation' have been pronounced relevant for study of class in India. The other observation is that caste is a 'real' phenomenon, whereas class is a category, an attributional construction. It may be stated that if caste is a 'real' phenomenon, then class is also equally 'real' and 'empiric'. Both caste and class are real and empiric in the same situations and human transactions. The two are interactional and hierarchical, and the one incorporates the other. Confusion regarding 'class' also emanates from its Marxist meaning. What about 'unity' and 'harmony' among patrons and clients, landlords and tenants, upper caste 'haves' and lower caste 'have nots'? This is not to undermine the role and significance of contradictions and consequent conflicts between the powerful and the lesser ones. But power is not a zero sum reality. Thus, to reduce the totality of social relations to two simple layers, namely, the top and the bottom, would be too crude a way of understanding the multilayered and intricate social formation of Indian society.

Since caste incorporates class and class incorporates caste, neither 'caste view' nor simply 'class view' would explain the totality of India's social reality. A perfect congruence between caste, class and power never existed in pre-British India.[40] Mobility and migration were quite normal activities particularly resulting from warfare for power, and protests against atrocities committed by the rulers and the upper-caste priests were also witnessed from time to time. In recent years, land reforms, adult franchise, and certain constitutional provisions have brought about incongruities in 'summation of statuses' which characterised the Indian society before independence.

Since 'caste view' has been accorded unwarranted and undue emphasis, it is quite appropriate to make a note of the 'class view' of Indian society. Kosambi analyses the Aryans in the post-Rig Vedic period from the perspective of their economic formation.[41] Thapar, Habib and Desai have analysed the class based character of Indian society in ancient, medieval and modern India, respectively.[42] Lamb reports the prevalence of class relations as early as 600 BC in India.[43] Material and

40. Stein, B., 1968, "Social Mobility and Medieval South Indian Sects," in J. Silverberg (ed.), op. cit.; and Panikkar, K.M. 1955, *Hindu Society at the Crossroads*, Bombay, Asia Publishing House.

41. Kosambi, D.D., 1958, *An Introduction to the Study of Indian History*, Bombay, Popular Prakashan, pp. 86–87.

42. Thapar, R., 1974, "Social Mobility in Ancient Indian Society," in R.S. Sharma (ed.), *Indian Society: Historical Problems*, New Delhi, Peoples Publishing House, pp. 95–123; Habib, I., 1974, "Social Distribution of Landed Property in the Pre-British India: A Historical Survey," in R.S. Sharma (ed.), op. cit., pp. 264–316; and Desai, A.R., 1948, *Social Background of Indian Nationalism*, Bombay, Popular Book Depot.

43. Lamb, H.B., 1975, "The Indian Merchant", in M. Singer (ed.), op. cit., pp. 25–34.

cultural traditions existed in a congruent form, and class transformation had been a vital fact in the form of new kingdoms, settled agriculture, trade, cities, and banking and guild organisations. Desai's approach is, however, of a different nature. Desai observes that caste inheres an underdeveloped but potentially explosive class character. He also analyses the character of the Indian State from the Marxist point of view, and calls it 'capitalistic' in essence and reality.

Both caste and class are real dimensions of India's social formation, hence inseparable. Class is not simply a conceptually abstracted category. It is not a construct based on certain attributes or indices, operationally arrived at. Classes of landowners, landless labourers, traders and moneylenders are not abstractions, but they are existential structural components of India's class structure. Interactional ties (both conflict and cooperation) between them refer to their life-situations.

Caste and class nexus is highlighted in the analysis of the mode of production as a social formation. Kathleen Gough finds interconnections of caste, kinship, family and marriage with forces of production and production relations.[44] Marxist ideologues Namboodiripad and Ranadive consider class relations as 'domain assumption' in the treatment of caste and kinship in India.[45] Even *varna* and *jajmani* systems have been explained in terms of class relations and modes of production.[46] A 'class view' of social structure and social relations is found in the analyses presented by Goran and Lindberg, Singh,

44. Gough, K.E., 1980, "Modes of Production in Southern India," *Economic and Political Weekly*, Vol. XV(AN), Nos. 5, 6 & 7, pp. 337–64.
45. Namboodiripad, E.M.S., 1979, "Caste Conflicts vs. Growing Unity of Popular Democratic Forces," *Economic and Political Weekly*, Vol. XIV(AN), Nos. 7 & 8, pp. 329–36; and Ranadive, B.T., 1979, "Caste, Class and Property Relations", *Economic and Political Weekly*, Vol. XIV(AN), Nos. 7 & 8, pp. 337–48.
46. Meillassoux, C., 1973, "Are there Castes in India?", *Economy and Society*, February, pp. 89–111.

Thorner, Saith and Tanakha, and Bhardwaj and Das.[47]

Caste and class represent to a large extent aspects of the same structural reality. Singh comments on caste and class nexus: "the situation corresponds to a 'prismatic' model of change where traditional sentiments of caste and kinship undergo adaptive transformation without completely being 'diffracted' into classes or corporate groups. Classes operate within the framework of castes."[48] Caste conflicts are also class conflicts as the gap between the upper and the lower castes is the same as one finds between the upper and the lower classes. Castes also function as classes as they are geared for performing their class-interests. Therefore, common class consciousness among members of a caste is mainly due to their common economic deprivations. Caste associations, particularly in the urban context, perform economic and political functions for the benefit of their respective members.[49] Thus, castes are interactional groups rather than attributional constructs. Mencher finds that caste is a very effective system of economic exploitation of lower castes.[50] Precisely due to this, the upper castes (in the garb of exploiting classes) have not allowed for the emergence of class consciousness among the lower classes as they feared a threat to their 'entrenched status' in India's social structure.

47. Goran, D. and J. Lindberg, 1975, *Behind Poverty: The Social Formation of a Tamil Village*, London, Curzon Press; Singh, H., 1979, "Kin, Caste and Kisan Movement in Marwar: Some Questions to the Conventional Sociology of Kin and Caste," *Journal of Peasant Studies*, Vol. 7, No. 2; Thorner, D., 1974, *Land and Labour in India*, Bombay, Asia Publishing House; Saith, A. and A. Tanakha, 1972, "Agrarian Transition and the Differentiation of the Peasantry: A Study of a West U.P. Village," *Economic and Political Weekly*, Vol., VII, No.14, pp. 712–23; and Bhardwaj, K. and P.K. Das, 1975, "Tenurial Conditions and Mode of Exploitation," *Economic and Political Weekly*, Vol. X, Nos. 5–7, pp. 223–33.

48. Singh, Y., 1968, "Caste and Class: Some Aspects of Continuity and Change," *Sociological Bulletin*, Vol. XVII, No. 2, p. 171.

49. Rudolph, L.I. and S.H. Rudolph, 1967, *The Modernity of Tradition*, New Delhi, Orient Longman.

50. Mencher, J.P., 1974, "The Caste System Upside Down, the Not-So Mysterious East," *Current Anthropology*, Vol. 15, No. 4, p. 469.

III

Marxist notions of class and class conflict have become the hallmark of studies on India's agricultural and urban-industrial structures. Marx wrote about caste and traditional ethos of village communities in two articles on India in the *New York Daily Tribune.* Initially, Marx thought of Asiatic mode of production by which he meant absence of private property in land and static nature of economy due to a certain tie-up between caste, agriculture and village handicrafts. However, Kurian observes that the analysis of Asiatic mode does not deny the role of class contradictions and class structures.[51] India's precapitalist economic formation was neither classless nor static. Social relations and exploitation were based on both caste and class. Now, it is firmly viewed that different forms of communal societies, forms of slavery and bondage, and feudal relations have existed in different combinations in the same areas and at the same time.

Two questions are relevant for a discussion on class: (1) how to analyse the class structure in Indian society?, and (2) what is class-caste nexus and its ramifications and interrelations in each region? The purpose of discussing these questions is not to accept or reject the Marxian approach for studying Indian society, but to understand the concept and reality of class in the Indian context, and to know how has it been different from or similar to the concept and reality of caste. Rudra, while analysing the class composition of the Indian agricultural population, observes that there are only two classes among them: one termed as 'the class of big landlords' and the other 'the class of agricultural labourers'.[52] These two classes are in antagonistic contradiction with each other, and this contradiction constitutes the principal contradiction in Indian

51. Kurian, K.M., 1980, "Class Analysis and its Relevance to the Study of Indian Society," *State and Society*, pp. 96–106.
52. Rudra, A., 1978, "Class Relations in Indian Agriculture—I", *Economic and Political Weekly*, Vol. XII, No. 22, pp. 916–23.

rural society. Rudra's view is similar to that of Desai.[53] Rudra and those who adhere to his view do not accept that class differentiation in terms of agricultural labourers, poor peasants, middle peasants, rich peasants and landlords exists today only, it even existed in medieval India.[54] Rudra emphatically argues that Indian agriculture has capitalist relations and capitalist development, hence there are two classes—'haves' and 'have-nots'. State in India has assumed property norms of capitalist society as the axis of developmental strategy. One of the implications of this formulation is that the frame of reference which applies to the rest of the capitalist world also applies very well to the Indian society. The other inference is that the dominant causality in Indian society is 'economic' in nature in all situations and contexts.

Kosambi accepts mode of production as the basis of understanding of class relations, but does not accept the hypotheses regarding 'economic determinism' and 'universal application' of Marxism as a monodimensional frame of reference.[55] Concepts specifically relevant for studying Indian society could be evolved from its historicity and experience. Mukerji and Thorner, for example, have used indigenous concepts drawing from agrarian relations and India's cultural heritage.[56] Even Utsa Patnaik, who uses notions of 'mode of production' and 'differentiation of peasantry', rejects a mechanical acceptance of Marx's model of study.[57] She observes that

53. Desai, A.R., 1948, op. cit.; *State and Society in India: Essays in Dissent*, 1975, Bombay, Popular Prakashan.
54. Sharma, K.L., 1983, "Agrarian Stratification: Old Issues, New Explanations and New Issues, Old Explanations," *Economic and Political Weekly*, Vol. XVIII, Nos. 42 and 43.
55. Kosambi, D.D., 1958, op. cit.
56. Mukerji, D.P., 1958, *Diversities*, New Delhi, Peoples Publishing House; and Thorner, D., 1974, op. cit.
57. Patnaik, U., 1972, op. cit., and also 1976, "Class Differentiation within the Peasantry: An Approach to Analysis of Indian Agriculture", *Economic and Political Weekly*, Vol. XI, No. 39, pp. A82–A101.

several modes of production coexist in India, and development of capitalism has not only been limited but distorted. Lin also makes a reference regarding interpenetration and integration of precapitalist and capitalist relations.[58]

Dandekar, while examining nature of class and class-conflict in Indian society, adds to a new dimension. Five major classes in India, according to Dandekar, are: (1) pre-capitalist (cultivators, agricultural labourers and household industry), (2) independent workers in capitalist society, (3) employers, (4) white-collar employees, and (5) blue-collar workers.[59] The main classes in contemporary India can also be referred to as: (1) agrarian, (2) industrial, (3) professional, and (4) business and mercantile. The emergence of these classes in modern India cannot simply be explained by the Marxist approach. Dandekar states that large-scale industry and monopoly capitalism have not been seen fully in terms of their implications in India. Marx did not think that capitalism would change due to trade unions and collective bargaining power of workers. Class antagonism is the kernel of Marxism, but class harmony is also a fact of life, and multiplicity of classes between the 'haves' and the 'have-nots' cannot escape our attention. There is a 'middle class' inevitably in all societies, and it has a class higher and a class lower to it—this has not received Marx's serious attention. The proletarian is propertyless, but he has also a chance for embourgeoisiement, and this is not stated by Marx. In India strikes by wage-earners is a very common feature, and they include those earning from Rs. 200 to Rs. 2,000 per month, hence wage-earners (proletariat) are a heterogenous category. About three-fourths of the total workforce are left out by the Marxian yardstick. Indian State, being a welfare state, is the largest employer today. Is the Indian State a capitalist,

58. Lin, S.G., 1980, "Theory of a Dual Mode of Production in Post-Colonial India", *Economic and Political Weekly*, Vol. XV, Nos. 10 and 11.

59. Dandekar, V.M., 1978, "Nature of Class Conflict in the Indian Society", *Artha Vjnana*, Vol. 20, No. 2, pp. 102–24.

exploitative and oppressive agency just like an industrialist or an employer of wage-earners? About 10 million workers are engaged in small-scale industries and family-owned concerns, and these workers generally do not witness class antagonism and strikes. The organised labour in India is one-ninth of the total workforce. Can we accept the Marxian approach in toto in view of these vital facts mentioned by Dandekar? Besides these points, overlapping of class, caste and occupation, and elite conflict, pressure groups and factions, influence of middle classes, and prevalence of 'mixed classes' like 'gentleman farmers' are some other important points to be taken into account for a serious analysis of India's class structure.

IV

Gough has analysed conflicts and litigations based on economic inequalities between different castes in a Tanjore village.[60] The 'mix' of caste and class in East Bengal,[61] class genesis of caste structure in Bengal,[62] and changes from caste to class have been reported in the studies conducted by Misra, Béteille, Miller and Kolenda,[63] but none of them has studied resurgence of caste in the new situations with its multiple facets. Some scholars have undertaken a class analysis of India's social formation considering caste, religion, family and politics as subservient to class relations.[64] However, Harriss and Omvedt have analysed class

60. Gough, K.E., 1960, "Caste in a Tanjore Village," in E.R. Leach (ed.), op. cit., pp. 11–60.
61. Mukherjee, R.K., 1957, *Dynamics of a Rural Society*, Berlin, Akademie Verlag.
62. Bose, N.K., 1967, *Culture and Society in India*, Bombay, Asia Publishing House.
63. Misra, B.B., 1964, *The Indian Middle Classes*, Oxford, Oxford University Press; Béteille, A., op. cit., 1969; Miller, D.B., 1975, *From Hierarchy to Stratification: Changing Patterns of Social Inequality in a North Indian Village*, Delhi, Oxford University Press; and Kolenda, P., 1978, *Caste in Contemporary India: Beyond Organic Solidarity*, California, Benjamin Cummings Publishing Co.
64. Desai, A.R., op. cit., 1948; op. cit., 1975; and "Relevance of the Marxist Approach to the Study of Indian Society", Presidential Address, 15th

relations as a dominant causality within which they explain caste and other structural aspects in Indian society.[65] They have objected to the 'culturological determinism' as advocated by Srinivas,[66] Dumont[67] and several others of their persuasion. Parvathamma, while commenting on Srinivas' *Remembered Village*, writes: "In all the writings of Srinivas, the Brahmin-non-Brahmin values are juxtaposed."[68] Hierarchy based on pollution-purity remains intrinsic to Srinivas' thinking in regard to all aspects of human life even if it is actually not so pronounced. However, Bailey incorporates both cultural and structural dimensions in the definition of caste.[69] Class, as an analytic notion, is used by Béteille, Bhatt and Aggarwal as they draw a distinct line of demarcation between caste, class and power.[70] Methodological device is the main concern of these and other sociologists in drawing a distinction between caste and class.[71] Emergence of 'grades' within a caste has also been referred to as a class-like change within caste. Hypergamy within caste endogamy always refers to status distinctions based on economic position and parental heritage, and therefore, class grades have always been there as part of the caste system itself. Class is not a result of the new forces of change which have recently affected the caste system. Changes

---

Indian Sociological Conference, 2nd November, 1980; and Bettelheim, C. 1968, *India Independent*, London, MacGibbon and Kee Ltd.

65. Harris, J., 1982, *Capitalism and Peasant Farming*, Bombay, Oxford University Press; Omvedt, G., (ed.) 1982, op. cit.

66. Srinivas, M.N., 1952, *Religion and Society among the Coorgs of South India*, Oxford, Clarendon Press; Srinivas, M.N., 1976, *The Remembered Village*, New Delhi, Oxford University Press.

67. Dumont, L., op. cit., 1970.

68. Parvathamma, C., 1978, "The Remembered Village: A Brahminical Odyssey", *Contributions to Indian Sociology*, New Series, Vol. 12, No. 1, p. 91.

69. Bailey, F.G., 1963, op. cit., pp. 107–24.

70. Béteille, A., 1976, op. cit.; Bhatt, A., 1975, *Caste, Class and Politics*. Delhi, Manohar Book Service; Aggarwal, P.C., 1971, *Caste, Religion and Power*, New Delhi, Shri Ram Centre for Industrial Relations.

71. D'Souza, V.S., 1967, op. cit., pp. 192–211.

are in the traditional caste and class relations and not in caste alone paving way to emergence of class relations. Thus, classes are found as part of a system of social stratification in the same way as castes are rooted in the Indian society. There is no universal and monolithic nature of class, class relations and class conflict. There are certainly objective criteria of class identification and determination of class position. A class is certainly a concrete unit of interaction with other units.

Caste in India is mistakenly projected as a system of harmonic relations. Caste inheres numerous problems related to economic domination and subjugation, privileges and deprivations, and 'conspicuous waste' and bare survival. Class relationships are treated as a domain assumption in the treatment of caste and kinship in India. *Jajmani* system can be explained in terms of class relations and the mode of production. Morton Klass hypothesises that class exchanges women, whereas caste system exchanges goods without exchanging women.[72] According to Klass, India has ecosystems in which people have different modes of life, and within these systems caste adapts itself to the nature and economic conditions.

V

Some empirical studies reveal a high concentration of socially backward castes among tenant cultivators. The study by Reddy and Murthy shows that as many as 73 per cent of the pure tenant-cultivators belong to the backward castes, and of the owner-cum-tenant cultivators 70 per cent belong to these backward castes.[73] The backward castes tenant-cultivators are predominant in the small and medium size groups. The socially backward castes in Andhra Pradesh consist of Settibaliji and

72. Klass, M., 1980, *Caste: The Emergence of the System in South Asia*, Philadelphia, Institute for the Study of Human Issues.
73. Reddy, V.N. and C.S. Murthy, 1978, "Backward Castes and Tenancy: A Village Study", *Economic and Political Weekly*, Vol. XIII, No. 26, pp. 1061–76.

Harijan, and the socially advanced castes consist of Brahmin, Kapu, Devanga and others. Thus, most of the tenants of small and medium size belong to the economically and socially depressed castes, and pure rent-receivers, except 12 per cent, belong to the dominant castes. Mukherjee cites the example of caste riots to explain the unidimensionality of caste, class and religion. He writes: "Caste riots are frequent in those areas where the castewise 'social' deprivations are manifestly correlated with the classwise economic deprivations, such as in Bihar, Maharashtra, Tamil Nadu, etc."[74] According to Mukherjee, these caste contradictions are due to inherent class contradictions in the caste system. Vagiswari observes that the Harijans have proletarianised between 1950 and 1970, while the non-Harijans have improved their economic standing during the same period.[75]

The *dalits* have been attacked, murdered, their womenfolk raped and put to indignities. Sinha in a despatch to *Economic and Political Weekly* observes that it is 'class war' against Harijans, and not atrocities.[76] In another despatch Sinha mentions that "in the villages of Bihar, the rise of a rich peasant class has driven agricultural labourers of all castes—Chamars, Dusandhs, Kurmis, Yadavas, Bhumihars and so on, to forsake their caste organisations and fight along trade union lines."[77] This shows that 'class war' cuts across caste lines. But, the fact is that a Harijan or Chamar agricultural labourer cannot be equated with his Brahmin or Bhumihar counterpart simply because the two have the same position in the class structure. The real situation in post-independent India is that a class of

74. Mukherjee, R., 1981, "Realities of Agrarian Relations in India", *Economic and Political Weekly*, Vol. XVI, No. 4, p. 112.
75. Vagiswari, A., 1972, *Income Earning Trends and Social Status of Harijan Community in Tamil Nadu*, Madras, Institute of Development Studies.
76. Sinha, A., 1977, "Bihar's Violence Against the Poor", *Economic and Political Weekly*, Vol. XII, No. 15, pp. 2037–40.
77. Sinha, A., 1978, "Bihar's Advancing Class Interests in the Name of Caste", *Economic and Political Weekly*, Vol. XIII, No. 16, pp. 675–76.

rich peasants from the backward castes is at the top of class hierarchy. This class is struggling against the social and political domination of the upper castes. The backward classes received encouragement for accelerating their struggle against the upper castes during the Janata government regime in Bihar. The upper castes are upper class in an overall sense of the term and in effect the lower castes are lower class. The backward classes are at intermediate level in the caste hierarchy and so is their position in class structure. The Janata rule brought about a shift in the structure of dominance in Bihar having implications for the political economy of the state. Brahmins lost heavily their political dominance. A study of a village in Andhra Pradesh, as mentioned earlier, shows that the four tenurial categories, namely, pure tenants, owners-cum-tenants, pure rent receivers and owners-cum-rent receivers are concomitant with caste divisions. Most of the tenants of small and medium sizes belong to economically and socially depressed castes, namely, Settibaliji and Harijan, whereas the dominant sections of all tenurial categories belong to socially advanced castes, namely, Kapu, Brahmin and Devanga.

The incidents of massacre, loot and rape of the scheduled castes in Belchi, Agra, Pantnagar, Marathwada and Bajitpur, among other places, show the role of the caste system *vis-à-vis* class struggle and class organisation as reported by Atyachar Virodhi Samiti.[78] The Samiti investigated the nature and extent of repression of scheduled castes in Maharashtra. The SCs were also poor peasants and agricultural labourers. The specific oppression and exploitation of women among the rural poor both sexually and as a class, particularly of the dalit women, have been highlighted in the report by the Samiti. The findings and observations of the Samiti on caste are quite meaningful as caste is seen as a relation of production. The following points may be noted:

78. Atyachar Virodhi Samiti, 1979, "The Marathwada Riots: A Report", *Economic and Political Weekly*, Vol. XIV, No. 19, pp. 45–52.

(1) The caste system functions as an extremely oppressive method of economic exploitation. The dominant class also acquires political power and social prestige which further perpetuates and consolidates caste hierarchy. Thus, cast hierarchy reflects ownership of land, and economic hierarchy is closely linked with social hierarchy.

(2) Caste determines a definite relation to the means of production and subsistence specially in rural areas. Caste riots reflect conflict of class interests.

(3) Caste also refers to the relations of production as it controls the access of groups and individuals to the conditions of production and to the resources and provides the social framework for politico-ritual activity.

(4) B.R. Ambedkar rightly observed that the caste system was not merely division of labour, but also a division of labourers. However, caste prevents labourers from being a class-for-itself. Hence, caste is to be viewed as an ideology.

(5) Caste and religion are used to perpetuate a particular class structure.

(6) Caste persists as a part of feudal ideology.

The view of the Samiti lends support to our discussion on caste and class nexus, its continuity and change. "Caste is one of the most important aspects of Indian society. It represents a specific form of oppression at the level of relations of production. To say that there are only class issues, and nothing like questions pertaining to caste, is totally absurd, because of the material reality that caste divisions beyond purely 'economic' classes do still persist. So issues around specific caste questions must be taken by all the progressives and leftists, *dalits* and non-*dalits* and organisations".[79] The reality today is of caste oppression and class exploitation particularly in villages. A report from a village in Punjab by Singh shows that

79. Ibid., p. 52.

farm workers and rich farmers are Jat Sikhs.[80] The principal demand of the village workers is for an increase in the wage rates. The big and middle peasants are united in opposition to the agricultural labourers. Thus, both class and caste are found as non-distinct aspects of a given situation.

Convergences of caste and class have been reported in Gujarat by Bose[81] against reservation of seats for post-graduate medical courses, and in Bihar against reserving 44 per cent of government jobs for the backward classes. Scarce resources and employment opportunities are the main cause of caste-class convergence. The Mandal Commission for Backward Classes (1978–80) was faced with the problem of caste and class convergence. It thought that caste and class hierarchics went together, and therefore, caste was considered as the basis of determining backwardness of a given member of society. Again, in the context of Bihar, Das[82] observes that apparently the phenomenon of caste is found in its virulent form, but to ignore the concept of class is to undermine the concrete conditions of the state. Caste is not a simplified entity having only non-class social elements. Class is not an abstract, mechanical construct; it is a politico-economic concept; it refers to an active process and not to a catalogue category. A 'class analysis' of Bihar situation even in terms of expressions through caste idioms is essential.[83]

Classes are found in India in caste idiom. A Marxist explanation of this statement is quite relevant here. Caste should be analysed in regard to its nature, its material basis in the past and in the present, and its role in politics. It is

80. Singh, A.P., 1979, "Farm Workers vs. Rich Peasants: Class and Caste in a Punjab Village", *Economic and Political Weekly*, Vol. XIV, Nos. 42 and 43, pp. 1753–54.

81. Bose, P.K., 1981, "Social Mobility and Caste Violence: A Study of Gujarat Riots", *Economic and Political Weekly*, Vol. XIV, No. 16, pp. 713–16.

82. Das, A.N., 1984, "Class in Itself, Caste for Itself: Social Articulation in Bihar", *Economic and Political Weekly*, Vol. XIX, No. 37, pp. 1816–19.

83. Ibid.

imperative to know which castes are the ruling ones, and which ones own land and capital, employ wage-labourers and extract surplus. Caste divisions hamper progress and unity among the oppressed classes. According to this view, all classes are defined by the relations in which the various sections of society are found related to the means of production, and castes are a carryover of the feudal class divisions. The 1979 Annual Number of *Economic and Political Weekly* on 'Class and Caste in India', includes essays such as 'Dialectics of Caste and Class Conflicts', 'Caste and Class: An Interlinked View', 'Caste Conflicts versus Growing Unity of Popular Democratic Forces', 'Caste, Class and Property Relations', 'Caste and Class in Maharashtra', 'Class and Caste in Tribal Movement', 'Caste, Class and Economic Opportunity in Kerala: An Empirical Analysis', 'Caste and Class in Bihar', and 'Class and Jati at Asthapuram and Kanthapuram'. All these studies report caste and class nexus, use of caste, class and religion for gaining political power, emergence of an elite class in every caste, an interlinked view of caste and class, realisation of caste idioms in power game, role of caste in agrarian and social movements.

VI

Extreme viewpoints have been expressed about caste and class. One such view is that the two are polar opposites and antithetical to each other. The other view is that caste represents ideational and normative aspect whereas class refers to basic economic relations.

The nexus between these two systems of social stratification and its continuity and change has been discussed here as a conceptual framework. Such an approach is based on the premise that there is a caste basis of class and also a class basis of caste. A given caste association, for example, is not simply an organisation of the members of that caste group, but it is also an organisation of unskilled workers or potters or traders.

Structural aspects of caste, namely, economic and political dimensions have remained underestimated, whereas the cultural aspects of social stratification can provide a deeper understanding of India's social formation because the two are, in fact, inseparable from each other. Both are conceptual constructs as well as empiric phenomena. Thus, caste and class represent, to a large extent, though from different angles, the same social reality. Classes function within the contexts of castes. Caste conflicts are also class or agrarian conflicts. The rifts between the upper and the lower castes to a large extent correspond with conflicts between landowners and share-croppers or agricultural labourers. Hence, an overemphasis on either ideological or on structural aspects would provide an incomplete view of social reality.

2 Rethinking Inter-Caste Relations as the Basis of Social Stratification

I

Cliches such as tradition and modernity, continuity and change, hierarchy and stratification, organic and segmentary structures instead of providing an understanding of the semblance of the persisting social inequalities and changes in the structure of Indian society, have led to unfounded conceptualisations of a resilient and harmonic society. Along with this thesis a continued emphasis is laid on caste as a homo hierarchicus, culture-bound, change-resisting system of social stratification. A number of other studies from the mid-sixties onwards have focused mainly on the weakening of the caste as a system of social stratification by highlighting on what Béteille mentions as the emergence of "differentiated institutional structures of various kinds".[1] Along with 'ideas', 'interests' have emerged in the shaping of the pattern of social stratification.[2] A new 'caste-free occupational structure' and modern education have created a non-traditional basis of social relations

1. Béteille, André, 1966, 'Closed and Open Social Stratification in India', *European Journal of Sociology*, Vol. VII, pp. 224–46.
2. Béteille, André, 1969, 'Ideas and Interests: Some Conceptual Problems in the Study of Social Stratification in Rural India', *International Social Science Journal*, Vol. 21, No. 7, pp. 219–35.

weakening traditional inter-caste relations.[3] 'Multiple status hierarchies', 'attributional' criteria of caste ranking, 'new castes', 'levels of social mobility', 'downward social mobility', 'obverse structural process of social change', 'structural criteria of dominance', 'new status images', etc., as expressions of change are indicative of caste-class and country-town nexuses and fading out of the old cognitive constructions and orientations.[4] A new discourse on social stratification reflecting distantiation from caste as the fundamental basis of social relations and stratification is echoed unhesitatingly not by the upper and upper middle castes alone but also by the erstwhile

3. Sharma, K.L., 1974, *The Changing Rural Stratification System*, New Delhi, Orient Longman Ltd.

4. Indian society is being seen even today through caste and religious categories. Interest in such a culturological/indological framework, undermining the relevance of structural criteria, is though an old one, but its recent revival in the wake of pronounced phenomenal changes seems somewhat puzzling. Caste simply as a system of 'ideas and values' and hierarchisation, ignoring the historical and the contextual contexts of change, lends credence to the cognitive constructions and categories which have failed to explain the ground reality, namely, inter-caste and intra-caste relations, which are the fundamental basis of caste as a system of social relations and inequality. Louis Dumont, M.N. Srinivas, McKim Marriott, Jonathan Parry and several others have not only used the culturological framework, but have also expressed a hope for continuity of the caste system in India in future.

Dimensional studies of social stratification distinguishing analytically between 'caste, class and power,' and then finding out congruence/incongruence between them were taken as a step forward from the structuralist and the earlier functionalist interpretations of caste. Since these studies were devoid of historical depth, emphasis on India's social formation as a whole lacked in them. Culture and language as instruments of power substituting explanations such as the structuralist, the functionalist and the structural-historical have been focused in some recent studies based on the common sense cognitions and perceptions of the people. But connections of such perceptions with everyday life and contingent situations have not been established in the neo-structuralist formulations. 'Caste for itself' and caste as an everyday life phenomenon are two different aspects, generally unrelated to each other. In the first case caste is an episodic, metaphoric and goal-oriented phenomenon; in the latter case it is discrete, personalised and family-specific behavioral phenomenon, Both the modalities are not in agreement with the 'caste model' of Indian society.

depressed sections of rural society. Caste has paved a way for family in reproduction of inequality,[5] breaking the traditional barriers to social mobility, and in becoming a major unit of status evaluation.

Thus, three patterns are clearly discernible from available literature: (1) caste continues to be an *avtar*[6]; (2) caste is a resilient and adaptive institution capable of absorbing modern changes[7]; and (3) caste today has lost its significance as a fundamental mechanism of status determination[8]. I intend to focus on the last point by highlighting on the fact that the withering away of inter-caste relations has led to fading out of caste-based social stratification. A new pattern of alliances and configurations across caste boundaries reflecting status dynamics and power equations has replaced the old pattern of social ranking. However, caste is lingering on in the non-essential social domains and discrete personal relations. Such structural changes have always occurred, but the process has considerably accentuated since independence.

II

Though caste has continually been studied to arrive at reliable and convincing conceptualisations and explanations, yet certain ambiguities and loose ends persist in its construction as a system of social stratification. Two reasons have generally been attributed to such a rather confusing state of affairs: (1) variation in the practice of the caste principle from caste to caste and area to area; and (2) impact of the caste of the

5. Béteille, André, 1991, 'Caste and Family', *Anthropology Today*, Vol. 8, No. 1, pp. 13–18.
6. Srinivas, M.N. (ed.), 1996, *Caste: Its Twentieth Century* Avatar, New Delhi, Viking, Penguin.
7. Singh, Yogendra, 1968, 'Caste and Class: Some Aspects of Continuity and Change', *Sociological Bulletin*, Vol. XVII, No. 2, pp. 165–86.
8. Kolenda, P., 1984, *Caste in Contemporary India: Beyond Organic Solidarity*, Jaipur, Rawat Publications.

observer-analyst and that of the observed on the conceptualisation. Another point may also be stated here. 'Caste model' for studying Indian society in general and the village community in particular has been applied as an unquestioned approach in most studies conducted in the 1950s and 1960s. And related to this is the study of 'inter-caste relations' generally at the expense of the understanding of 'intra-caste relations', and this which has resulted into reinforcing of constructions relating to hierarchy and its allied extensions and networks. This implies operation of a 'mindset' on the one hand, and exploration of half-truths on the other. Adequate explanations of status and power in conjunction with caste, and also independent of it, have been relegated to the background because of the perfunctory discussion on the nature of social stratification. Inter-caste relations were observed in the light of the ideology of caste and its actualisation. Caste structured interrelations, economy, polity and religion were reported in most village studies in the first two decades after independence. Thus, justification and rationalisation of the 'caste model' were the hallmark of these early studies.

Such undue emphasis on the significance of caste emanates from the perception of a perfect adjustment of the individual to the universe and from his adaptation to the laws that control the universe, and the proclivity to view everything as hierarchically structured.[9] S.C. Dube believed that these were found in both thought (text) and activities (context) of the group.[10] Unifying and harmonising principles as such are quite strong. Based on the ritual distance castes are stratified irrespective of their ritual, economic and occupational pursuits. Antinomies such as man/woman, educated/uneducated, urban/rural, childhood/youth/old age and cooperation/conflict along with caste structured inequalities which further

9. Opler, Morris Edward, 1955, 'Foreword,' *Indian Village*, by S.C. Dube, London, Routledge & Kegan Paul.

10. Dube, S.C., 1955, *Indian Village*, London, Routledge & Kegan Paul.

strengthened the system of social stratification. Though Dube enlists six major factors such as religion and caste, landownership, wealth, position in government service and village organisation, age and distinctive personality traits which contribute to status differentiation, yet in several spheres of life, caste has resonance in controlling the village community.[11] Society continues to be caste structured as caste is desideratum in social, economic and ritual organisation.[12]

However, Dube is not as rigid about the centrality of caste as are Dumont and Srinivas. Dube, while describing 'levels of standard of living', mentions about the rich, well-to-do, average and poor people.[13] He also refers to the gendered division of labour besides caste-based allocation of economic and occupational activities.[14] Ultimately, Dube, though not so succinctly, considers 'poor' as central to status differentiation.[15] He writes: "Superior caste can dominate inferior caste; the rich dominate the poor; those in authority dominate those who lack it. Age, kinship status, wealth and authority, together with caste status, determine superior and inferior statuses".[16] Democratic institutions have also led to some adjustments and modifications in the nature of hierarchy and tone of domination.

Hierarchical arrangement of castes is reported in some other studies as well.[17] Inter-caste relations, for example, are described through *jajmani* relations between a Thakur and the castes which serve his family on the occasions of birth, *mundan*, marriage and death.[18] Besides Majumdar, Oscar Lewis

11. Ibid., p. 201.
12. Ibid., p. 225.
13. Ibid., p. 167.
14. Ibid., pp. 170–72.
15. Ibid., p. 234.
16. Ibid.
17. Majumdar, D.N., 1958, *Caste and Communication in an Indian Village*, Bombay, Asia Publishing House; Mathur, K.S., 1964, *Caste and Ritual in a Malwa Village*, Bombay, Asia Publishing House.
18. Majumdar, D.N., ibid., pp. 36–54.

also analyses group formation and centres of authority within and between various castes.[19] Inter-caste relations permeate beyond village due to marked variations in the composition and structure of caste in India. A holistic morphology of caste regions based on the caste data of the 1931 census incorporating the variables, such as locally dominant caste, degree of dominance, degree of ramifications of the system as a whole, rate of rise in the number of castes within increasing village size, and relative heterogeneity of caste structure within the villages of particular locality, are of special importance.[20] The view regarding defilement of inter-caste relations among Hindus in terms of 'relational pollution' follows Louis Dumont's well-known thesis of caste as a system of ideas and norms based on the principle of pollution-purity.

Realising the difficulties of an attributional index McKim Marriott also prefers a 'transactional model' of caste ranking.[21] The perceptions of the villagers (of Kishangarhi) studied by Marriott are validated by their resemblance to the realities and presumed potentialities of the ranking established by food transfer.[22] The multilateral system of transfers is an objective fact for all villagers, hence differences of caste participation and individual membership become insignificant in influencing their opinions.

Marriott stretches this thesis too far to explain almost every aspect of the caste system including the role of wealth and power in social mobility. He writes: "The multilaterality of interests in food transactions appears to be a principal reason for the conservation of the system. A change in the transactions

19. Lewis, Oscar, 1958, *Village Life in Northern India*, Urbana, The University of Illinois Press.
20. Schwartzberg, Joseph R., 1996, 'Caste Regions of the North Indian Plain', in Milton Singer and Bernard S. Cohn (eds), *Structure and Change in Indian Society*, Jaipur and Delhi, Rawat Publications.
21. Marriott, McKim, 1996, 'Caste Ranking and Food Transactions: A Matrix Analysis', in Milton Singer and Bernard S. Cohn (eds), *Structure and Change in Indian Society*, Jaipur and Delhi, Rawat Publications.
22. Ibid., p. 169.

of any one caste may affect the relative standing of any other caste, and a change of relative rank can never be in the interests of everyone".[23] Reciprocity is so well founded in the food transaction that it restrains change between castes in many pairs. Wealth and power find their manifestation outside the transactional domain. Marriott presents his model as an instrument to understand access to dominance by feeding others or by being fed. It is an explanation of being 'high' and 'low', as it is a model of stratified transactions and representations of the constituents of a given caste structure.

Several conclusions follow from this explanation of caste ranking. Since inter-caste relations become the bedrock of society, an organic model for understanding it gains pre-eminence. The supremacy of a normative approach embodied in the notions of pollution-purity, ritual distance and hypergamy subordinates an independent inquiry into crucible of caste. So strong is the facade of this particular point of view that everything is viewed holistically and functionally. Though antinomies or polarities like 'high' and 'low', 'pure' and 'impure', 'pollution' and 'purity', are accepted as 'binary opposition', but the principle of the superiority of pure over impure engulfs all aspects of social life as subordinate phenomena. The entrenchment of this framework into the minds of the proponents of an exclusive Indian ethnosociology calls for a heretical imperative to know the real face of the caste system.

Some studies even of the 1970s and 1980s have lent support to the culturological explanation of caste. In these studies too, commensality and rules of marriage remain central features in caste ranking. Jonathan P. Parry, in his study of caste and kinship in Kangara, observes that each caste is associated with a set of customs and a style of life of greater or lesser purity and prestige governing inter and intra caste relations.[24] The whole of Kangara society is seen by Parry in

23. Ibid.

24. Parry, Jonathan P., 1979, *Caste and Kinship in Kangra*, London, Routledge & Kegan Paul.

terms of a series of oppositions such as junior/senior agnates, wife-givers/wife-takers, low castes/high castes, and men/gods. The 'encompassing' ideology of hierarchy permeates every sphere of social life including the subordination of the tenant to his landlord and of the subject to his ruler.[25] However, unlike Dumont, Parry argues that hierarchy inevitably implies equality within the hierarchically ranked units.[26] But this enchantment for inherent equality in inequality is somewhat superficial because hierarchical relations overshadow egalitarian ties. Though segmentation and equality coexist, but the two are ideologically subordinated to the superior principle of hierarchy. Such a frame of reference, namely, give and take or what Gloria Goodwin Raheja calls *len-den,* and *dan* (gift) remains central to the understanding of the nature of caste dominance, caste hierarchy and inter-caste relations.[27] This is why at the end of the 20th century caste is found as an *avatar*, subordinating women, economy, political power, religion, social movements, etc., by its stupor in all domains of Indian society.[28] Such a story of the 'super-organic' nature of caste is fondly repeated in several studies of social stratification despite what Marriott calls the uneven 'elaboration' of the caste system in different regions of India.[29]

III

It is undeniably admitted today that a 'caste model' of Indian society is not only inadequate to embrace its social reality, it has also become defunct as an ideological framework to map

25. Ibid., p. 6.
26. Ibid., p. 315.
27. Raheja, Gloria Goodwin, 1988, *The Poison in the Gift, Ritual, Presentation, and the Dominant Caste in a North Indian Village*, Chicago, The University of Chicago Press.
28. Srinivas, M.N., 1996, op. cit.
29. Marriott, McKim, 1960, *Caste Ranking and Community Structure in Five Regions of India and Pakistan*, Poona, Deccan College.

the ground level situation. Caste as a 'resource' has gained acceptance across the country. Violation of commensal regulations and even connubial norms in certain quarters is being tolerated without infliction of punitive measures.[30] Inter-caste competition and rivalry noted by Leach almost forty years ago have reached unprecedented heights.[31] Inter-caste solidarity has disappeared. Intra-caste economic and political disparities and inequalities have not only weakened the ideational foundation of the caste system, but have also paved a way for the formation of both new alliances and boundaries in the village community. It is not simply a change *in* inter-caste relations, but a change *of* the system of inter-caste relations.

As an empirical reality caste needs to be located in specific contexts as a source of social placement and as an instrument of identity. Some questions follow from this. Is caste an interest group? Can common interests bring together smoothly men of different castes from various regions than those of the same caste? What are the modalities being practised for using caste as an instrument of socio-cultural and political mobilisations? Are caste conflicts also class conflicts and vice versa?

The caste-class nexus approach assumes caste and class as mutually inherent phenomena. The preceding questions could be responded to, by focusing on the understanding of structure, culture, history and dialectics of India's social formation. The word 'nexus' refers to a set of ties/connections effecting structural and cultural changes. "Nexus does not

30. Sharma, K.L., 1986, *Caste, Class & Social Movements*, Jaipur Rawat Publications; Sharma, K.L., 1986 (ed.), *Social Stratification in India*, New Delhi, Manohar Publications; and Sharma, K.L., 1997, *Social Stratification in India: Issues and Themes*, New Delhi, Sage Publications.

31. Leach, E.R., 1960, 'Introduction: What should we mean by caste?', in E.R. Leach (ed.), *Aspects of Caste in South India, Ceylon and North-West Pakistan*, Cambridge, Cambridge University Press, pp. 1–10.

imply a correspondence or symmetry between caste and class. Interdependence, contradictions, symmetry and hegemony of social relations are integral features of nexus as a frame of reference."[32] Formulations of caste stratification such as a system of 'ideas and values',[33] as a 'closed system',[34] and as an 'unique system'[35] reaffirm the colonial perception[36] of the caste system as a functional and harmonic arrangement of social relations. A few studies focusing on the 'multiple criteria',[37] 'levels of caste dominance',[38] and 'levels of mobility in the caste system, structural process of change and downward mobility'[39] have shattered the facade of the ideological canopy of the caste system.

Caste-class nexus approach also brings out the inter-connections of caste, kinship, family and marriage with the forces and relations of production.[40] Caste conflicts are

32. Sharma, K.L., 1996, *Rural Society in India*, Jaipur and Delhi, Rawat Publications; Sharma, K.L., 1996, 'Conceptualisation of Caste-Class Nexus as an Alternative to Caste-Class Dichotomy', in A.R. Momin (ed.), *The Legacy of G.S. Ghurye: A Centennial Festschrift*, Bombay, Popular Prakashan, pp. 130–46.
33. Dumont, Louis, 1972, *Homo Hierarchicus*, London, Paladin, Granada Publishing Ltd.
34. Bailey, F.G., 1963, 'Closed Social Stratification in India', *European Journal of Sociology*, Vol. 4, No. 1, pp. 107–24.
35. Srinivas, M.N., 1952, *Religion and Society among the Coorgs of South India*, Oxford, Clarendon Press; Srinivas, M.N., 1959, 'The Dominant Caste in Rampura', *American Anthropologist*, Vol. LXI, No. l, pp. 1–16; Srinivas, M.N., 1962, *Caste in Modern India*, Bombay, Asia Publishing House, Srinivas, M.N., 1996, op. cit.; Mathur, K.S., 1964, *Caste and Ritual in a Malwa Village*, Bombay, Asia Publishing House; and Marriott, McKim, 1960, op. cit.
36. Hutton, J.H., 1946, *Caste in India*, Oxford, Oxford University Press.
37. Hazlehurst, Leighton, W., 1968, 'Multiple Status Hierarchies in Northern India', *Contributions to Indian Sociology* (n.s.), No. II, pp. 38–57.
38. Dube, S.C., 1968, 'Caste, Dominance and Factionalism', *Contributions to Indian Sociology* (n.s.), No. II, pp. 58–81; Gardner, Peter M., 1968, 'Dominance in India: A Reappraisal', *Contributions to Indian Sociology*, New Series, No. II, pp. 83–97.
39. Sharma, K.L., 1969, 'Stresses in Caste Stratification', *Economic and Political Weekly*, Vol. IV, No. 3.
40. Gough, Kathleen, E., 1980, 'Modes of Production in Southern India', *Economic and Political Weekly*, Vol. XI, Nos. 5, 6 & 7.

taken as class conflicts.[41] Manifestations like caste as an effective system of economic exploitation[42], and as a means of access to political power[43] are indicative of the weakening of the inter-caste relations. Contextualisation of caste[44] rather than its grandiose application highlights the ramifications of its practice.

At times it becomes difficult to distinguish between caste and class dimensions. Elsewhere I have noted that Jat Sabha, Kishan Sabha, Vaishya Sabha, Kshatrsiya Mahasabha and Bhooswami Sangh[45] in Rajasthan connote both caste and class. Jat Sabha is simultaneously both a caste association and a peasant organisation. Kisan Sabha though seems to be a wider forum of peasants, but in the Shekhawati region of Rajasthan it had overwhelmingly Jat members; hence it functioned as a caste organisation. Bhooswami Sangh was formed in the early 1950s in Rajasthan to protect the interests of the landed people in the wake of land reforms, but it restricted its membership to Rajputs, hence, it was a caste organisation. Such a logic applied to other organisations as well, namely, Vaishya Sabha and Kshatriya Mahasabha.

41. Namboodiripad, E.M.S., 1979, 'Caste Conflicts v/s Growing Unity of Popular Democratic Forces,' *Economic and Political Weekly*, Vol. XV (AN), Nos. 5, 6 & 7, pp. 329–36; Ranadive, B.T., 1979, 'Caste, Class and Property Relations', *Economic and Political Weekly*, Vol. XV (AN), Nos. 5, 6 & 7, pp. 337–48; and Singh, Hira, 1979, 'Kin, Caste and Kisan Movement in Marwar: Some Questions to the Conventional Sociology of Kin and Caste', *Journal of Peasant Studies*, Vol. 7, No. 2.
42. Mencher, Joan P., 1974, 'The Caste System Upside Down, or The Not-so Mysterious East', *Current Anthropology*, Vol. 15, No. 4.
43. Rudolph, Lloyd, I. and Rudoplh, Hoeber Susanne, 1967, 'The Modernity of Tradition', *Political Development in India*, Chicago, Chicago University Press; Rudolph L.I. and Rudolph, Hoeber Susanne, 1987, 'In Pursuit of Lakshmi', *The Political Economy of the Indian State*, Bombay, Orient Longman Ltd.; Kothari, Rajni, 1970, *Politics in India*, New Delhi, Orient Longman Ltd.; and Kothari, Rajni, (ed.), 1970, *Caste in Indian Politics*, New Delhi, Orient Longman Ltd.
44. Searee-Chatterjee, M. and Sharma, U.M., 1994, 'Introduction', in M. Searee-Chatterjee, and U.M. Sharma (eds), *Contextualizing Caste Post-Dumontian Approaches*, Oxford, Blackwell.
45. Sharma, K.L., 1996, op. cit.

Caste and class divide was never rigid even in ancient India because society was not rigidly structured.[46] The existence of 'mixed castes' and the hiatus between 'actual status' and 'ritual status' made social mobility possible in ancient India. Status incongruities in the ancient period[47] and emphasis on production rather than kinship[48] signified not only the dynamic nature of Indian society; but an urge for equality and social mobility was well conceived by the people both in thought and action. No debate on inequality can ignore the element of equality as an important component of all human societies and of social movements therein.[49] Efforts to delegitimise and derecognise the established and exclusive institutional mechanisms and privileges have a long trajectory in the form of social movements and legislations. A systematic account of discontinuities, breakdowns, contradictions and changes can bring out the 'relational' character of both inequality and equality *vis-a-vis* caste and class dimensions.

Both inequality and equality were built into the ideology and practice of the caste system. Some balancing mechanisms as devices were incorporated in the caste system. For example, both Brahmins and some lower and untouchables castes were required to perform certain rituals on specific occasions, and both were paid as 'priests' in cash and kind for services they rendered. The priest (Brahmin) and the 'contra-priest'[50] were involved in the ritual performances,

46. Thapar, Romila, 1974, 'Social Mobility in Ancient Indian Society', in R.S. Sharma (ed.), *Indian Society: Historical Probings*, New Delhi, Peoples Publishing House, pp. 95–123.
47. Chakravarti, Uma, 1985, 'Towards a Historical Sociology of Stratification in Ancient India: Evidence of Buddhist Sources', *Economic and Political Weekly*, Vol. XX, No. 9.
48. Kosambi, D.D., 1958, *An Introduction to the Study of Indian History*, Bombay, Popular Book Depot.
49. Sharma, K.L. (ed.), 1994, *Caste and Class in India*, Jaipur, Rawat Publications.
50. Gould, Harold A., 1967, 'Priest and Contrapriest: A Structural Analysis of Jajmani Relations in the Hindu Plains and the Nilgiri Hills', *Contributions to Indian Sociology* (n.s.), No. 1.

though of an unsimilar nature, hence a sort of 'equality' prevailed. But then they have remained Brahmin and lower caste, pure and impure or not so pure, high and low, hence inequality was a legitimised phenomenon. The two performances were also unequally valued. However, both were seen as essential to the community.

The actual functioning of *kamins* (lower caste functionaries) is another example of the semblance of inequality and equality in the caste system. Was this facade of 'equality' created to legitimise caste as an icon of the lower castes? Though the *kamins* such as barbers, carpenters, blacksmiths, washermen, potters were inferior to their upper caste *jajmans* (patrons), but at the same time the patrons could not annoy and dissatisfy the *kamins* by way of violating established norms of payment and *inam* (reward) in lieu of their services. Several instances of withdrawal of services by *kamins* have occurred due to inadequate and irregular payments and humiliation by the patrons.[51] The *biradaris* of the *kamins* would not allow substitution of services by other fellow functionaries. Generally, an agreement would follow on the terms and conditions favourable to the aggrieved functionaries. Such aspects relating to inequality-equality intrigue, violation of norms, tensions and conflict resolutions require deeper analysis.

IV

A comparative study of six villages in Rajasthan[52] selected two each from Sikar, Jaipur and Bharatpur districts based on historical, cultural and structural variations and multiple status determinants show that caste, class and power hierarchies were visibly independent of each other. Family and its influential members rather than caste were ranked having high and low status rather than caste/*jati* as a whole. Some families were

51. Sharma, K.L., 1974, op. cit.
52. Ibid.

considered equal or more equal than others across the caste boundaries. Access to economic, political and cultural sources of status and prestige were more crucial than birth, ascription and ancestory.

The example of Roopgarh, a remote village (one of the six villages), situated at a distance of 35 kilometres south of Sikar town may be cited. In the mid-1960s the village was not linked by road with the district and *tehsil* headquarters. Traditional means of transport were in vogue. However, some government institutions and offices started functioning in the village in 1953. The first one was a single teacher primary school. About 1,500 people of the village (including the twin village of Tehat) belonged to 16 castes, of which Jats, Regars (shoemakers), Balais (an untouchable caste), Brahmins, and Kumhars were numerically preponderant in the descending order. Being a former *jagirdari* village, the Thakur and Bhomias enjoyed immense status and power till 1954 when the *jagirdari* system was abolished. With the exception of some Banias and Brahmins most families of other castes had no *pucca* houses until the 1950s. The ex-jagirdar *also known as Sardar/Thakur Saheb*, being the chief of his *jagir*, owned a citadel on the hilltop, a palace (*mahal*) in the foothills, and another vast mansion in the outskirts of the village. Most castes lived in segregated enclaves. *Jajmani* relations were the pivot around social and economic life of the village revolved. But by the mid-1960s cracks in the functioning of the system had become quite visible.

Rajputs, Banias, and Jats never served other castes as constituents of the *jajmani* system. Though the Brahmins served as priests for all the castes except 'untouchables' and some very low castes and Muslims, but they were never equated with the *kamin* castes like carpenters, potters and barbers. When some of the functionary castes served other equal or inferior castes on the basis of *jajmani* arrangements they were not treated as *kamins*. Exchange of services among functionary castes was also a socially recognised reciprocity. *Jajman-kamin* relations despite being an essential element in the village community were not the sole basis of ritual ranking or caste stratification. Functional inevitability of reciprocal exchanges and *jajmani* relations could be explained in terms of the absence of requisite markets and means of transport and communication. The superior castes enjoying urban contacts and resources depended less on the local arrangements.

During the last two and half decades the scene in Roopgarh has acquired a new look. Except the Nai (barber), no other functionary caste is found working in the village. The barber too serves minimally to a select group of families. Most of the members of the extended clan of barbers have moved out of the village as far as Ahmedabad to work in cotton mills and saloons in the nearby towns. Potters and carpenters have switched to commercial transactions even on the occasions of marriage and death. Migration from among the lower castes such as Balais and Regars has led to their economic betterment. Most of them today own *pucca* houses. The fact is that it is rare to find a *kuchcha* house in Roopgarh.

For the last several years Roopgarh is linked with the district and *tehsil* headquarters by tarred *pucca* road. The village primary school has been upgraded to a senior secondary school. A private middle school as well as a government primary school also function in the village. The institutional complex has expanded. Some families of the middle and lower castes have settled down on the roadside. Two tea stalls have come up. Education has spread far and wide among various castes, whereas earlier it was restricted mainly to Brahmins and Banias. About ten school teachers belong to the Regar community (an untouchable caste of shoemakers). A couple of years ago a Jat student from the village was President of the Government Postgraduate College at Sikar. Currently, another postgraduate student, son of a Regar school teacher, is General Secretary of the Students Union in the same college.

In the 1960s there was one postgraduate and three graduates in the village. Today, there are several postgraduates, graduates, engineering graduates and two PhDs. The boom in higher education has brought about migration and social mobility. Exodus among upper castes, in particular, to nearby towns, seeking government jobs, has witnessed a phenomenal expansion. Earlier, upper caste members, though not highly educated, used to migrate to far off towns such as Calcutta, Guwahati, Kanpur, Ahmedabad and Bombay to work as shop-assistants (*munims*). A good number of early migrants have settled in these places. The second generation of migrants is a mixed group consisting of highly educated, and college and school drop-outs. The highly educated upper caste members have generally been in lucrative jobs such as civil services, engineering service, teaching and research, trade and commerce, whereas the less educated ones after failing to secure government jobs, migrated to remote places using their traditional Marwari connections to work as assistants in the private establishments. Some members of the latter category have, however, become sub-contractors and independent small-scale traders and businessmen.

Strains in the *jajmani* system, as well as in the ideology and practice of caste were visible even in the mid-1960s. The abolition of the *jagirdari* system and a complete withdrawal by the ex-*jagirdar* from village affairs severely affected the functioning of the system. Out-migration by Brahmins and Banias marginalised the upper caste patrons as receivers of functional services from the *kamin* castes. Except one, all the Jain-Banias migrated to far off places such as Kanpur, Patna, Calcutta, Ranchi and Raipur. One family shifted to the salt town of Sambhar. All of them have so far done very well in establishing independent enterprises. They have built modern houses, established factories, companies, etc. and have now stopped visiting the village. This has happened in the last twenty-five years. Similarly, the Brahmins, with lucrative government services, have settled down in towns like Sikar, Jaipur, Kota and Ajmer. The educated among the peasant and lower castes have not succeeded in settling down outside the village. However, some of them have accumulated property in the village in the form of ornaments, *pucca* houses, agricultural land and equipments like tractors and jeeps.

Electrification of the village nearly twenty-five years ago brought about 'green revolution' in the village. Several electric pumpsets were installed. Five Brahmins took advantage of this new facility. Besides wheat, gram and mustard, some cash crops are grown. The biggest beneficiaries are, however, the Jats. Education, white-collar employment and migration still elude the Jat peasants. Economic prosperity and political power enjoyed by the Jats is disproportionate to their numerical strength. Intellectual achievement among the Jats of the village is almost negligible.

The structure of both inter-caste and intra-caste relations is no more the basis of caste hierarchy, division of labour and asymmetrical power relations. About forty-five years ago an upper caste family was ostracised on account of presumed illicit relations of a woman with her father-in-law. After a gap of nearly fifteen years the family was allowed to rejoin the caste. No such action has been taken in the village since this incident. But splits, mainly based on political equations and alignments, have occurred followed by severance of social interactions such as attending rituals relating to marriage and death. The factional splits are not just an intra-caste phenomenon, the village has remained divided vertically due to splits in the major castes, namely, Brahmins, Jats and Regars. Extensions of the divides could be seen in their alignments with the political parties such as Congress, BJP and CPI(M).

The changed political scene has repercussions on the intra-caste relations. Two Brahmins and one Jat (a *de jure* nominee of the dominant Brahmins) controlled the *panchayat* for nearly thirty years from 1953 to 1973. In the last fifteen years, two Jats, representing two factions, have been competing for power in local institutions. A Brahmin settled in Sikar tried in vain, as a nominee of one of the Jat leaders to capture the office of Sarpanch. He was opposed by members of his own lineage being on the other side of power politics. Not only intra-caste rivalries but open intralineage oppositions have become a way of life in the power game.

Such structural changes affecting the traditional pattern of inter-caste and intra-caste relations could be witnessed from the advent of village panchayat in the early 1950s. Sanskritisation has never been a visible and strong process of change in the village. Discarding of traditional occupations such as removal of carcass, midwifery and shoemaking is the only instance of the so-called process of sanskritisation. Recently, some of the very well off Jats imitated Brahmins in regard to dowry and marriage reception. Whether cultural change is followed by manifest or latent structural change or structural change is followed by cultural change—needs to be thoroughly explored. Are they not complimentary phenomena? The present scenario in Roopgarh relating to inter-caste and intra-caste relations may throw light on the caste-class divide and the caste-class complementarity/ segmentation.

It seems that caste has lost much of its aura and appeal due to a multiplicity of factors. Family-centred relations within and between castes have replaced the inter-caste and intra-caste relations. Each separate caste has undergone a noticeable process of social and economic differentiation. Among the Brahmins such a differentiation has been caused by modern education, white-collar jobs and effective urban connections. Banias and Brahmins have moved up substantially in the economic field, but without corresponding social honour and recognition. Since the white-collar government jobs are diverse and differentiated in regard to social honour and emoluments, corresponding 'class configurations' have emerged among the upper castes. Such social and economic gradations have also been witnessed among the Jats. A small number of 'tractor capitalists'[53] have emerged among the Jat peasants. Below them are the 'bullock capitalists'[54]. Due to availability of tractor on hire bullocks have disappeared. A similar pattern of gradation characterises the Regars of Roopgarh. Employment in the Gulf countries, benefits accruing from reservation policy, and enhanced viability of the traditional occupation of shoemaking have brought about class-like gradations among the Regars.

V

The traditional pattern of inter-caste and intra-caste ties is being realised as an anachronistic and superfluous institution particularly by the middle and lower castes. The formation of political and social alliances based on the intra-caste economic and social configurations speak volumes for redundancy of inter-caste relations. Status rivalries and aspirations for political power have contributed to such a formation. Extension of patronage and distribution of favours attract people to join these configurations. The gatherings on social occasions are, therefore, not restricted to members of one's own caste. It is a common sight to observe practically members of all castes attending celebrations at the houses of the leaders of such alliances.

Conspicuous expenditure on marriage processions, feasts, and festivals rewards social recognition, which the people tactfully translate into political gains. Bourdieu rightly characterises such a situation by transformation of 'social capital' into 'political capital'.[55] A new pattern of stratification demonstrating empirically its class, status, and power dimensions

53. Rudolphs, 1967, op. cit.

54. Ibid.

55. Bourdieu, Pierre, 1991, *Language and Symbolic Power*, Cambridge, Polity Press.

in place of caste as an ideological all-encompassing construction has become a part of everyday life. Caste 'for itself', as a means of social mobilisation based on primordial sentiments, is still persisting with an illusory vision of inter-caste and intra-caste relations. But the intra-caste differentiations and family-based social and political configurations put limits on such primordial mobilisations. Caste-based support or caste-centred exclusivity not only restricts broadening of social base of individuals and families in a given context, but are also incongruent with the demands of the present-day status determinants.

How does a given caste move up in social hierarchy? The illustration of Kanbis from Jan Berman's study of South Gujarat (1985) is partly in consonance with my argument. The Kanbis were earlier ordinary peasants with a caste-based organisation, but they are known today as Patidars and enjoy rural dominance. A new organisation—Yuvak Mandal—organised activities such as the spread of education, initiation of social reforms and steps for abolishing harmful customs and traditions, mobilisation and cultivation of public opinion and protection of the interests of farmers. None of these activities were concerned with the revival and rejuvenation of declining practices relating to the Kanbis as a caste. Kanbis are a typical upwardly mobile caste. The Mandal organised caste gatherings, an *ashram* (hostel) for students at Surat, and started the publication of its own magazine. Breman rightly refers to the Kanbi *patidars* as a class in a caste-setting, a caste 'for itself'. Caste-class divide or antinomy loses its significance in such a situation. Caste 'for itself' and the incorporation of the Kanbis into the world market as producers of cotton were found in considerable harmony.

A couple of years ago, one of the Jats in Roopgarh, after having consolidated his economic standing, entered the political arena. He became Sarpanch of the village panchayat, and the president of the cooperative society. An influential Brahmin, who had carved out a niche for himself as a leader, supported the Jat leader. In course of time the Jat leader became an acknowledged political figure in the panchayat samiti. His rise in politics, besides his elevated economic standing, accentuated rivalries within the ranks of his own caste. Two young leaders who were far more educated started opposing him. Ultimately, the two opponents combined, though they claimed affinities with two diagonally opposed political parties, namely, the BJP and the CPI(M). Coming together of these two Jat leaders with the support of another Brahmin led to the defeat of his nominee, an SC woman for the office of the Sarpanch in the panchayat elections (held after the implementation of the 73rd Constitutional Amendment).

From the situation in Roopgarh two inferences can be drawn: (1) inter-caste and intra-caste relations no more provide a fundamental basis for social stratification, networking of social relations go beyond caste and lineage ties; and (2) power alliances tend to ignore both party affiliations and caste allegiances at the village level. Besides social and economic standing, other important status determinants are: lifestyle, political networks, connections with bureaucrats and influential people at the block, district and state levels. The successful Jat leader mentioned above spent conspicuously on the marriages of his sister and daughter. Items like motorcycle, Maruti car, gold ornaments, television, refrigerator, etc., were given in dowry. A typical Brahmin-Bania pattern of conspicuous expenditure was reflected in some of the recently organised social events in upwardly mobile Jat families as well as in some other communities. The 'tractor capitalist' Jat leader encashing on his political networks and connections with officials has acquired Public Works Department contracts to construct roads. Besides owning a jeep for his personal use and a fleet of tractors for hire, he has acquired some property, namely, a plot of land and shops in the district town. He is getting his children educated outside the village.

Narain Singh, a Congress MLA and DCC chief and formerly a cabinet minister and president of Zila Parishad, blessed him in his political endeavours. The local influential Brahmin family's support has proved to be a real political initiation for social mobility. A contest for the post of Vice-President of the District Cooperative Bank, which he unfortunately lost by just one vote, was a pinnacle of his political trajectory. Here is a person with only primary-level education who has risen socially, economically and politically much ahead of others, many of whom were ahead of him on several counts.

Some time ago, three elderly Brahmins died in the village. Elaborate death feasts were arranged inviting all the villagers irrespective of their castes, and some chosen families of different castes from the nearby villages were also invited. Some members of other castes and the Jat leader and his followers were active in making arrangements. Even the lineage members were relegated to the background. The persons active on these occasions were on the side of the Brahmins. The others who tried to come to the front stage were outclassed by their opponents. It was clearly an enactment of power-game. Likewise, the influential Brahmins play a leading role on such occasions in the families of other castes. Thus, dominance and reciprocity characterise the emerging pattern of social stratification.

VI

"What should we mean by caste?"[56] is the persisting perennial question. The systems of social stratification in South India, Ceylon and North-West Pakistan are referred by Leach as caste systems because all of them are similar in certain very fundamental ways to the ideal pattern of Hindu caste organisation.[57] Leach, while agreeing with Frederick Barth,[58] observes that the

56. Leach, E.R., 1960, op. cit.

57. Ibid., p. 5.

58. Barth, Frederick, 1960, 'The System of Social Stratification in Swat, North Pakistan', in E.R. Leach (ed.), *Aspects of Caste in South India, Ceylon and North-West Pakistan*, Cambridge, Cambridge University Press, pp. 113–146.

similarity of the three regions or rather situations is a matter of structure rather than culture.[59] There is no syndrome of common cultural traits. While disagreeing with Barth's view regarding caste as a structural phenomenon having world-wide application, Leach considers caste as a particular species of structural organisation indissolubly linked with a pan-Indian civilisation. Leach concurs with Dumont's view that the specific character of caste system lies in the peculiar nature of the systematic organisation itself. Leach may be right in his observation that caste as a structural phenomenon is context-specific rather than a worldwide phenomenon. But his formulation regarding inter-caste relations is not convincing. He writes: "In fact, a caste does not exist by itself. A caste can only be recognised in contrast to other castes with which its members are closely involved in a network of economic, political and ritual relationships. Furthermore, it is precisely with these inter-caste relationships that we are concerned when we discuss caste as a social phenomenon."[60] Thus, according to Leach, caste is an organic system, a system of division of labour and economic interdependence stressing upon hierarchy and the exclusiveness of caste separation. The class organised societies, social status and economic security go together, whereas in a caste society, status and security are polarised.[61]

Leach, like many other western scholars, is wrong as he too posits caste and class as antithetical polar opposite systems. He observes: "My own view is that wherever caste groups are seen to be acting as corporations in competition against like groups of different castes, then, they are acting in defiance of caste principles."[62] Thus, for Leach "caste is a system of interrelationship and that every caste in a caste system has its special privileges".[63] Leach along with the

59. Leach, E.R., 1960, op. cit., p. 5.
60. Ibid.
61. Ibid., p. 6.
62. Ibid., p. 7.
63. Ibid., p. 10.

contributors of the volume ignores the historical fact of status incongruities within the members of a caste and between different castes.[64] Rivalries for status and power, feuds and fights, and migration and mobility were not uncommon in ancient, medieval, and the British periods.[65]

Numerical preponderance along with overwhelming control of land determined dominance of a caste.[66] Widely ramifying connections in most spheres of life, extending right upto some of the most powerful positions within the state, provided opportunities for social mobility. But Harriss also falls in line with the sociologists of the earlier genre. He writes: "People in Random village still experience the world primarily in terms of caste: for caste is a structure in the empirical sense that it defines actual groups of people and supplies norms which guide their interactions; while it also underlies the systems of meaning through which they interpret the world and perceive themselves in relation to it."[67] After having said all this Harriss states that 'caste' may not be the only system of meaning, but it is a dominant one giving coherence to the totality of relationships. Meillassoux[68] criticises not only such structural-functionalist and structuralist analyses, but also believes that within a class society, 'caste system' persists in the form of status relationships and status ideology. The code and substance of caste need to be seen separately to know the nature of caste interactions at the ground level. Harriss does

64. Ibid.

65. Thapar, Romila, 1974, op. cit., pp. 95–123; Stein, Burton, 1968, 'Social Mobility and Medieval South Indian Sects', in James Silverberg (ed.), *Social Mobility in the Caste System in India*, The Hague, Mouton Publishers, pp. 78–94; Panikkar, K.M., 1955, *Hindu Society at the Cross Roads*, Bombay, Asia Publishing House.

66. Harriss, John, 1982, *Capitalism and Peasant Farming, Agrarian Structure and Ideology in Northern Tamil Nadu*, New Delhi, Oxford University Press, pp. 42–56.

67. Ibid., p. 214.

68. Meillassoux, C., 1973, 'Are there castes in India', *Economy and Society*, Vol. III, No. 1, p. 108.

not ultimately consider even departures from the dominant meaning system of caste. The opposition of purity and pollution provides the logic of caste interactions. Class relations are also important in actual structure of social relationships. Caste structure rests upon relations of appropriation of surplus by the dominant caste. The relations of production are given a particular meaning in caste ideology, hence they are included within the caste structure.[69]

The analysis by Breman[70] considerably resembles with my own observations. According to Breman, economic differentiation has led to incongruity between caste and class position lending to an indeterminate and disintegrated character to social organisation.[71] Recognition of the *ujliparaj*, the high-caste moneylenders and landlords, differentiation of peasantry, Halpatis, and differentiation of the top and the bottom economic strata, overshadowing of caste identity by class position, caste-class nexus, and aspirations for social mobility—make Breman's study of south Gujarat relevant in the context of change in the theory and practice of caste.

Today, people in Roopgarh identify themselves as very rich, rich, well-off, not so poor, and poor. Another mode of recognition is found in their perception as 'powerful' and 'weak' families or as 'superior' and 'inferior' people. But, more distinctly, they identify themselves as people engaged in lucrative and prestigious government jobs, as middle and lower level government servants, businessmen, shopkeepers, self-employed, big, middle and small farmers, masons and manual workers. In everyday life every time people do not identify themselves as Brahmins, Rajputs, Banias, Jats, Regars, etc. Caste identities have become increasingly personalised realisations rather than public expressions. The new identities are related to

69. Ibid., p. 227.

70. Breman, Jan, 1985, *Of Peasants, Migrants and Paupers, Rural Labour Circulation and Capitalist Production in West India*, Delhi, Oxford University Press, pp. 361–79.

71. Ibid., p. 362.

the caste/religious affinities and not vice versa, necessarily. A school teacher is identified as such and then he is referred as a Regar, a Khati (carpenter), a Brahmin, etc. Inter-caste relations do not find a platform to stand on in such a situation of identities and perceptions of status.

Economic status, esteem and power are clearly the underlying criteria in these new evaluative expressions of social stratification. Short-lived, episodic and inconsequential expressions of 'casteism', however, could be witnessed, which, in no way, throw light on enduring inter-caste and intra-caste relations. Social relations and equations could simply be disturbed, for example, in favour or against one or other 'configuration' due to election of a member of legislative assembly belonging to a particular political party or as a result of the government headed by a given party at the state level.

Studies of social stratification in the 1960s and the 1970s became problem-oriented. The problems of caste and class exploitation, domination, poverty, alienation and distributive justice were taken up in several studies of social stratification. The main concern was patterning of social relations among people based on a new set of norms and practices going beyond mere caste-based structuring of social ranking.[72] A number of essays[73] highlight on the contradictions within the caste system and the influence of external forces of change ruling out the possibility of caste as homo hierarchicus system. A long history of resilience, discontinuities, breakdowns, contradictions and change in the caste system negates caste as organic, holistic and all-encompassing system. Inequality and equality were built into the ideology and practice of the caste system. Several balancing mechanisms were an inherent feature

72. Sharma, K.L., 1986, op. cit., pp. XI-XXVI.
73. Sharma, K.L., 1994, op. cit., and Béteille, André, 1996, 'Caste in Contemporary India', in C.J. Fuller (ed.), *Caste Today*, New Delhi, OUP, pp. 150–179.

of the system. The *kamin* castes had certain safeguards to protect themselves against the injustices meted out to them by the upper caste patrons. Additionally, anti-upper caste movements lent a support to such balancing mechanisms. Most of these essays address the new form of caste, both intended and unintended changes in the ideology and practice of caste, caste-class nexus, social mobility (both upward and downward), and new constructions of caste such as 'forward', 'backward', 'dalit', etc. Emergence of a 'rich peasant class', white-collar employment, accentuation of the country-town nexus, politicisation of caste identity, varying patterns of social mobility,[74] and continuity of tradition and simultaneous emergence of modernity, determination of social relations, nature and direction of social change, and co-existence of the value frame, structure and process of social inequality[75] are some of the trends reported in various studies from all over the country.

VII

Thus, caste is no more an object or an end in itself. It has become a dormant and passive phenomenon in everyday life; but on certain given occasions momentarily it becomes active, a sort of means for mobilisation, and a resource for having access to political power. Hence, an appropriate

74. Sharma, K.L., 1994, op. cit.
75. Sharma, K.L., (ed.) 1995, *Social Inequality in India*, Jaipur and New Delhi, Rawat Publications; Béteille, André, 1996, 'Caste in Contemporary India', in C.J. Fuller (ed.), *Caste Today*, New Delhi, OUP, pp. 150–179; Gupta, Dipankar, 1991, 'Continuous Hierarchies and Discrete Castes', in Dipankar Gupta (ed.), *Social Stratification*, New Delhi, Oxford University Press, pp. 110–42; Dirks, N.B., 1992, 'Caste of Mind', *Representations*, Vol. 37, pp. 56–78; Mayer, Adrian, 1996, 'Caste in an Indian Village: Change and Continuity, 1954–1992', in C.J. Fuller (ed.), *Caste Today*, New Delhi, Oxford University Press, pp. 32–64; Orenstein, Henry, 1996, 'Toward a Grammar of Defilement in Hindu Sacred Hindu Law', in Milton Singer and Bernard S. Cohn (eds), *Structure and Change in Indian Society*, Jaipur and Delhi, Rawat Publications.

reconceptualisation of such a situation is inevitable to break the monotony of the conventional meanings attributed to 'caste', 'class' and 'power'.

The 'forwards', the 'upper backwards', the 'lower backwards', the minorities, the scheduled castes, the scheduled tribes, the dalits, the Bahujan Samaj, etc., are a sort of new 'symbolic productions' aiming at redemption from the traditional forces. Such constructions impart the message of opposition to the established hierarchisation. A message of threat and challenge is implicit in the new language to oust the entrenched sections. The path of sanskritisation has become barren as a means of struggle for seeking status and power.

In Roopgarh not even a slightest effort is visible for imitating the upper castes by the Jats and the Regars. Most of the Brahmins have been seeking status and power outside the village and their success in the village is largely dependent upon their networks and resources. The crucible of caste is located in the multi-faceted determinants and situations which are far away from the ideology of pollution-purity and binary-opposition.

Caste clusters rather than individual castes, and multi-faceted conflicts between such clusters in Maharashtra,[76] caste-class nexus in Bihar,[77] the pre-eminence of the principle of division more than the principle of hierarchy[78] are some of the recent observations hinting at the need for a rethinking on the nature of the caste system in India. Pauline Kolenda, based on her restudy of a village in west Uttar Pradesh, analyses changes

76. Kamat, A.R., 1980, 'Politico-economic development in Maharashtra: a review of the post-independence period', *Economic and Political Weekly*, Vol. XV, No. 39, pp. 1627–30, and No. 40, pp. 1669–75.

77. Prasad, Pradhan H., 1979, 'Caste and Class in Bihar', *Economic and Political Weekly*, Vol. XIV (AN), Nos. 1 & 8, pp. 481–84; Das, A.N., 1984, 'Class in itself, Caste for itself: Social Articulation in Bihar', *Economic and Political Weekly*, Vol. XIV, No. 37, pp. 1616–19.

78. Shah, A.M. and Desai, I.P., 1988, An Overview of Caste in Gujarat, *Division and Hierarchy*, Delhi, Hindustan Publishing Corporation.

in the caste system in terms of what she calls 'micro-ideology and micro-utopia'.[79] *Varna* ideology functions merely as a social practice.[80] Desai recognises type of society, role of political power, and social mobility as significant factors to understand social and educational backwardness.[81] Caste plays a minor role in the occupational field. Desai remarks that our minds are possessed by caste. Kolenda[82] examines caste in its totality, and attributes structural factors to the change in the caste system.[83] Hierarchy, hypergamy and endogamy along with difference and competition characterise the caste system.[84] Desai, in his critique of A.M. Shah's view, argues for an empirical view of the caste system. Caste is disintegrating, getting secularised, hence it is a new system of social stratification.

A forceful alternative viewpoint put forward by Kolenda[85] focuses on the changes in discourse on caste over the past three decades. Earlier people used to debate on the issues relating to educational and occupational access for the lower castes and untouchables. The ideas related to equal etiquette and equal rights, inter-caste marriage, utility of the caste system itself and social change are being discussed today by the

79. Kolenda, P., 1989, 'Micro ideology and micro-utopia in Khalapur: Changes in the discourse on caste over thirty years,' *Economic and Political Weekly*, Vol. XXIV, No. 32, pp. 1833–38.
80. Franco, F., Chand, Sherry and Sarvar, V., 1989, 'Ideology as Social Practice: The Functioning of Varna', *Economic and Political Weekly*, Vol. XXIV, No. 47, pp. 2601–12.
81. Desai, I.P., 1984, 'Should 'caste' be the basis for recognising backwardness?', *Economic and Political Weekly*, Vol. XIX, No.
82. Kolenda, Pauline, 1984, op. cit.
83. Kolenda, P., 1986, 'Caste in India since independence', in Dilip K. Basu and Richard Sisson (eds), *Social and Economic Development in India: A Reassessment*, New Delhi, Sage Publications, pp. 106–28.
84. Shah, A.M., 1982, 'Division and hierarchy: An overview of caste in Gujarat', *Contributions to Indian Sociology* (n.s.), Vol. 16, No. 1; 1988, 'A Response to the Critique on 'Division and Hierarchy', in A.M. Shah and I.p. Desai, *Division and Hierarchy*, Delhi, Hindustan Publishing Corporation, pp. 92–133.
85. Kolenda, Pauline, 1989, op. cit., pp. 1833–88.

villagers in a village in west Uttar Pradesh. In Roopgarh very recently two inter-caste marriages in a dominant Brahmin family took place, though both the marriages were solemnised in Jaipur, kinsmen, relatives, caste members and villagers attended the marriages. Hardly anyone tried to make it an issue of a 'grave' violation of the marriage rules. Commensal violations by Brahmins have become quite frequent. Discourse today in Roopgarh centres on the issues relating to salaried government jobs, status and power, education, migration and upward mobility and some other related issues. Caste becomes a feable point of discussion in such a discourse on mundane, everyday life issues. Inter-caste relations have come to an end. A lip service is sometimes paid to such relations without aiming at the realisation of the formal actions.

3 Caste and Class in the Emergence of Dalit Identity and Movement

I

Asymmetry with regard to distributive process implies a scarcity of social goods and services. Inequality emanating from the legitimisation of this distribution of scarce goods and services causes social unrests, upheavals and even overthrow of such a system. Social movements all over the world, in essence, despite their varying forms, aim at the delegitimisation of the inequalitarian distributive processes and the establishment of a desired type of society which can ensure egalitarian and humanitarian social order. Thus, all social movements strike for a new 'social language', in fact, for new parameters for sustaining the altered social relations. A threat to the persisting 'social stock of knowledge' through an advocacy of new cognitive categories and orientations is seen by the forces of status quo as well as by the harbingers of new ideological moorings. Ultimately, the objective of a new social language is to produce new forms of power and dominance by altering and rejecting the persisting polity and society.

A new social language equips the aspiring groups of people with new beliefs, values and norms. A powerful conceptual tool is thus created for examining dominance in everyday life in all aspects. A social movement is successful if its ideological/cognitive apparatus is powerful enough to bring about commensurate structural changes in society. Hiatus between cognitive and structural processes of change would mean both the power of the status quo forces to persist and to resist the new ideologues, and the limitations of the latter to challenge effectively the entrenched power-wielders.

II

Bryan S. Turner writes about the contemporary situation in South Africa: "The forms of equality we enjoy in modern democracy are to some extent the consequences of violent or radical reaction on the part of subordinate groups to achieve a more equitable distribution of wealth and power."[1] Quintessentially, this may be true about the movements launched by the weaker sections and the other backward classes in India. But, the change has not simply been there due to movements and struggles energised by these sections. India's national movement and its leadership, legislations and the Indian State after independence have made significant contribution in attacking the established socio-cultural, economic and political hierarchies in India. The contemporary efforts towards 'equality' can be seen mainly in terms of 'social consciousness', which is produced historically and nationally.

No debate on inequality can ignore the importance of equality as component of all human societies and social movements therein. Legal derecognition of power and privileges based on birth and caste rank created a sense of equal citizenship and equality of opportunity. Such a major step had a history of 150 years of struggle against the British Raj. The Indian nation-state too gets mirrored through this constitutional provision. A check on the traditionally privileged people

1. Turner Bryan S., 1986, *Equality*, Tavistock Publications and Ellis Howood Ltd., New York, p. 11.

on one hand and encouragement to the sections aspiring for equality to demand their share in national resources on the other have become salient features of the post-independence era. So long as the institutions of private property, family inheritance and recognition of social honour remain, inequality would continue to emanate from them despite constitutional safeguards and provisions for the betterment of the weaker sections. A new vocabulary—a language of equity has considerably made equality as a value,[2] that the achievement of equality is desirable and feasible for the future of Indian State and society.

However, the debate about equality is not a recent one. 'Equal exchange' or 'just exchange' were in a way part of the traditional arrangement of socio-economic ties. Despite patron-client or *jajman-kamin* relations, there were 'contra-priests'[3], who signified the role of the lower caste functionaries and value of their relative equality and power of bargaining. The question was: How they were treated by their patrons? If the expected positive treatment was not meted out to them, what steps they could take to safeguard their social honour. Thus, despite rigidity of caste-based inequality, there were some inbuilt mechanisms for grievance redressal in the system. All anti-caste movements during last one hundred years or so have sought destruction of the established hierarchies and hegemony of the erstwhile privileged sections of society. Replacement of the persisting social order is being sought by a new distributive process and empowerment of the depressed castes and communities by alienating the entrenched groups of people from positions of power and privilege. Can this be done? How it can be done? What has been our experience since 1950? What are the stumbling blocks in the creation of a desired type of society?

2. Ibid., p. 18.
3. Gould, Harold A., 1967, "Priest and Contra-Priest: A Structural Analysis of Jajmani Relationships in the Hindu Plains in Nilgiri Hills", *Contributions to Indian Sociology*, New Series, No. 1.

Let us understand the meaning of inequality. Jean-Jacques Rousseau in his *magnum opus*, *The Social Contract and Discourse on the Origin of Inequality*, observes that 'freedom' is an instrumental value, and it ensures man's happiness.[4] He writes: "The independence of *natural man* assured his freedom and his happy existence. The imposition of society on this natural man created a situation of conflict, inequality, distorted values, and misery."[5] The 'natural man' of Rousseau is considerably similar to Sigmund Freud's 'libido', the innate energy in man, which can prosper if 'culture' keeps itself away from him in the form of an alien control. Such a *spontaneity* is seen as a virtue in man's reflections towards his objects. Articulation of innate consciousness for achieving equality can be realised against oppressive collectivities and individuals.

Rousseau discusses the origin and foundation of inequality among men. He observes: "I conceive two species of inequality among men; one which I call natural, or physical inequality, because it is established by nature, and consists in the difference of age, health, bodily strength, and the qualities of the mind, or of the soul, the other which may be termed moral or political inequality, because it depends on a kind of convention, and is established, or at least authorised by the common consent of mankind. This species of inequality consists in the different privileges, which some men enjoy, to the prejudice of others, such as that of being richer, more honoured, more powerful, and even that of exacting obedience from them."[6] For Rousseau, "morals and politics are inseparable. Both become politics, and every phenomenon has a

4. Rousseau, Jean-Jacques, 1967, *The Social Contract and Discourse on the Origin of Inequality*, edited and with an Introduction by Lester G. Crocker, Washington Square Press, New York, p. XIV. See also K.L. Sharma, *Caste, Class and Social Movements*, 1986, Rawat Publications, Jaipur.

5. Ibid., Introduction.

6. Ibid., p. 175.

political significance. Nothing is neutral or indifferent."[7] Thus, Rousseau emphasises on 'social contract' as a way out for conflict and misery created by political inequality.

R.H. Tawney's observations about inequality seem to be relevant to understand the position of the underdog in the Indian society. He writes: "There are certain gross and crushing disabilities—conditions of life injurious to health, inferior education, economic insecurity with those not similarly afflicted."[8] Certain services can mitigate crucial disabilities to a considerable extent to bring about equality. Turner identifies four types of equality: (1) ontological equality, as the fundamental equality of persons, (2) equality of opportunity to achieve desirable ends, (3) equality of condition(s) of life equal for relevant social groups, and (4) equality of outcome or equality of result.[9] All these forms of equality imply totality of equality in social life. However, the last one refers to the practice of the first three prescriptive formulations, namely, equality of all men, equality of opportunity and that of condition(s). The last refers to the outcome of all the above three postulates. What is tangible or measurable in some way is the equality of outcome/result.

III

In Marxian sense, a dalit can be seen as a 'class' emerging from the dissolution of all classes, a class in civil society and not a class of civil society.[10] Such a class has a universal character because its sufferings are universal, the 'wrong' done to it is also general and not a particular wrong. Such a class has no

7. Crocker's Introduction to Roussean, p. xxi.
8. Tawney, R.H., 1931, *Equality*, Allen Unwin, London, cited from Turner, op.cit., Chapter 2.
9. Turner, op.cit., p. 35.
10. See an intensely argued debate on this in Gail Omvedt, 1994, *Dalits and the Democratic Revolution, Dr. Ambedkar and the Dalit Movement in Colonial India*, New Delhi, Sage Publications, Chapter I, pp. 21-58.

'traditional' status but only a 'human' status. It is a class which seeks a total emancipation from the chains of domination and control. This particular class is known as the proletariat. Although consciousness is determined by the existence and not vice versa, and yet consciousness becomes a means of uniting and mobilising the proletariat. Does such collective consciousness commensurate with the existential conditions of the proletariat? Luckacs puts this point as follows: "For a class to be ripe for hegemony means that its interests and consciousness enable it to organise the whole of society in accordance with those interests. The crucial question in every class struggle is this: Which class possesses this capacity and this consciousness at the decisive moment? This does not preclude the use of force. It does not mean that the class-interests destined to prevail and thus to uphold the interests of society as a whole can be guaranteed an automatic victory. On the contrary, such a transfer of power can often only be brought about by the most ruthless use of force ... But it often turns out that questions of class consciousness prove to be decisive in just those situations where force is unavoidable and where classes are locked in a life-and-death struggle."[11] Can one perceive the dalits and caste Hindus in such a situation of class struggle? In recent years the questions of 'social justice' and 'empowerment' of the weaker sections and the OBCs by providing reservations in jobs have been made central concerns of power politics in India. Social divides and tensions, arising out of the articulation and the opposition of these questions, have tormented the Indian political scene. Social and cultural deprivation of the backward sections of society prevented them from having access to their anticipated share in the national resources and heritage.

Can dalits be treated as a thing, a component of Indian

11. Luckacs, Georg, 1971, *History and Class Consciousness*, London, Merlin Press, pp. 52–53.

society? Gandhi gave the name 'Harijan' to the 'untouchables'. A sense of compassion and empathy is reflected through the use of the word 'Harijan' as they are God's gift like any other human beings. Compassion and sympathy, though are not taken kindly by the leadership of the Harijans, helped them immensely by way of the policy of 'protective discrimination' and special provisions for their advancement. Thus, Gandhi's Harijans, a human entity, became a legal entity, namely, the scheduled castes. A new class of beneficiaries ('creamy layer') emerged from among them. The articulate leadership of the scheduled castes thought it necessary to create ideological and political militancy, hence dalitism. The word 'dalit', thus, refers to ideological transformation of the scheduled castes indicating their heightened protests against the upper caste domination by way of rejection of the upper caste cognitive paradigms and creation of their own cultural idioms, literature and ethnic harmony.

Though it is quite unclear whether the dalits can be referred as a 'class', but if they are understood as such, what E.P. Thompson observes about 'class' seems to be relevant for analysing the emergence of dalits. He writes: "By class I understand an historical phenomenon, unifying a number of disparate and seemingly unconnected events, both in the raw material of experience and in consciousness. I emphasise that it is a *historical* phenomenon. I do not see class as a 'structure', or even as a 'category', but as something which in fact happens (and can be shown to have happened) in human relationships."[12] Dalits imply a notion of a class (social) in terms of historical relationship. Thompson observes: "This relationship must always be embodied in real people and in a real context."[13] He further writes: "And class happens when some men, as a result of common experiences (inherited or shared),

12. Thompson, E.P., 1984, 'Class Consciousness', in R.S. Neale (ed.), *History and Class*, Oxford, Basil Blackwell, p. 114.

13. Ibid., p. 114.

feel and articulate the identity of their interests as between themselves, and as against other men whose interests are different from (and usually opposed to) theirs. The class experience is largely determined by the productive relations into which men are born or enter involuntarily. Class consciousness is the way in which these experiences are handled in cultural terms: embodied in traditions, value systems, ideas, and institutional forms."[14]

For dalits their relationship with the upper castes/classes, who have socio-economic and political dominance, determines their interests and consciousness. However, interests and consciousness are not the same phenomena, nor they have one-to-one relationship. At different times and places consciousness may differ despite interests remaining the same. In the context of dalits, consciousness is different from what one can see in the case of the scheduled castes and Harijans. Consciousness is now being projected as a main instrument of assertion of the rights of the oppressed people through cultural objects and activities. The question is not simply of bread and butter for the scheduled castes, *izzat* (social honour), lifestyle or social standing, and life chances[15] have become serious concerns of the dalits. Dalits may be referred as a *consciousness community*.[16] Though, Mahars, Mangs and Chamars, for example, have never enjoyed the same status before or after Independence, nor they have been benefited in an equal measure. Since they constitute the class of dalits, hence dalits as a class are not a monolith. However, it does not imply that class and status are unrelated phenomena either conceptually or substantively. What is important to note is that a new 'field of cultural production', 'symbolic goods', mental structures, in

14. Ibid., p. 115.
15. See Max Weber, 1970, "Class, Status and Party", in *From Max Weber: Essays in Sociology*, edited with an introduction, by H.H. Gerth and C. Wright Mills, London, Routledge & Kegan Paul Ltd., pp. 180–95.
16. Max Weber discusses how common class interests can pave a way for communal/community consciousness and action.

other words, what Bourdieu[17] calls 'symbolic power', 'symbolic capital' and 'cultural capital' are being created by the dalits to enhance their economic and political empowerment.

IV

The question of 'social status', at least apparently, has been central with regard to 'untouchables', though their economic standing and political power continue to remain substantive issues in determining their position in Indian society. According to Louis Dumont and several other scholars the principle of purity-impurity is a scaler yardstick, and it operates to keep different castes separate from one another.[18] Differences in the degree of pollution thus create closed segments in terms of inclusion of some and exclusion of other members.[19] All interactions and ties—commensal and connubial, are guided by the principle of pollution-purity. Anti-caste movements were launched initially against such pollution-purity based hierarchisation of caste groups. Violation of the cultural restrictions imposed upon various lower castes resulted into the imitation of the styles of life of the upper castes by the lower castes, and this process of imitation is characterised as sanskritisation.[20] What norms could be violated and to what extent? Who came forward among the 'untouchables' to imitate and thereby threaten the dominance of the upper castes? What was the reaction of the upper castes to such moves of the lower/'untouchable' castes? What were the structural, manifest as well as latent, implications of such symbolic acts for both the upper and the lower

17. See Pierre Bourdieu, 1993, *The Field of Culture Production*, Edited and Introduced by Randal Johnson, Cambridge, Polity Press, Chapters 1 to 3.
18. See Louis Dumont's well-known work, *Homo Hierarchicus*, 1972, London, Paladin.
19. Kolenda, Pauline, *Caste in Contemporary India*, 1984, Rawat Publications, Jaipur, pp. 66–67.
20. See M.N. Srinivas, 1966, *Social Change in Modern India*, Berkeley, University of California Press.

castes? These and some other questions still remain to be analysed adequately.

A study of two villages by Jan Breman (1979) in South Gujarat highlights caste-class nexus and patterns of social mobility among the landowning and the landless communities.[21] Traditionally, there were ideal patron-client relations between the landowning Anavil Brahmins and the landless Dublas, a tribal caste, also known as *halpati*. After the disintegration of the *halpatipratha*, the Dublas are mostly employed as farm servants. Anavil Brahmins have also diversified their occupational base. Dublas have changed much less than their masters. Depersonalisation and depatronisation have occurred as the Anavils are lured by urban occupations and salaried jobs. The traditional right of the Dublas to remain attached to their Anavil landlords is no more considered legitimate. The social security guaranteed by the landlords has disappeared. The Dublas have been changed from subjects to objects.[22] But dependence and subordination of the Dublas persist *vis-à-vis* the Anavil landlords. Breman writes: "The Dublas are increasingly aware of the fact that their subjection is one of the main causes of their low social status. Economic disadvantages aside, weakness and dependence are looked upon as dishonourable and deplorable."[23] They resist the inhuman treatment meted to them and their womenfolk, and yet they feel constrained to remain under the control of the dominant landlords. Subjection of the lower castes has become particularly the main object of contention in the recent dalit movement. Today untouchability and economic exploitation are not the main issues as they used to be before and around the time of independence. What is being asked is empowerment and social justice as a right for the dalits and other backward sections of society.

21. Breman, Jan, 1979, *Patronage and Exploitation: Changing Agrarian Relations in South India*, Manohar, New Delhi.
22. Ibid., p. 221.
23. Ibid., p. 226.

V

'Untouchables' account for about 16 per cent of India's population. The disabilities imposed on them in the past included residential segregation, confinement to polluting and menial occupations and denial of access to temples, wells and other civic amenities.[24] The Constitution of India, under Article 46, promotes educational and economic interests of the weaker sections of the people. Article 17 abolishes the practice of untouchability.[25] Béteille (1992) mentions about three principal rights to equality. These are: (1) equality before the law; (2) prohibition of discrimination on grounds of religion, race, caste, sex or place of birth; and (3) equality of opportunity in matters of public employment.[26] The most important of the three is equality of opportunity. But this becomes a value where a high value is placed on the individual,[27] but this has not been the case in Indian history and society. Hence, there are quotas in education and employment for the weaker sections in Indian society. Equality is therefore more a 'policy' than as a 'right'. Equality as a policy requires special case for its implementation with regard to the depressed sections of society. It is this policy which finds its execution in the constitutional provisions for the welfare of the scheduled castes and the scheduled tribes.

No lower ('untouchable') castes are willing to accept their lower status in the caste hierarchy, but all of them have accepted special favours for their upliftment. In fact, movements have been launched for securing more quotas in education and employment by the scheduled castes and the scheduled tribes.[28]

24. Béteille, André, 1992, *Society and Politics in India: Essays in a Comparative Perspective*, Delhi, Oxford University Press, p. 198.
25. See Durga Das Basu, 1990, Introduction to the Constitution of India (13th edition), New Delhi, Prentice-Hall of India.
26. Béteille, André, op. cit., p. 199.
27. Ibid., p. 202.
28. Freeman, James M., 1986, "The Consciousness of Freedom among India's Untouchables", in Dilip K. Basu and Richard Sisson (eds), *Social and Economic Development in India*, New Delhi, Sage Publications, pp. 153–71.

The same provisions are now being made for the Other Backward Castes as per the recommendations of the Mandal Commission Report.[29] Marc Galanter considers the compensatory discrimination policies as systematic departure from norms of secular equality, a departure from formal equality.[30] The preferences have been extended on a 'communal basis', or as what Beteillè considers equality as policy, and not as a right, has found preference in post-independent India. Galanter refers to three basic types of preferences: (1) reservations, (2) programmes or provision of services, and (3) special protections.[31] Certain such preferences and provisions for the depressed sections attack frontally the causes of the persisting system of social stratification, and hence the structure of the distributive system is inflicted upon by the dynamics of the distributive processes.[32] Is all this enough? If not, what is more? Why has this pattern emerged and come to stay? These questions constrain us to go deep into the debate on India's ex-untouchables.

Discourse on untouchability, Harijans, the scheduled castes and dalits brings Gandhi and Ambedkar in centre. Gandhi was accused of subverting the Hindu social order by way of patronising the Harijans, and was accused by Ambedkar for making only token concessions to the untouchables.[33] Gandhi is blamed for advising the Harijans to find solutions to their problems by remaining under the fold of Hinduism.

29. See Report of the Backward Classes Commission (B.P. Mandal Commission), 1981, Government of India Publications.
30. Galanter, Marc, 1986, "Pursuing Equality: An Assessment of India's Policy of Compensatory Discrimination for Disadvantaged Groups", in Dilip K. Basu and Richard Sisson (eds), op. cit., p. 130. See also Marc Galanter, 1984, *Competing Equalities, Law and the Backward Classes in India*, New Delhi, Oxford University Press.
31. Ibid., pp. 130–31.
32. See, for example, Gerhard Lenski, 1966, *Power and Privilege: A Theory of Social Stratification*, New York, McGraw-Hill Book Company, Chapters 3 & 4.
33. Parekh, Bhikhu, 1989, *Colonialism, Tradition and Reform: An Analysis of Gandhi's Political Discourse*, New Delhi, Sage Publications, p. 207.

Opposition to a separate electorate for the untouchables was vehemently criticised by Ambedkar. Lack of earnestness and sincerity, encouragement to the Hindu hegemony, hypocrisy are attributed to Gandhi with regard to his treatment of the Harijans. Ambedkar, himself an 'untouchable', a talented lawyer, the father of India's Constitution and India's first Law Minister, had serious differences with Gandhi on the question of the Harijans and the strategies for their upliftment. Ambedkar died on December 5, 1956. Before his death, he adopted Buddhism along with hundreds of thousands of untouchables particularly from the state of Maharashtra. The Buddhist movement and the neo-Buddhism are mainly an offshoot of Ambedkar's disenchantment with Hinduism in general and Gandhi's perception of India's 'untouchables',[34] in particular.

Untouchability was essentially perceived by Gandhi as a moral problem, and hence it could be mitigated by changing the heart and mind of the caste Hindus. Gandhi thought of untouchability as a matter of 'shame', 'guilt' and 'sin' for the upper castes rather than simply an ordinary evil. Struggle against untouchability was more than securing equal rights and economic betterment; it was a moral and spiritual struggle.[35] Gandhi asked the caste Hindus to undertake activities for the upliftment of the untouchables to minimise this guilt/sin. Thus, Gandhi was not so much in favour of legislations for the upliftment of the untouchables as he was for regeneration of the value of equality. The organisations and newspapers such as Harijan Sevak Sangh and *Harijan* founded by Gandhi are testimony to this effect.[36] Bhikhu Parekh writes: "Gandhi's contribution was considerable and greater than that of any other Indian leader. No one before him had mounted a frontal attack on untouchability and launched a vigorous

34. Ibid., pp. 207–46.

35. See, for example, Bhikhu Parekh, op. cit. and M.S. Gore, op. cit.

36. Gandhi founded several organisations and newspapers such as Harijan Sevak Sangh and Harijan, etc.

national campaign."[37] He combined moral, religious and political appeals and his own personal example in creating an anti-untouchability ambience. But Gandhi failed to shake social, economic and political roots of untouchability.[38] One can infer that Gandhi was not for bringing in militancy in the anti-untouchability movement, and in fact, he preferred moral and social programmes rather than legislative enactments for the upliftment of the Harijans. However, in post-independent India, the policy of protective discrimination has become a corner stone of India's Constitution.[39]

The shift from the moral and spiritual explanation of untouchability given by Gandhi is seen in the constitutional safeguards and subsequent amendments therein and other legislative enactments. The discourse has acquired a cultural and political character. Competing claims for furtherance of 'Ambedkarism' by different political parties more for political mileage have surfaced during last one decade or so. The nearly forgotten Ambedkar has suddenly become politically alive and vibrant. He is now everywhere, in parliament, political parties, central secretariat, universities, research institutes and NGOs. Statues of Ambedkar have mushroomed in both small and big towns. Efforts are on to monopolise Ambedkar by one political party or other, by one group or other. Distortions in the discourse have throttled creativity and reflection with regard to a thinker, ideologue, reformer and activist. The hypocritical showering of praises on him has done a great harm

37. Parekh, Bhikhu, op. cit., p. 241.

38. Ibid., p. 241.

39. Initially reservation policy was implemented for a period of ten years. After the expiry of the initial term, it has been extended continually till date. All the political parties have extended support to the reservation policy for the SCs and the STs.

Support to the recommendations of the B.P. Mandal Commission for 27% reservation in jobs for the OBCs, after a great deal of controversy, has now been extended by all the major political parties. In case, total reservation exceeds 50%, an amendment in the constitution may be brought about in near future.

to him and to the cause for which he fought during his life-time. Humiliating observations about Gandhi have been equated with the promotion of Ambedkarism. Kanshi Ram, the supremo of the Bahujan Samaj Party (BSP), once observed: "What has Gandhi done? He fought tooth and nail against the interests of the down-trodden people. In September 1932, he went on fast against reservations. Later it was propagated that Gandhi was responsible for reservations. He was a great hypocrite, to my mind. He lived in a sweeper's colony and he told them: "Your job is a very good job, you are doing a very good job. If I am to be born again I would like to be born as a sweeper." He was told: "If you want to be a sweeper, you can fulfil your desire in this life. Come on." But he never came. He was a hypocrite just fooling innocent people."[40]

Similar rather more harsh observation was made by Mayawati, a prominent leader of the BSP. She gave a call for finishing Gandhism, and described Gandhi as the biggest enemy of dalits. By coining the name 'Harijan' for the oppressed class, he did the maximum damage to them. If the word 'Harijan' meant the 'children of God', then Mahatma himself was the 'son of a demon' (*shaitan*). Why leaders like Gandhi, Nehru and Pant did not add 'Harijan' to their names, she asked in a raised voice. Mayawati roared for finishing Gandhism and asked for introducing Ambedkarvaad.[41]

Though the BSP was not an effective political party until recent assembly elections in Uttar Pradesh; its militant anti-upper caste articulations and expressions, particularly against Brahmins, Rajputs, Vaishyas and Kayasthas, lured the lower castes towards it in these elections. In Maharashtra, however, the dalits still comprise of the ex-untouchable castes. The non-dalit lower castes are, however, getting attracted

40. See, Kanshi Ram, in Bhikhu Parekh, op. cit., p. 209.

41. See *Hindustan Times* of March 10, 1994, for Mayawati's statement on Gandhi, issued in a press conference at Lucknow. The statement shocked many political leaders, and was condemned in parliament.

towards the BSP. Ambedkar's efforts to transform the 'untouchables' were less reactive and more constructive, whereas the above two assertions by Kanshi Ram and Mayawati are merely reactive. In fact, Ambedkar in essence agreed with Gandhi. He said: "Rights are protected not by law but by the social and moral conscience of society."[42] Ambedkar also said: "If social conscience is such that it is prepared to recognise the rights which law chooses to enact, rights will be safe and secure."[43] Further he mentioned: "If the rights are opposed by the community, no law, no parliament, no judiciary can guarantee them in the real sense of the world."[44]

VI

Dalit movements are, in fact, the Harijan/scheduled castes' movements. The word 'the oppressed' is closest to the word 'dalit'. As it has been stated earlier—from 'Harijan' to 'scheduled castes' and from 'scheduled castes' to 'dalit' marks the process of the emergence of the word 'dalit'. Thus, dalits are the SCs and they constitute nearly 16 per cent of India's population. Most of them are manual and agricultural workers. Many of them are engaged in their traditional occupations, and some are engaged in white-collar government and public sector jobs.[45] In Maharashtra, Ambedkar mobilised the Mahars and other 'untouchables' for launching a socio-political movement against their persisting depressed status. Some scholars have compared the dalits of India with the blacks of the USA.[46]

42. Radhakrishnan, P., 1991, "Ambedkar Legacy to Dalits, Has the Nation Reneged on its Promises?", *Economic and Political Weekly*, Vol. XXVI, No. 33, p. 1920.
43. Ibid., p. 1920.
44. Ibid.
45. Shah, Ghanshyam, 1990, *Social Movements in India*, New Delhi, Sage Publications, pp. 107–20.
46. See, for example, Sidney Verba, B. Ahmad and Anil Bhatt, 1971, *Caste, Race and Politics*, Berkeley, Sage Publications.

Barring some studies such as by Bharat Patankar and Gail Omvedt[47] and Ghanshyam Shah[48], most studies have emphasised on the process of sanskritisation among the SCs.

Ghanshyam Shah has classified dalit movements as (1) reformative, and (2) alternative. The reformative movements focus mainly on the study of changes in the caste system and the institution of untouchability. The issues related to conversion to other religions (for example, Buddhism, Islam, Christianity) and education, economic status and political power are taken up in the study of the alternative movements.[49] However, Patankar and Omvedt mention that the dalit movements are: (1) caste-based, and (2) class-based.[50] In essence all the dalit movements are anti-Brahmins, anti-upper castes and anti-castes. The movements such as the Satyashodhak Samaj, the Self-Respect, the Adi-Dharma, the Adi-Andhra, the Adi-Hindu, the Namashudra, the Nadar, the neo-Buddhist, etc., emphasised on discarding of Brahminical ways of life and practice of untouchability. In the process of these movements the 'untouchables' discarded their traditional occupations too for claiming social status equal to the 'clean castes'. In fact, sanskritisation has been observed as the main consequence, not clearly intended of most of the dalit movements.

The most significant consequence of the dalit movements is the formation of various voluntary organisations for the welfare of the poorest of the poor from among the dalits. Some of these are: Rural Community Development Association, Harijan Labourers' Association, Agricultural Workers' Movements, Rural Harijan Agricultural Development

47. Patankar, Bharat and Omvedt, Gail, 1979, "The Dalit Liberation Movement in Colonial Period", *Economic and Political Weekly*, Annual Number, Vol. XIV, Nos. 7 & 8. See also Gail Omvedt, 1994, op. cit.

48. Shah, Ghanshyam, 1980, "Anti-untouchability Movements"; Vimal Shah (ed.), *Removal of Untouchability*, Ahmedabad, Gujarat University; see also M.S. Gore, 1993, *The Social Context of an Ideology: Ambedkar's Political and Social Thought*, New Delhi, Sage Publications.

49. Shah, Ghanshyam, op. cit., pp. 108–13.

50. Patankar and Omvedt, op. cit.

Association, Association of Rural Poor, etc. The main objective of these organisations is to mobilise the agricultural poor from among the dalits to make them conscious of their socio-economic and cultural oppression and subjugation. For Peter Robb, all the movements of labourers both tribal and non-tribal (including SCs) are dalit movements.[51] These organisations have so far remained active in the states of Andhra Pradesh and Tamil Nadu.

The message which Ambedkar gave to the *bhikkhus* was of becoming as models of 'self-culture and self-service'. The supporters of Ambedkarite Buddhism and the dalit movement consider Ambedkar's writings on Buddhism as a 'religion of the oppressed', or a form of 'liberation theology'.[52] Ambedkar's contribution is seen as a shift in the debates from religious to secular discourse having the emancipatory exercise at its core. 'Ambedkar cult' is perhaps in the making. A sense of liberation and freedom through the act of conversion to neo-Buddhism has captured attention of dalits more than any other idea. Impact of Kabirpanth and Jyotirao Phule on Ambedkar created a sense of repulsion and hatred in him against Hinduism and traditional caste hierarchy. He distanced from Gandhi and closeted with Marxism.[53]

Since the early 1970s, the word 'dalit' has become "a positive, assertive expression of pride in untouchable heritage and a rejection of oppression,"[54] 'dalit' refers to all forms of social and economic oppression and it also applies to other oppressed groups like tribals, religious minorities, women and the economically oppressed of all castes.[55] Many scholars,

51. See Peter Robb (ed.), 1993, *Dalit Movements and the Meanings of Labour in India*, New Delhi, Oxford University Press.

52. Rodrigues, Valerian, 1993, "Making a Tradition Critical: Ambedkar's Reading of Buddhism", in Peter Robb (ed.), op. cit., p. 301.

53. Ibid., pp. 299–338.

54. Joshi, Barbara R., 1986, Untouchable: Voice of the Dalit Liberation Movement, New Delhi, Select Book Service Syndicate, p. 3.

55. Ibid., pp. 3–4.

however, prefer to use the term 'untouchable' rather than 'dalit'.[56] Ambedkar's message for the downtrodden was: 'be a lion', 'be your own light'.[57] He attacked the established Indian order by giving a call for destroying culturally defined inequality and persisting economic inequality.[58] Creation of a counter-culture, a culture of protest was his goal. Ambedkar's strong advocacy was for a cultural revolution and a radical social democracy.[59] Labour must control government and not the people inspired by self-serving individualism. He asked for protection against exploitation as a fundamental right.[60] Gandhian moral reform, orthodox Marxism, western economic developmentalism (both the capitalist and the socialist types) even put together would not equal to an indigenous dalit tradition. It represents a "community of communication within which individuals and organisations argue and evolve."[61]

VII

Two distinct approaches are found with regard to Ambedkar's basic formulations about Indian society. As illustrations of these approaches we propose to highlight briefly the views of M.S. Gore[62] and Gail Omvedt[63]. Gore analyses Ambedkar's thought system from the functionalist standpoint of knowledge, whereas Omvedt examines the dalit revolt from the historical materialist viewpoint. Gore and Omvedt have published more or less at the same time, in 1993 and 1994, respectively. Let us sum up the salient points of their perspectives on Ambedkar.

56. Ibid. Joshi herself prefers the word, *Harijan*.
57. Ibid.
58. Ibid., pp. 26–28.
59. Ibid.
60. Ibid., p. 140.
61. Ibid.
62. See M.S. Gore, 1993, op. cit.
63. See Gail Omvedt, 1994, op. cit.

Gore considers Ambedkar's thought and action as an 'ideology of protest'. According to Gore, Ambedkar clearly identified the outcaste untouchables distinct from the intermediate castes of Marathas and Kunbis, and the backward castes of Telis, Tambolis, Barbers and Artisans.[64] Before the Simon Commission, he declared that the 'depressed classes' referred to untouchable caste groups as well as tribal communities, but he preferred to plead on behalf of the untouchables only. He was also aware of the fact that the untouchables had several sub-castes as unequal status groups within Maharashtra and elsewhere. Despite intra-untouchable distinctions based on language, cultural context and economic standing, Ambedkar tried to create a sense of common identity among the untouchables of India. Ambedkar identified Brahmins as the real adversary of the untouchables as they not only were priests, they were most important elite group in society controlling public life by holding positions in education, administration and professions. A counter-protest from the Brahmins was a natural consequence in the defense of the established social order.[65]

Ambedkar hinted at the 'graded' inequality in Indian society as the root cause of persisting oppression of the lower sections. Gore applies the Mertonian paradigm of sociology of knowledge to the understanding of the Ambedkar ideology and to its social context.[66] The 'communication paradigm' is also found useful by Gore in addressing questions like—who protests against whom, for what reasons, with what objectives, and with what means. The nationalist/larger political context inspired mobilisation, but the internal division and stratification among the untouchables created obstacles in the movement.[67]

The main aim of Ambedkar was to evolve a definite

64. Ibid., p. 52.
65. Ibid., p. 55.
66. Ibid., pp. 65–66.
67. Ibid.

perspective on the problems faced by the untouchables of India. To register their protest and to seek an effective participation in the power structure of Indian society were his main concerns. The untouchables of India were seen by Ambedkar different from the underdog elsewhere all over the world. To elevate the untouchables from the underdog position, Ambedkar emphasised on the role of both 'law' and 'moral order'.[68]

Omvedt focuses on the dalit movement as a part of a broader anti-caste movement in the colonial period. The dalit and non-Brahman anti-caste movements can be classified as 'anti-systemic movements', or as 'value-oriented movements' as opposed to 'norm-oriented movements'.[69] Omvedt writes: "That is they (movements) challenged and sought to transform the basic structure of the Indian social system, replacing caste and the accompanying social oppression, economic exploitation and political domination by an equalitarian society."[70] There were also reformist trends in the anti-caste movements particularly represented by Gandhi, Jagjivan Ram, etc. The anti-caste dalit movement imparts a revolutionary message, a will to act against expolitation, a rise from oppression, from death to life, from darkness to light.[71] Thus, the spirit of militant Marxism and Naxalism is close to the ethos of the dalit movement. The dalits for steering such a movement must have the power of thought to challenge and destroy Brahminic hegemony and Hindu nationalism. Anti-caste radicals are thus distinguished from reformers.[72]

According to Ambedkar, the Indian National Congress was controlled by upper castes and capitalists (as 'Brahmin and bourgeois'). Phule gave 'rulers' the name of 'the *Irani Arya-bhats*', and later on others called them as

68. Ibid.
69. Ibid., pp. 9–10.
70. Ibid., p. 10.
71. Ibid., p. 11.
72. Ibid.

'*Shetji-Bhatji*' or 'Brahmin-Bania' raj.[73] The left-dalit unity having workers and peasants as a core base only could bring about the empowerment of the exploited sections of the society. Dalit Panthers mention in their Manifesto: "We don't want a little place in Brahmin alley. We want the rule of the whole country."[74] Dalit movement is seen by Omvedt as 'diversionary', and not simply in 'class' terms or as a second fiddle of the Congress-dominated national movement.[75] Omvedt suggests for formulating "a revised historical materialist understanding not only of the linkage between the 'economic base' and the 'superstructure', but economic processes themselves."[76] Alongwith 'economic subordination' Omvedt discusses the role played by cultural/community forms and force and violence in the agenda she sets for the understanding of the anti-caste and dalit movements.[77]

Omvedt's study provides a systematic socio-historical account of the dalits and their movements in the states of Maharashtra, Andhra Pradesh and Karnataka from a well-knit neo-Marxist viewpoint. With regard to the patterns of dalit mobilisation and Ambedkarism, the following points may be mentioned:

(1) The dalit movement emerged in all regions as a result of Ambedkar's leadership with similar trends, though having varying degrees of strength.

(2) The movement was genuinely anti-caste, and not merely a caste reform movement.

(3) Dalits as exploited workers, peasants and agricultural workers were involved with economic or 'class' issues everywhere, in all regions.[78]

73. Ibid.
74. See for Dalit Panther Manifesto (Bombay, 1973), Lata Murugkar, 1991, Dalit Movement in Maharashtra, Bombay, Popular Prakashan, pp. 232–37.
75. Omvedt, Gail, 1994, op. cit., p. 14.
76. Ibid., p. 17.
77. Ibid., pp. 9–20.
78. Ibid., pp. 12–67.

Omvedt further says: "The dalit movement emerged as a political force and at the same time as the non-Brahmin movement and as a source of inspiration for the working class and peasantry as they were creating their organisational forms."[79] With all this, 'Ambedkarism' is considered by Omvedt as 'the theory of dalit liberation'.[80] 'Ambedkarism' outlines the following:

(1) An uncompromising dedication to the needs of the dalits, which required total annihilation of the system and the Brahminic superiority it embodied.

(2) An almost equally strong dedication to the reality of India—denial of the imposition of a 'Hindu' identity.

(3) A conviction that the eradication of caste required a repudiation of Hinduism as a religion, and adoption of Buddhism as an alternative religion.

(4) A broad economic radicalism interpreted as 'socialism' mixed with and growing out of Ambedkar's democratic liberalism and liberal dedication to individual rights.

(5) A fierce rationalism.

(6) A firmly autonomous dalit movement having the socially and economically exploited (dalits and Shudras, workers and peasants in class terms) as an alternative political front to the Congress party which he saw as the unique platform of 'Brahminism' and 'capitalism'.[81]

In 1949, Ambedkar hinted in the Constituent Assembly that we were entering into a life of contradictions. "In politics we will have equality and in social and economic life we will have inequality ..."[82] Ambedkar was so disgusted with the situation that once he said: "I myself will burn the

79. Ibid., p. 165.
80. Ibid., pp. 223–59.
81. Ibid., pp. 224–25.
82. Cited from Gail Omvedt, p. 324.

Constitution."[83] In the 1970s, the followers of Ambedkar threatened to desecrate the national flag, burn the Constitution as well as the *Manusmriti*. Ambedkar declared once Nehru to be 'just another Brahmin'.[84] Dalit movement is 'class-caste struggle'.[85] It is a movement for establishing an alternative identity which is explosive and revolutionary.[86] Creation of a new consciousness pertaining as a quality related to the existence and assertion of the dalits is the ultimate goal of the dalit movements. Dalit literature and dalit writers have come to the centre stage in creating a sense of self-respect and dignity. A couple of years ago and also quite recently, the controversy and ensuing conflicts (including killings and suicides) over the issue of renaming the Marathawada University as Dr. B.R. Ambedkar University could be seen as an example of the ongoing power struggle between the upper castes and the dalits.[87]

VIII

The notion of 'dalit' is not the same as those of 'Harijan' and 'scheduled castes'. The terms 'Harijan' and 'scheduled castes' connote 'socio-cultural' and 'legal' meanings, respectively. The word 'dalit' symbolises 'knowledge' and 'power' of the oppressed people particularly belonging to the untouchable castes/ communities. It refers to the genesis and expression of their consciousness. 'Identity' of the 'oppressed people' is central to the term 'dalit'. Thus, the emergence of the identity of the dalit has created a new social language, a language of protest and struggle, of deconstruction and reconstruction of meanings of social situations, contexts and status parameters. It is an 'oppositional' side in creation of new cognitive structures.

83. Ibid., p. 325.
84. Ibid.
85. Ibid.
86. Ibid., p. 340.
87. See for details Lata Murugkar, 1991, op. cit.

Dalitism sets a new agenda for an equalitarian social order, new distributive just processes. 'Equality of outcome/result' is the most concrete and measurable yardstick of the envisaged new social order.

Dalitism is a historical phenomenon. Dalits as a class can be seen only in terms of human relationships, and not as a category, a thing or as a fixed 'structure' at a given point of time. Dalitism implies ideological and political militancy of the dalits. They could be referred as 'consciousness community'. Acquisition and control of knowledge and power is treated as the most potent resource by the dalits. Thus, Ambedkarian discourse on dalits and untouchability is said to be an alternative perspective to the Gandhian view about Harijans.

Dalit movement may be seen in terms of (1) the sociology of knowledge and communication paradigms, and (2) neo-Marxist view emphasising the class-caste approach. In the first case, the social context of Ambedkarism is highlighted, whereas in the second approach emphasis is on the understanding of the broad situation of the underdog mainly in class terms without loosing the sight of the specific caste situation in India. As such, dalit movement is an anti-systemic movement. Both manifest and latent consequences of the dalit movement are observable in socio-cultural, political and economic spheres of life. Dalitism implies an 'ideology of protest', but of varying degrees and intensities.

Finally, 'caste' is the central phenomenon in the discourse on 'dalitism', but 'class' is also inherently present in it. Caste is used as an idiom for waging a 'class war' against the established and entrenched hierarchies of power and domination. However, dalits are not just a constellation of untouchable castes, they are seen also as actual exploited workers, peasants and agricultural labourers in all parts of India. Emphasis is laid on their emancipation from economic bondage by bringing about 'economic radicalism' (socialism). Despite all these elements, which we have put together, the notion of 'dalit' is a new arrival; it is an ad hoc concept; it is a culture-bound construction; it is a reactive and not a generative 'concept'. Squeezing between caste and class reduces its 'atomistic' existence as a concept. It has more emotional and effectual appeal than rational and logical message. Lastly, it is a concept in making.

4 The Peasant Movement and Caste-Class-Power Nexus in Shekhawati

I

Jats are the principal agricultural caste in Shekhawati, they, therefore, not only formulated the 'peasant question', but also directed the peasant movement and set parameters of interaction between themselves on one hand, and Rajput landlords, other upper castes, non-principal middle and lower agricultural castes, on the other. Despite differentiation of landlords and peasants the mode of production in agriculture was influenced by feudalism and caste of peasants. Jagirdars and bhomias incessantly interfered with actual agricultural production to appropriate maximum share for themselves. No caste was as dependent on agriculture for livelihood as the Jats in Shekhawati. They were also numerically more preponderant than other castes in the region. The brunt of the jagirdars' power was experienced by the Jats. Thus, excessive dependence on agriculture, dehumanisation and numerical strength prompted them to oppose the excesses and atrocities of Rajput rulers.

Alienation of other intermediate and lower agricultural castes from the mobilisation against Rajput jagirdars and their kinsmen was the natural corollary of such a situation.

Increased ethnicisation of the Jat-kisan movement distanced other castes and communities. Proximity of the non-Jat castes with Rao Raja of Sikar distanced Jats from the latter. Jat-kisan leaders even sought alliances with those who were declared opponents of their immediate rulers.

Questions relating to the peasant movement in terms of caste-class-power nexus have been analysed in this essay drawing mainly from indigenous accounts of the peasant movement of 1920s and 1930s. Various accounts of this period indicate that the 'peasant' and the 'caste' questions got meshed up. The two were not independent of the Maharaja of Jaipur State, Rao Raja of Sikar thikana, and chhutbhaiyas and bhomias. Hence, not only peasantry (class) and caste were intertwined, 'power' was never independent of caste and class. Ultimately, to have control over land and power was the main item on the agenda of the Jat-peasant mobilisation and movement.

Though the facts presented here are descriptive, but their implications for redefining the 'dimensional approach' to the study of social formation are significantly transparent. The two upper castes, namely, Brahamins and Banias figure scantily in the entire peasant movement. In no way, superiority of the Brahmins is manifested in the movement. On the contrary, the established supremacy of Rajput landlords was threatened and challenged by Jat peasantry in particular, and in retaliation landed groups did their best to reaffirm their power and authority. The role of the British and the state of Jaipur was contingent upon the interests they had in relation to the local feudal order.

II

Peasants have been found nowhere as a monolithic stratum of society. Peasants as well as owners of land have had institutionalised patterns of gradations, and high and low positions.

'Agrarian hierarchy' existed in the form of autonomous chieftains, intermediary zamindars and primary zamindars.[1] Mooreland discusses in detail the village hierarchy consisting of rulers, intermediaries (landlords), peasantry, landless labourers, village servants, recipients of charity, etc.[2] All zamindars, jagirdars and ryots were intricately linked to definite socio-ceremonial and communal as well as economic and political roles.[3] Uneven structures of landlords, tenants and peasants also existed in the princely state of Rajputana at the time of the advent of the British in India.[4] Grantees, sub-grantees, bhomias, occupancy tenants, tenants-at-will, sharecroppers and sub-cultivators were quite common stratificational entities in villages of Rajputana.

Besides landed classes there were also merchants and artisans. British rule in India created 'new classes' as new modes of polity and administration, trade and commerce, industry, education, etc., were introduced by the Raj. Professional classes in particular were the most significant and visible addition to Indian society. Impact of colonialism and capitalism could be seen simultaneously on society, culture, economy and polity.

Land was no more the primary determinant of socio-economic status and power. Education and white-collar employment in particular not only provided new sources of

1. Hasan, S. Nurul, 1979, 'Zamindars under the Mughals', in Robert Eric Frykenberg (ed.), *Land Control and Social Structure in Indian History*, Delhi, Manohar Publications, pp. 17–31. See also Irfan Habib, 1963, *The Agrarian System of Mughal India* (1556–1707), Delhi, Asia Publishing House, p. 180; Bernard S. Cohn, 1979, 'Structural Change in Indian Rural Society', in R.E. Frykenberg (ed.), op. cit., p. 77.
2. Mooreland, W.H., 1968, *The Agrarian System of Moslem India*, Delhi, Munshi Ram Manoharlal.
3. Embree, Ainslie, 1979, 'Landholding in India and British Institutions,' in R.E. Frykenberg (ed.), op. cit., p. 47.
4. Sharma, K.L., 1982, 'Land-Tenure Systems, Social Structure and Change: Some Reflections on Land Reforms in Rajasthan', in S.K. Lal (ed.), *Sociological Perspective of Land Reforms*, New Delhi, Agricole Publishing Academy, pp. 95–132.

livelihood but also became bases of status and honour. Differentiation of peasantry in terms of zamindari and ryotwari systems in British India and approval of jagir and khalsa systems of land tenure in feudal/princely India was the most glaring change brought about by the British. However, hierarchies of jagirdars, zamindars and bhomias and peasants were quite complex as there were 45 types of jagirs and 175 types of cesses and taxes in operation[5] in the Shekhawati region. And then, there were distinct dissimilarities between zamindari and ryotwari areas in British India, and between jagir and khalsa areas in princely India.[6]

To examine the peasant question today, we have to know about the nature of tenancy, reliance on cultivation as the main occupation and social background (mainly caste) of peasantry. The question of tenancy is quite complex and it varies from area to area. Even with regard to sharecropping, for example, there are: concealed tenancy, commercial tenancy, crop-sharing tenancy, fixed-rent tenancy, and fixed-product or fixed kind-rent tenancy.

In the case of Rajasthan unity and continuity between feudalism and capitalism have existed. The prevalence of jagirdari, khalsa, zamindari and bhomichara systems of land tenure created uneven and inequitous categories of peasants having corresponding uneven differential consequences for the peasantry. Today, new structures of inequality are transformed forms of the traditional modes of production and differentiation of peasantry. The state of Jaipur, the thikanas of Shekhawati, grantees of thikanedars, chhutbhaias, maufidars and bhomias, in fact, refer to the layers of feudalism prevalent in the princely state of Jaipur. Caste played an important role in the hierarchy of landlords. All those who held land grants and belonged to the caste and clan of the durbar and thikanedars enjoyed superior status and honour than those

5. Ibid., p. 106.
6. Ibid., pp. 103–11.

grantees who belonged to other castes including Brahmin. Several lower castes like Nai, Balai (shoe-maker) and Dholi (drum-beater) had land grants as *inams* (rewards) in lieu of their services to the jagirdar, and sometimes their lands were cultivated by superior castes like Brahmins and Jats. But, the interactional ties were different in comparison to the ties between the upper-caste landlords and the lower-caste tenants.[7] Jats were never favoured by jagirdars in Shekhawati. Land-grants were never given to Jats. However, those Jat peasants who helped the jagirs in collection of land revenue were honoured with the title of Patel or Chaudhary, and were given some concession, with regard to the payment of land revenue.

The study of peasantry in the Shekhawati region of Rajasthan raises several questions: Can we treat peasantry as a class, a constructed stratum in the village community? Can we consider peasantry synonym with a caste community? What was the nature of social differentiation within the peasantry? What factors could be attributed to such a system of stratification? Were peasants merely an economic category? Was the peasant an isolated entity confined to his farm and family?

Several cross-cultural studies of peasantry have found a marked system of stratification and class relations. In some cases peasants are found to be synonymous with the village community as a whole, and in some a given caste/community is taken as peasantry in the village. Differentiations within the peasantry are reflected, for example, in terms of (i) non-cultivating owners and tenure-holders, (ii) owner-cultivators and cultivating tenants, and (iii) sharecroppers and agricultural labourers. These categories are based on the relations that individuals and families have with agriculture and ownership of land.

However, one can talk about some other segments of village community without such constructions. More

7. Sharma, K.L., 1974, *The Changing Rural Stratification System*, New Delhi, Orient Longman. See also R.E. Frykenberg (ed.), op. cit.

convincingly, we can talk about Rajputs, Charans and Jats rather than landlords, maufidars and peasants. In the Shekhawati region, Rajputs, Charans and Jats were landlords, sub-grantees and peasants, respectively, but some other castes too constituted these categories, and these castes were not reducible to such economic categories in certain important respects. This particular point can be discussed with regard to the Jat peasantry in the Shekhawati region.

III

The main social groups (castes) in Sikar district of Shekhawati are Brahmins, Rajputs, Mahajans, Jats, Gujars, Ahirs, Minas, etc. There are also several functionary castes such as Khati, Luhar, Sunar, Nai, Dhobi, Darzee, Teli, Lakhera, Rangrej, Tamboli and Thathera. Besides several groups of Muslims such as Kayaomkhani, Sayyad, Pathan, Shaikh, there are also a large number of scheduled castes and scheduled tribes. Groups like Brahmins, Rajputs, Mahajans and Jats are divided among several sub-castes and classes. Jats are the major cultivators in the district.

Rajputs, Brahmins and Mahajans belonged to the upper stratum, whereas Jats, Ahirs, Malis, artisan castes like Sonar and Khati and some groups of Muslims (who were rulers in the medieval period) formed the second layer of the social hierarchy. According to the 1903 census, in the state of Jaipur, the major backward castes could be classified into the following categories:

1. Castes dependent on agricultural labour.
2. Agricultural castes.
3. Castes dependent on animal husbandry.
4. Mendicant castes.
5. Castes engaged in cottage industries.
6. Artisan castes.

7. Castes engaged in social functions.
8. Castes dependent on the jagirdars and the state.[8]

However, in a broad sense, all castes can be divided into agricultural and non-agricultural castes, and further agricultural castes can be classified into principal agricultural castes and other agricultural castes. Unless every caste in a given context is seen in relation to its dependence directly on agriculture for livelihood, 'caste' and 'peasant' questions remain unrelated. There is an intermixing of the two questions, but the two are also not necessarily in direct relation to each other. However, in some cases the peasant question is also the caste question. In the context of Jats of Shekhawati such a nexus has been found historically and contextually.

By all accounts Jats in Shekhawati, Torawati and other parts of the Jaipur State were the principal agricultural caste, and Jats also had numerical preponderance over all other principal agricultural castes. Besides Jats the other main caste was of Rajputs in the Shekhawati region. Though Rajputs were the ruling community, they could not be treated as 'bourgeoisie'. Similarly, Jats were not only cultivators, they worked under severely oppressive rule and command of the Rajput jagirdars and landlords, but they were not 'proletariat'. Jats were at the top of the non-*dwij* principal agricultural castes. They were ranked below Brahmins, Rajputs and Mahajans. Their numerical strength equalled all *dwij* castes. Being at the top of the intermediate castes, Jats took their dehumanised oppressive and exploitative situation seriously and mobilised themselves as a peasant force against Rajput jagirdars and bhomias. Jats became synonymous with peasantry, and Rajputs were treated as a symbol of cruel rule to which Jats were subjugated.

On the whole the common man had limited ambitions in life, such as coarse foodgrains, milch cattle, and functional

8. Arya, Harphool Singh, 1987, *Shekhawati Ke Thikanon Ka Itihas Aiwan Yogdan*, Jaipur, Panchsheel Prakashan, pp. 158–65.

housing. The feudal system was such that even these minimum necessities for survival were made unavailable to peasants and other sections of society. For example, the thikana of Sikar had an annual revenue of Rs. 5,50,000 in 1925, but it spent only Rs. 20,000 on health facilities and Rs. 15,000 on education. Unscientific and arbitrary systems of collection of land revenue like *batai, kunta, ijara*, etc. and innumerable lagbags (taxes and cesses) impoverished peasants beyond redemption. These cesses were imposed to meet expenses incurred on marriages, guests, tours, leisure activities of the jagirdar's family members and kinsmen. Forced labour or *begar* was a routine activity. Even help extended to landlords in genuine crisis situations was transformed into perpetual forced labour in normal situations. Most functionary castes like Balai, Bhangi, Naik, Regar, Nai, Khati, Kumhar had to render *begar*. Non-functionary castes such as Jat, Ahir and Mali too had to offer *begar* in the form of manual labour and cultivation of the jagirdar's personal farms.

In 1941, there were 136 lagbags in the Marwar region of Rajasthan. Hira Singh lists a number of such lagbags in the region, and observes that *begar, bigori/hasil,* and lagbags were three main sources of *zulum* (atrocities and injustices) committed on the common man and peasantry.[9] Only Rajputs and Brahmins were spared from rendering *begar*. However, if a Brahmin showed disrespect to the jagirdar or violated established norms and rules of the thikana, he too, had to render *begar*, as punishment. Certainly, punishment used to be much less for a Brahmin than a lower caste man for the same offence.

The main reason of discontent in Shekhawati was the dehumanised existence inflicted upon the peasants by the jagirdars and bhomias. Social degradation, economic enslavement, political oppression and terror and insecurity created by feudal lords had reduced the people and particularly the peasantry to a level of nothingness. A class of parasites and

9. Singh, Hira, 1981, Decline of Feudalism: Marwar from 1870s to 1940s, Ph.D. thesis (mimeo), Department of Sociology, University of Delhi.

sycophants evolved around the jagirdars, and they too, contributed to the miserable plight of the people.

IV

A caste-class nexus was clearly visible in Shekhawati. Jat Sabha, for example, was a caste association as well as an organisation of peasants. This may be true about Rajput/Kshatriya Mahasabha or Bhooswami Sangh and also about Vaishya Mahasabha or Traders' Association. In case of these organisations it would not be easy to disentangle caste from class or class from caste. However, it does not imply that caste is nothing but simply class, and class is just a replica of caste. The two, i.e., caste and class, are not reducible to each other. Caste is a given interactional social and cultural phenomenon, whereas class is both an attributional construction and interactional reality.

The caste-class nexus in case of Jat peasants in the Shekhawati region demands a thorough probity. Often Jats and peasants have been equated with each other and also treated synonymously. It is invariably reported that the peasantry, particularly Jat peasants, were maltreated by Rajput jagirdars. But non-Rajput grantees/sub-grantees and maufidars (including Brahmins) never maltreated Jat kisans. In case the non-Rajput landlords had problems with their Jat tenants, they sought the 'good offices' of the Rajput jagirdars to settle their disputes. No other caste except Jats demanded social equality with Rajputs. However, they never demanded social equality with Brahmins and Banias. Jats demanded that they be allowed to ride horses and elephants like the Rajputs on the occasion of marriage. Several castes, lower to the Jats of Shekhawati, were not subjected to as much inhuman treatment as it meted out to Jats. Some of the members of lower castes being functionaries and servants under the thikanas enjoyed some privileges too. On behalf of the jagirdars and bhomias they at times ill-treated the Jat peasants, and this further added to their agony. Jats being at the top of the principal agricultural castes, in terms of their superior rank, numerical strength and sole dependence on agriculture, were perceived as a major threat by the Rajput rulers. Jats, taking advantage of these factors, were generally hostile to their Rajput landlords.

Autocratic conduct of the Shekhawati thikanedars can also be attributed to their near-autonomy from the state of Jaipur. Rudolph and Rudolph observe: "Shekhawati was Jaipur's Burgundy or Wales: its obstreperous thakurs bore their obligations to Jaipur lightly and were indifferent to the writ of the maharaja."[10]

In fact, so much was the defiance of the authority of the durbar by the thikanedars of Shekhawati that the Maharaja of Jaipur State appointed a committee under the chairmanship of C.U. Wills to ascertain rights and obligations of the Shekhawati thikanedars *vis-à-vis* the state of Jaipur.[11] One of the reasons for claiming autonomy and independence from the state of Jaipur by the Shekhawati thikanedars was their *tazimi* status under which the durbar was under obligation to receive them with due respect and cordiality, and they were exempted from appearing in courts in person. The peasantry were the obvious direct victim of the autonomy and freedom enjoyed by the thikanedars. There was hardly any scope for formal/legal appeal or complaint against the injustices and cruelties committed on the peasants by the jagirdars.

The question of caste-class nexus finds a mention in some studies of peasant movements in Rajasthan.[12] Ghasi Ram

10. Rudolph, S.H. and Rudolph L.I., 1984, *Essays on Rajputana, Reflections on History, Culture and Administration*, New Delhi, Concept Publishing Co.
11. Wills, C.U., 1933, *The Report on Land Tenures and Special Powers of Certain Thikanedars of the Jaipur State*, Delhi, T.M.H. Press.
12. Ram, Ghasi, 1987, *Rajasthan Mein Kisan Andolan Ka Udai aur Vikas, Shekhawati Ke Vishesha Sandarbh Main: 1893 Se 1947 Tak*, Ph.D. thesis (mimeo), Department of Political Science, Rajasthan University, Jaipur, pp. 151–58.

observes that due to some misgiving peasant movement in Shekhawati is referred as a Jat movement. According to Ram, Jats, despite being numerically preponderant among the peasants, were worst affected by the inhuman feudal rule in the region. Due to these factors Jats were ahead of other communities and they also led the peasant movement. Thus a peasant movement cannot be described as a Jat movement.[13] There were peasants among the Rajputs but they had more facilities and concessions than the Jat peasantry. At the same time, Ghasi Ram admiringly states that on caste basis organisation formation becomes easy. The movement, therefore, he admits, looks like a Jat movement, and the opponents are hence thakur-bhomias and Jats, the former being the exploiter and the latter the exploited. The underlying fundamental reality is of exploitative economic relations and consequent unequal social strata constituted of Rajputs and Jats.

The Shekhawati movement in its form was a movement of peasants but in essence it was overwhelmingly a Jat movement. From the class point of view of Jats, there was no class struggle between the rich and the poor or between the bourgeoisie and the proletariat. So much was the casteist complexion of the movement that peasants from other castes such as Brahmin, Gujar, Ahir, Meena, etc. were neither encouraged to participate in the movement nor they thought it fit fearing their marginalisation. Glorification of Jats as the best peasantry also proved to be a deterrent factor for other castes and communities in joining the mainstream of the movement. Organisation spearheading the movement too had the stamp of Jat leadership. Leaders like Harlal Singh, Ladu Ram Kisari, Chaudhary Ghasi Ram, Chaudhary Desh Raj, Sir Chhotu Ram, Net Ram Singh, Hardeo Singh Patsari, Bharon Singh Togra, Begraj Singh Mandori, etc. (all Jats) actively led the movement and the Jat Sabha. The message went out to the

13. Ibid., p. 159.

people was that the whole movement was a Jat affair, and it was a fight between the Rajputs and the Jats. Those who belonged to other communities and had sympathy for the peasant cause even did not feel psychologically comfortable to join the leadership as well as rank and file of the movement.

Kisan Sabha and Kisan Panchayat were in effect Jat Sabha and Jat Panchayat. These organisations were in the beginning caste associations but later on for tactical reasons the word 'Kisȧn' was added in the nomenclature of these organisations. Some concerned leaders and workers from other castes also joined the movement despite its 'Jatish' character in form and substance both.

The peasant movement in Rajasthan aimed at the overthrow of the feudal system. The agenda of the movement included demands for 'occupancy tenancy' for the peasants, land settlement, proper assessment of land revenue and its payment in cash. Demand for according 'social honour' to the Jats was also at the top of the agenda of the movement.[14] Brahmins, Mahajans and Kayasthas were involved in the administration of the State, jagirs and thikanas, and this certainly discouraged them to participate actively in the movement. Secondly, the 'Jatism' had taken over the movement in leaps and bounds, and therefore, others did not see a place of significance and honour for themselves in the orbit of the movement. Some functionary castes and groups did not join the movement partly due to their marginal dependence on agriculture and partly on the thikanas for their livelihood.

Jat religious saints undertook tours of the region and also organised fairs and festivals. In 1920s All India Jat Mahasabha became active in Rajputana alongwith the states of Uttar Pradesh and Punjab. Inspired by this organisation, the

14. Sisson, Richard, 1969, 'Peasant Movements and Political Mobilization: The Jats of Rajasthan', *The Asian Survey*, No. 9, p. 12. See also Richard Sisson, *The Congress Party in Rajasthan: Political Integration and Institution-building in an Indian State*, Berkeley, University of California Press.

first conference of kisans was organised in Khandela in 1925. In 1930s Shekhawati Jat Mahasabha was formed on the pattern of the All India Jat Mahasabha. Another organisation, to educate the Jat youths, was established by the name of Jat Shiksha Samiti. Jat Vidyarthi Parishad, a Jat Student's organisation, was also active during this period. In several thikanas of Shekhawati, Jat panchayats and Jat Sabhas were formed. In 1932, a grand conference of All India Jat Mahasabha was held at Jhunjhunu, and in January 1935 at Sikar, Jat Prajapati Mahayagya was organised. Both of these events boosted morale of the Jats with regard to their claim for social equality particularly with the Rajputs. The mahayagya provided a new identity and communitarian feeling to the Jats of Shekhawati. It was apparently a sanskritic act on the part of the Jats of the area, but in effect it was more of a political mobilisation against the Rajput jagirdars and bhomias. At the conclusion of the mahayagya, a procession on elephant was taken out violating the restriction on the use of elephant and horse by the non-*dwij* castes.

These events were taken as social mobilisations of the Jats in the Shekhawati region. In 1938, in Pushkar *mela* (fair) an organisation by the name of Jat Krishak Sudharak was also formed. Jat peasant leadership was so overwhelmed by these oganisational and movemental efforts that they started a campaign of 'no taxes' and 'no lagbags and *begar*' to the thikanedars be paid by the kisans. Literature glorifying the 'Jat power' started appearing during the late 1930s. Thakur Desh Raj's book, *Jat Shakti Ka Itihas*[15] (History of the Jat Power) is the most popular book of this period regarding the Jats of Shekhawati in particular. Jat hysteria was at its peak as reflected

15. See Desh Raj, 1961, *Shekhawati Ke Jan jagran Aivam Kisan Andolan Ke Char Dashak*, Jaipur, Rajasthan Printers. See also Kalu Ram Sharma, 1974, *Unniswin Sadi Ke Rajasthan Ka Samajik Aivam Aarthik Jiwan*, Jaipur, Rajasthan Hindi Granth Academy, Jamana Lal Bajaj, *Patra-Vyavahar*, 1958–1969, eight volumes, published and edited by Ram Krishan Bajaj, New Delhi, Sasta Sahitya Mandal.

in the mahayagya. Jat leaders, journalists, advocates, writers, teachers—all participated in the mahayagya. Sir Chhotu Ram and Thakur Deshraj were the leading lights of the day.

The thikanedars retaliated against the massive show of strength by the Jats by arresting and externing the eminent leaders and activists. In a memorandum submitted by about 200 kisans to the Prime Minister of Jaipur State, alongwith other demands, it was stated that the Jats be accorded priority and encouragement in the services in thikanas, they should be given social status and privileges equal to Rajputs, and all the partisan orders, customs and practices against the Jats must be abolished.[16]

According to another agreement, the Kisan Panchayat's legitimacy was accepted by the state of Jaipur.[17] The Rajput style of nomenclature had become quite common among the Jats by this time. Jats would suffix 'Singh' with their names along with the prefix of 'Chaudhary'. This was perhaps done to show victory of the Jats over the Rajputs after the abolition of the jagirdari system. The leaders arrested after the submission of this memorandum were all Jats including Prithvi Singh, Haru Singh, Tej Singh and Ishwar Singh.[18]

When despite several memoranda and agreements arrived at thereupon no concrete reliefs were effected to the peasantry. In fifteen villages of Shekhawati the kisans took a vow that if any Jat kisan paid land revenue to the thikana, he would be ostracised, and kisans of other castes who violated this decision would face social boycott. As a result of this decision several violent encounters occurred between the bhomias and the Jats. Meanwhile, the C.U. Wills report on the Shekhawati thikanas declared the thikanedars and jagirdars of Shekhawati as ijaredars of the state of Jaipur, as the latter was ijaredar of the British. Since this challenged the autonomy and

16. Ram, Ghasi, op. cit., pp. 189–90.
17. Ibid., p. 193.
18. Ibid.

freedom of the Shekhawati chiefs, it was rejoiced by the Jat kisans. Expression of satisfaction and happiness, by the Jat kisans with regard to the Wills report, invited again the wrath and crushing hand of the Rajputs against the Jats. Jat leaders were arrested; their organisations were banned. The schools run by the Jat organisations were demolished. Jat processions and demonstrations were ruthlessly crushed. Police firings and killings of Jats at Khoori and Kudan villages are still afresh in the memory of the people. Except some leaders at the regional level, no leaders and activists at the village level were arrested and tortoured belonging to any other caste other than Jats. In fact, people from other castes at the village level were never active in the Jat-kisan movement.

Acute and intense Jat-Rajput conflict is revealed in the incidents in 1935 which occurred at Khoori and Kudan villages of Sikar thikana. On March 20, 1935, at the time of the marriage of a Jat girl, it was decided to take the groom on horseback to the bride's place, but the Rajput bhomias objected to this as the non-twice-born castes were never allowed to ride on horse/elephant. When the Jats attempted to take out the procession with bridegroom riding on a horse, the Rajputs obstructed it. Jats lodged a protest against this to the Sikar thikana officials, but instead of taking action against the erring Rajputs, the officials arrested a relative of the Jat bridegroom. Two days after this incidence, Chaudhary Ratna was murdered in broad day light by the bhomias. As a consequence of this Rajputs and Jats found themselves in a situation of confrontation. On March 27, 1935, Captain Webb, an officer of Sikar thikana, ordered both Jats and Rajputs to leave Khoori as they had gathered there in large numbers. A brutal lathi-charge was ordered in which about one hundred persons were wounded and two of them died later on.

Another brutal incident of police firing took place in May 1935 in which 12 Jats were killed. Akhil Bhartiya Jat Sabha and other organisations condemned this as a barbaric inhuman act committed again by Captain Webb. Jat leaders from Uttar Pradesh in particular condemned this incident. Again, about 300 Jats were ill-treated and beaten up when they demanded concession in the amount of land revenue due to drought in Shekhawati. And finally, when they refused to pay land revenue to the thikanas, they were arrested. Main leaders involved in the agitation were Jats, and they included Ishwar Singh, Hari Singh, Hardeo Singh, Prithvi Singh, Ganesh Ram, Panne Singh, Goru Singh, Devi Singh Bochlia and Master Chandra Bhan Singh.

Some instances of feudal atrocities may be mentioned. Chaudhary Ram Bux's belongings were taken away by the officials of the thikanedar. He, his wife, and children were forced to stand in scorching heat for hours. Even agricultural implements were looted from his house. Master Chandra Bhan was taken out in the streets of Laxmangarh and Fatehpur while being beaten up with shoes. Chaudhary Ishwar Singh's wife was beaten up in Bhainrupura village. In village Khoru Master Chandra Bhan and Biram Jat were beaten up. Many Jats who visited Sikar were caught and beaten up. One elderly Jat died due to the torture inflicted upon him by the thikana officials.

Rubin observes: "There is a tradition of conflict between Rajput and Jat in the Rajput ruled areas. The Jat cultivators produced an agricultural surplus which the Rajput rulers expropriated to maintain their durbars and equip their troops."[19] Many Jat leaders toured other parts of India to inform the people about the barbaric treatment meted out to the Jat peasantry. Newspapers highlighted the oppressive archaic hegemonic rule of the jagirdars obviously pleading for emancipation of the underdog.[20]

The 1938 Sikar agitation in the Jaipur State was an

19. Rubin, Barnett R., 1983, *Feudal Revolt and State-Building: The 1938 Sikar Agitation in Jaipur*, New Delhi, South Asian Publishers, p. 20.

20. See Ghasi Ram, op. cit., pp. 205–14.

event which further substantiated the role of caste-class nexus in the peasant movement in Shekhawati. This agitation by the people of Sikar in favour of their Rao Raja Kalyan Singh against the durbar of Jaipur State brings out several issues including caste-class nexus, political power, nature and magnitude of feudalism and primordialism. It is known that the Jat-kisan movement was 'anti-feudal' in essence. The Jats were subjected to myriad taxes and lagbags, whereas the Rajputs/bhomias were free from such inhuman excessive pressures and hardships. Thus, caste was present in the Jat movement too in this particular manner.

Broadly speaking, with regard to the Jat movement, we may discern four social components in Shekhawati. These are: (1) Rajputs (jagirdars and bhomias), (2) Jats (peasants), (3) upper castes other than Rajputs (literati and economic dominants), and (4) lower castes (artisans and functionaries). In the Jat-kisan movement only leadership and the rank and file of the movement barring some exceptions remained with Jats. The Rajputs resisted the movement as it was against them, and therefore, their strategies were defensive as well as counter-offensive. The other two categories of castes/groups were disinterested onlookers.

The situation regarding the 1938 agitation was quite different. The jagirdars were always taken as a threat by the durbar as the former claimed independence and autonomy from the state of Jaipur. The British too in their own interest accorded recognition and status to the jagirdars and it was also not liked by the durbar.

V

Intra-caste/intra-clan clash due to sharing of power was the main cause in the Sikar agitation of 1938. The durbar was unable to effect the administration of Sikar and other *tazami* thikanas of Shekhawati. Shekhawati thikanas had control over three-fifth of the total area of Jaipur State. Sensing impending negative consequences of the nationalist and the local agitations against the State of Jaipur, the durbar desired to bring about reforms in the State, if necessary, even depriving the jagirdars of their political power in certain respects.[21] The durbar required institutional and legal support for realising this goal, and this was provided by the C.U. Wills Committee Report which declared thikanedars and jagirdars simply ijaredars of the state of Jaipur implying reduced powers and autonomy of the jagirdars.[22] Another point in the Wills Report was the establishment of a Court of Wards under a British Officer which enabled the durbar to interfere in the jagirs just as the British interfered in the princely states.[23] The Wills Report pictured the jagirdar status order as no more than the creation of a sovereign ruler.[24] Wills established in every respect the authority of the durbar over the Shekhawati chiefs and thikanedars.

The Wills Report shook seriously the Shekhawati chiefs, thikanedars and bhomias as it challenged the legitimary, autonomy and independence of their rule. They thought that their *izzat* (honour) was at stake, and encroachment on their fiefdoms would become a regular practice. The thikanedars in their reply, submitted to a Committee of Inquiry constituted by the durbar with regard to the Wills Report, argued that the "Mughal ijaras had nothing to do with the establishment of the thikanas or the powers of the thikanedars."[25] The thikanedars pleaded that their rule was based on their conquest, and their lands were considered 'ilaqa ghair'.[26] The arguments submitted

21. Rubin, Barnett R., op. cit., p. 29.
22. See C.U. Wills, op. cit., on *igaredars*, pp. 10–13.
23. Rubin, Barnett R., op. cit., p. 29.
24. Ibid.
25. Ibid., p. 33.
26. Ibid., p. 34. See James Tod, 1990, *Annals and Antiquities of Rajasthan*, 3 Vols., Delhi, Low Price Publications, pp. 1378–80. The first edition of Tod's seminal work on Rajasthan was published in 1829.

by the thikanedars remained unheaded. In 1935, when the report was submitted to the durbar, the Jat agitation had also reached to its peak. Thus, the jagirdars were doubly at the receiving end, one from the durbar and second from the Jat kisans. It was considered as a "decisive defeat for the Shekhawats."[27]

In this hour of crisis the jagirdars showed exemplary unity with the Rao Raja of Sikar. The dispute between the Rao Raja and the durbar was regarding Hardayal Singh, son of Rao Raja, who at the age of 12 years had been engaged to the daughter of the Maharaja of Dharangadhra in 1933. According to an order issued in 1937 by the durbar the responsibility for Hardayal Singh's upbringing was entrusted to the Maharaja. The Maharaja postponed the marriage which was originally scheduled to be held in the summer of 1938. Maharaja wanted to send the young boy to Cambridge in England for higher education.[28] This was not taken kindly by the Rao Raja and also by the thikanedars and the people of Shekhawati.

Kalyan Singh, the Rao Raja of Sikar, spoke local dialect, and that too restricted to a few words and sentences. I had opportunities to see the Rao Raja while I was a student at the local college at Sikar in the late 1950s. The Rao Raja was usually invited on certain occasions by the principal of the local college which was named after him. He would simply give a mock audience to the students and teachers and offer some money for sweets for the students. Despite his proven inabilities and limitations the Rao Raja was a man down to earth anxious about the erosion of his authority and autonomy.

Barnett R. Rubin writes: "Amar Singh (the thakur of Kanota) had a very low opinion of the Rao Raja's personal ability and integrity, but for the sake of the friendship between

27. Rubin, Barnett R., op. cit., p. 35.
28. See Rudolph S.H. and Rudolph, L.I., 1984, op. cit. Barnett R. Rubin, op. cit., pp. 42–47.

the two families he undertook many thankless efforts on the Rao Raja's behalf. He was also emotionally unstable having paranoid symptoms, and was also alcoholic."[29]

VI

The Sikar agitation of 1938 could be characterised in terms of primordial, regional and caste alliances on one hand and the Jat kisans question on the other. The Rao Raja had wired the thakurs of the big thikanas of Khur, Nawalgarh, Dundhlod and Mandawa to come to his rescue against the tirade launched by the durbar. Hundreds of Rajputs arrived daily at Sikar from all over Shekhawati and even from Marwar and Bikaner regions.[30] "They insisted that they would not let the Rao Raja go unless his powers were restored."[31] The Rajputs had taken over the command of the situation. They would not allow the Rao Raja to take a decision on his own, and perhaps he did not want either to take any decision. A couple of times the big Rajputs tried to take out the Rao Raja from his palace, but the crowd which consisted of small Rajputs in a large number did not allow.

The Rajputs, barring some big ones, were generally unlettered and rustic. Their chivalry and tribalism were known all over the world. The notion of honour was central to their existence. The thikanedars and even common Rajputs were upset seriously on the Wills Report that they were simply ijaredars of durbar and did not have autonomy and freedom which they had been claiming for a long time. Perhaps, this was also one of the strong reasons for extending all the possible help and cooperation to the Rao Raja of Sikar against the

29. Rubin Barnett R., op. cit., p. 44, fn.4., and p. 36, fn. 13. See S.H. Rudolph and L.I. Rudolph, 1975, 'A Bureaucratic Lineage in Princely India: Elite Formation and Conflict in a Patrimonial System', *Journal of Asian Studies*, Vol. 34, No. 3. Rudolphs observe that Amar Singh, thakur of Kanota, had a very low opinion of Rao Raja's personal ability and integrity.

30. Rubin, Barnett R., op. cit., p. 48.

31. Ibid., p. 48.

durbar and the British as the latter were also on the side of the durbar. Rajputs in general had earned a lot of notoriety and ill-will of the people due to the patterns of personal life which they had set for themselves. They were known for drinking, meat-eating, womanising and for such equally bad ways.[32] In general, Rajputs as a community had never been forward-looking. *Purdah*, orthodox practices regarding marriage, rituals, disinterestedness in education, drug use, female infanticide, clan rivalry, vanity, etc. are some of the known retrograde practices found among them.[33] In many parts of the Rajput stronghold today one can find illiterate, semi-employed and pauperised Rajputs in large numbers mainly due to the abolition of the jagirdari system. Thus, they were 'culturally backward' in the past due to their exalted status, and after the abolition of the jagirdari system they have become backward due to withdrawal of status.

The main question ultimately bogged down to rivalry between Sikar chieftainship and Jaipur durbar. The thikanas of Shekhawati considered themselves as *ilaqua ghair* (foreign territory) in several respects. They claimed that the durbar had no right to interfere in their administration. The Wills Report was believed to be taken by the durbar as the basis of his legitimacy to rule over the Shekhawati region. In the name of land reforms, like survey and settlement, the durbar, as it was imagined by the Shekhawat rulers, was encouraging the Jat peasants to rise against them. The Shekhawat rulers took the Wills Report as their defeat. Due to this reason too, the Shekhawat thikanedars thought of joining hands with the Rao Raja of Sikar against the durbar of Jaipur.

Apparently, one gets the impression that the entire Shekhawati turned against the Jaipur State and its durbar. A committee, known as Sikar Public Committee, was formed, and it was headed by a Bania, Badri Narain Sodhani. It had

32. Ibid., p. 19, fn. 6.
33. Ibid., p. 30.

representatives of big and small Rajputs, influential Banias and Kayasthas, and it had some workers and sympathisers from the local Praja Mandal.[34] The Sikar Public Committee was in touch with the Praja Mandal and with the Congress Committee in Ajmer. The agitation was taken in effect as a rebellion against the State of Jaipur and the British paramountcy. The Banias (seths) working outside Rajasthan at Bombay, Calcutta and elsewhere expressed their sympathy with the Rao Raja and also extended support to the agitation. Jamanalal Bajaj, a well-known Congress leader of national stature too, sympathised with the Rao Raja, and worked towards a compromise between Sikar and Jaipur. There was another committee known as Sikar Subjects Committee. This committee was organised by the Sikar seths in all cities of India outside Rajputana.

The Sikar Kayastha Sabha and some other groups too extended a helping hand to the Sikar Public Committee. June 19, 1938, the Rao Raja's birthday, was celebrated as All India Sikar Day. The Sikar Public Committee went all the way to Mount Abu, where Rao Raja was detained, to present a memorandum to the Resident for Rajputana with 40,000 signatures. Three main demands of the committee were: (1) the restoration of the Rao Raja to Sikar with full powers; (2) the retraction of the Jaipur order putting Sikar under the Court of Wards; and (3) removal of Captain Webb and Bafna, both officers working in the Sikar thikana.[35] The other demands included general amnesty for all actions until June 12, 1938, removal of Jaipur forces immediately, more time from the commission (inquiring into the Sikar agitation) for the people to appear before it.[36]

A deputation of the Jat Kisan Panchayat met the commission to extend support to the durbar for reforming the Sikar thikana. In fact, Wills Report and the agitation cheered

34. Ibid., p. 47.
35. Ibid., p. 60.
36. Ibid.

the Jat peasantry as these developments denigrated the Shekhawati thikanedars. The durbar also signalled that his policy was supported by the kisans. The Sikar Public Committee was simply an amorphous group of Rajputs, Kayasthas and Banias. The latter two were close to the thikana as members of these committees served it in different capacities. However, it is a fact that no Jat peasant was a member of the Sikar Public Committee. In general Jats had sympathy towards the durbar, but no Jat organisation joined the agitation against the thikana of Sikar. Besides Jamanalal Bajaj, other prominent leaders who contributed to the restoration of a normal situation were Heeralal Shastri and Haribhau Upadhyay. Even Kasturba Gandhi visited Sikar to find out an amicable solution of the problem.

The phenomena of 'caste alliance' as well as 'caste divide' surfaced during the Sikar agitation in a very significant and clear manner. Three to four thousand Rajputs gathered at Sikar, including the big thikanedars of Nawalgarh, Dundhlod, Mukandgarh, Mandawa and Khoor. They carried swords and muzzle loading guns. Some had sticks and some had nothing.[37] The Rajputs who gathered at Sikar were prepared to risk even their lives. The Rao Raja of Sikar was entirely in the hands of the Rajput mob. By April 26, 1938, there were 30,000 men in the fort.[38] Rajputs were considered to be so gregarious that once it was thought that if a Rajput company was despatched to Sikar, the local bhomias and thikanedars would not fight against their brethren. The following statements explicating caste sentiments are taken from the diary of Amar Singh, the thakur of Kanota:

1. The Rajputs had formed a circle around him (Rao Raja of Sikar) and were bringing him in spite of the crowd.
2. The mob (mixed groups) had rescued the Rao Rajajee from the Rajputs and were taking him back to the Gadh (fort).

37. Ibid., pp. 98–99.
38. Ibid., p. 48.

3. The Rajputs were very disgusted that they had given out that they were all going back to their homes.[39]

Certainly, there were other groups like the Mahajans and the Kayasthas who were involved in the agitation due to their deep roots in the affairs of thikanas in Shekhawati. In particular, the Sikar-born Banias, doing business in Calcutta and Bombay, were on the side of the Rao Raja, but preferred a compromise between Sikar and Jaipur.[40] Admittedly, Jats were out of the agitation as the Maharaja of Jaipur was found to be more sympathetic to their demands than the Rao Raja of Sikar.

However, the Rajputs were also unhappy with the Rao Raja of Sikar as they thought that he listened to Banias and Kayasthas and some Muslims and not to them regarding the agitation. The involvement of the Praja Mandal in the Sikar agitation was considered bad for all the Rajputs.[41] Amar Singh of Kanota thought that the leading Sardars of Shekhawati mainly helped in the agitation, and the public trusted them. Mangal Singh of Khoor was active in the movement, and gained a quite undeserved reputation as a violence-prone revolutionary. He had greater weight than anyone else. A number of Rajputs assembled at Sikar. Some came to Sikar from Reengus. They fired a few shots and killed a couple of policemen. In retaliation everyone of these Rajputs were shot down by the police.[42] The Jats were putting their heads up and holding big meetings with Mr. Young as President.[43] In other words, the sympathisers of the Rao Raja consisted of Rajputs, Banias and Kayasthas, indicating an alliance of the upper castes.[44] The Jaipur durbar lifted the externment order imposed earlier on the leaders of All India Jat Mahasabha partly to seek

39. Ibid., p. 108.
40. Ibid., p. 49.
41. Ibid., p. 119.
42. Ibid., p. 97, fn.28.
43. Ibid., p. 125.
44. Ibid., p. 133.

their goodwill and partly to create discomfiture for the Rao Raja.[45] Barring some individual Jats, no Jat organisation and Jats as a community joined the agitation in favour of the Rao Raja of Sikar. The durbar adopted the policy of divide and rule like the British by being liberal and sympathetic towards Jats. The Jats felt encouraged in protesting against the Rao Raja due to such an attitude of the durbar, and hence questioned the legitimacy of the Sikar Public Committee which supported the Rao Raja. They claimed that only the Banias and some Rajputs supported the Public Committee.[46] Rajputs came to the rescue of the Rao Raja due to the increasing role of the Praja Mandal in the region, and negative observations and recommendations made by C.U. Wills against the thikanedars of Shekhawati.[47]

VII

Peasants were differentiated socially and economically prior to independence. Agrarian hierarchy had socio-economic and political consequences for the peasantry in the Shekhawati region of Rajasthan. Structuring of society was clearly reflected in the treatment meted out by the jagirdars to the various sections of society. The peasant question was the caste question too. Both peasant and caste questions could be seen in terms of feudalism as a social formation, and as a mode of administration and polity.

Caste-peasantry nexus was differentiated at different levels of caste hierarchy. Its congruence existed mainly with regard to the principal agricultural castes. The nexus at times was so strong that it became quite problematic to disentangle caste from peasantry in the context of agrarian struggles and peasant movements in Shekhawati. The non-peasant castes were indifferent to the peasant question as their affinity with

45. Ibid., p. 61.
46. Ibid., pp. 66–67.
47. See C.U. Wills, op. cit.

land was sharply different from that of Jats. Hostility among the non-principal agricultural castes, functionary castes and the upper castes against the Rajput rulers was not much less compared to the Jats of the area. However, it also varied from caste to caste. The peasant castes (particularly the Jats) had extreme hostility towards the Rajput jagirdars and against the castes which aligned with them obviously due to the reasons discussed in this essay.

5 The Question of Identity and Sub-Nationality: A Case of Jharkhand Movement in Bihar

I

Prior to independence, three factors, namely, (i) administrative viability of the region; (ii) exploitation of the tribal people and of the mineral, material and forest resources by the *dikus* (outsiders); (iii) and ethnic distinctiveness of the *adivasis* (tribals) were forcefully articulated for the formation of the state of Jharkhand within the Indian Union.[1] These three factors continued to be the main basis for the demand for the state of Jharkhand. But, the character and complexion of the Jharkhand movement witnessed a sea-change in terms of leadership, electoral politics, discourse on ethnicity, class and power, intertribal ethnic and political linkages, and the question of identity and sub-nationality.

Our analysis in this essay is restricted to the dynamics of the movement in the post-independence period and covers

1. K.L Sharma, 1976, 'Jharkhand Movement in Bihar', *Economic and Political Weekly*, Vol. XL, No. 2. See also memorandum submitted to the States Reorganisation Commission by the Members of the Jharkhand Party in Bihar Legislature on the question of the formation of Jharkhand State with Indian Union, April 22, 1954. The points made in this memorandum were reiterated later on in two memoranda submitted to the Prime Minister of India, on March 12, 1973 and April 16, 1975.

details before the formation of the state on November 15, 2000. A mix of ethnicity, and class and power has persisted in the management of the Jharkhand movement right from its inception in 1938 with the formation of the Adivasi Mahasabha by the late Jaipal Singh, the great leader of the adivasis until the merger of the Jharkhand party with the Indian National Congress in 1963. Hindu zamindars and Bengali moneylenders exploited the adivasis of Bihar for a long time. Various tribal movements were launched against these exploiters. The British also joined the ranks of these non-tribal exploiters (dikus). The leadership of various movements prior to independence was provided by the tribal people of Bihar. This simple fact brings out the role played by ethnicity, class and power, explaining their 'mix' and the inherent contradictions between them.

To elaborate this point further, it would be appropriate to draw heuristic distinctions between class, ethnicity and power. But, at the same time, from the standpoint of the 'mix', lines demarcating the three get blurred. Since leadership of the tribal movements hailed mainly from among the tribals, it can be said that ethnicity and power coexisted. The exploiters were non-tribals, and they were not only economic dominants, but also enjoyed a great deal of patronage by the Raj. Thus, ethnicity, class and power had two contradictory formations as they were alliances comprising each other's opponents. It would be worthwhile to analyse the dynamics and dialectics of these contradictory formations in the context of the Jharkhand movement.

II

The proposed Jharkhand State, before November 15, 2000, was visualised having 28 districts, of which 18 came under Bihar, four each in Orissa and Madhya Pradesh, and two in West Bengal. It would have a population of more than 30 million, of which about 26 per cent are adivasis.[2] Despite geographical contiguity of these 28 districts the people of this region do not have a common written or spoken language or dialect. The State's Reorganisation Commission (SRC) in 1955 declined to accept the demand for the formation of the Jharkhand State mainly on the ground that the people of the region did not have a common language. The SRC had recommended the formation and redemarcation of states on the basis of 'common language' shared by the people living in a particular region.[3]

Thus, the number of states largely corresponded with the number of languages recognised as 'national' languages in India's Constitution. Ironically, during the last 50 years only one or two languages have been accorded the status of 'national' language, but contrary to this, more than ten new states have been carved out. None of the reasons such as administrative viability, common language, or even aspirations of the people have been considered as the basis for creating new states. Political expediency might have been the compelling force behind such a move from time to time.

Jharkhand had not been accepted as a separate state despite being a battlefield of uprisings, revolts and rebellions for more than 300 years against the zamindars, moneylenders, dikus, exploiters and the British. Prior to independence the tribal movements had two distinct features: (i) mobilisation of the masses against the appropriation of native resources such as forests and minerals, (ii) and social and cultural upliftment of the adivasis through various organisations such

2. See, for example, a report 'Demand for Jharkhand: Genesis,' *Times of India*, May 20, 1990; K.L. Sharma, 'Case for Jharkhand', *Hindustan Times*, December 14, 1989; and 'Genesis and Resurgence: Jharkhand Movement', *Hindustan Times*, April 27, 1988. Jharkhand was carved out as a new state on November 15, 2000 out of the existing state of Bihar. The other two new states formed besides the Jharkhand are Uttaranchal and Chhatisgarh from the states Uttar Pradesh and Madhya Pradesh, respectively.
3. Report of the States Reorganisation Commission, *Government of India*, New Delhi, 1955.

as Unnati Samaj and Adivasi Mahasabha.[4]

Prior to these reformative efforts, the Birsa uprisings at the end of the 19th century were most effective, widespread and composite endeavours against the Raj. However, more than being upheavals against an alien rule, these revolts proved quite effective in the revival of the lost status of the adivasis, restoration of their aboriginality and identity of the Chhotanagpur Raj. Use of force and symbols depicting tribal identity and unity was incorporated as the instruments of their goal attainment.

The net gains of the Birsa uprisings included tribal awakening, realisation of people's power, autonomy and forests as the lifeline of the tribals. It became evident that Chhotanagpur was a land of the adivasis, and they were never under the command of alien rulers. Another net gain was the emergence of a synthesis of tribal, Hindu and Christian cultures with pre-eminence of the tribal culture.

However, with the formation of the Unnati Samaj in 1914 the emphasis shifted from tribal autonomy to reformation in terms of abandonment of traditional customs and practices and adoption of education and new values. The Adivasi Mahasabha in 1938 in the form of a socio-cultural movement began with a certain degree of militancy for rejuvenating and revitalising the tribal society. In course of time, it got involved in the power game through elections. The Adivasi Mahasabha was rechristened as the Jharkhand Party in 1950 by its leader Jaipal Singh. The change in tone is evident from speeches by Jaipal Singh, who, as the President of the Adivasi Mahasabha, once told the adivasis:

> Arise and wake up. Recognise yourselves, you all who had been toiling and sweating under the exploiting wolves for the last hundreds of years... get this firmly nailed down in your heads that you have not been destined to cut grass and draw water for the *dikus* all your lives. You have to take your place in the society

4. K.L Sharma, op. cit., 1976.

on the basis of equality with others. So wake up, you are not inferior to any one. Assert yourselves, and fight for your rights.[5]

Exploitation, alienation and identity were the main concerns of Jaipal Singh in this emotional but realistic articulation. Keeping these points in view, he decided to fight for the cause of the adivasis politically, hence formed the Jharkhand Party.

III

Identity of Jharkhand as a distinct region was recognised as early as 6th century BC. It was known earlier as 'Khukhra' and 'Chhotanagpur'. The latter is still in vogue and it is a part of Bihar's administrative set-up. "Historical accounts corroborate the claim of administrative independence, cultural and ethnic exclusiveness, and autonomy of the region."[6] Before 6th century BC, according to B.C. Majumdar (1954), Jharkhand was known as 'Kalkavana'.[7] Majumdar writes: "I shall merely state here that the Santhal Parganas, Chutia Nagpur, the districts of Sambhalpur and the native states of adjoining Chutia Nagpur fall within Jharkhand." My own study of the Jharkhand movement suggests that until 1912 Chhotanagpur was with Bengal, and when Bihar was separated from Bengal in 1912, Chhotanagpur, Bihar and Orissa were formed as a separate state of Bihar. Further, in 1930, Orissa was carved out as a separate state and Chhotanagpur remained with Bihar.[8] It is in this way that Jharkhand remains divided in four states, namely, Bihar, Bengal, Orissa and Madhya Pradesh. Thus, a

5. In 1946 for the first lime Jaipal Singh declared—"We shall take Jharkhand". See the *Searchlight*, July 14, 1946. However, this demand was articulated vociferously at the time of the visit to Bihar of the States Reorganisation Commission in 1954.
6. B.C. Majumdar, *Aboriginals of Central India*, quoted from the States Reorganisation Commission, April 22, 1954.
7. Ibid.
8. S.C. Roy, *Mundas and Their Country*, 1912, Calcutta, City Bar Library.

major part of Jharkhand has remained with Bihar due to this intermittent bifurcation and realignment of states.[9]

S.C. Roy and several other scholars have acknowledged the uniqueness of the Jharkhand region and its people.[10] The recent history in terms of various movements, issues (raised) and organisations (formed) in the region also substantiate its claim for separate identity. The name 'Khukhra', as I have mentioned earlier, was attributed to Jharkhand before the British conquered India. In the year 1780 it was designated as the Ramgarh Hill Tract, and in 1833 it was renamed as the South-West Frontier Agency. The years 1811, 1818, 1820 and 1832 were years of uprisings against the Raj's atrocities committed on the tribal people. As a result of these upheavals the South-West Frontier Agency was rechristened as the Chhotanagpur Division with a view to create a sense of cultural and ethnic identity among the tribal people. Till recently, five districts of the Chhotanagpur comprised of this division. With an increase in the number of districts the Chhotanagpur Division has been bifurcated for administrative viability into North and South Chhotanagpur Divisions. The Santhal Parganas district has remained close to the Chhotanagpur both administratively and ethnically; it has maintained its separate identity since 1855—the year in which the famous insurrection shook the British administration.[11]

Ranchi, Palamau, Hazaribagh, Panchkot (Manbhum), Santhal Parganas of Bihar; Keonjhar, Bomai, Bambra, Gangpur and Mayurbhanj of Orissa; and Surguja, Jashpur, Udaipur, Korea and Changbharkar of Madhya Pradesh were never fully integrated with Bihar, and these districts on the other hand had

9. K.L Sharma, op. cit., 1976.

10. S.C. Roy, op. cit., and see also K.K. Datta, 1940, *The Santhal Insurrection of 1855–57*, Calcutta, University of Calcutta; R.R. Diwakar, 1959, *Bihar Through the Ages*, New Delhi, Orient Longman.

11. K.L. Sharma, op. cit., 1976; and 'Folk Culture of Jharkhand Region in Bihar', 1982, in Budhadeb Chaudhary (ed.), *Tribal Development in India: Problems and Prospects*, New Delhi, Inter-India Publications.

the geographical contiguity, ethnic homogeneity and administrative viability to come together as one state like any other state of Indian Union. All these areas were under the 'Chhotanagpur Raj' before the British took over India. Constrained by this solidary fact the Simon Commission declared Chhotanagpur and Santhal Parganas as 'partially excluded areas' in 1930. The President of India declared some areas as 'Scheduled Areas' and set up a Tribal Advisory Council.

The Hindu zamindars, Bengali moneylenders and the British rulers, besides being dikus, also impinged on the autonomy of the tribal people by adversely affecting their social organisation. The 'forest rules' and 'agricultural taxes' were used not only for oppressing and exploiting the tribal people, they also implied a process of diminishing of the tribal society itself in terms of its identity and exclusivity. Tribals valued their autonomy and freedom more than anything else, hence these movements. Being ruled by the alien people was taken as an attack on their culture, social organisation, polity and economy. Thus, most of the tribal movements including the Birsa uprisings aimed at the restoration and re-establishment of their lost status and identity.[12]

The main reformative revolts were as follows:

1. Rajas of Dalbhum, 1769–74.
2. Chuar Tribe of Midnapur, 1799.
3. Bhumij Chaur of Mahbhum, Chottanagpur and Santhal Parganas, 1795–1800.
4. Tana Revolt, 1820.
5. Kols, Hos and Mundas of Chhotanagpur, 1831–32.

12. See K.S. Singh, 1966, *The Dust-Storm and the Hanging Mist: A Study of Birsa Munda and his Movement in Chhotanagpur* (1874–1901), Calcutta, Firma, K.L. Mukhopadhyay; S.P. Sinha, 1964, *Life and Times of Birsa Bhagun*, Ranchi, Bihar Tribal Welfare Research Institute.

6. Santhals of Bihar, 1855–56.
7. Bhokta Uprising and Rai Movement, 1857.
8. Sardari Larai or Mulki Larai, 1857.
9. Kharwar Movement, 1871.
10. Birsa Uprisings, 1895–1900.
11. Bhagat Movement, 1902.
12. Kol Insurrection, 1931–32.[13]

These and several other uprisings and revolts were the result of a state of 'relative deprivation'. Economic exploitation by an alien unjust administration under the pretense of the ideal of having a just social order, became unbearable. And all the movements have exhibited abundantly the ethnic character of the people on the one hand and by waging wars against their oppressors, a sort of 'class struggle', on the other. Precisely, due to such a situation ethnic homogeneity was more or less a replica of the similarity of class background of the tribal people. It was a monolithic structure of ethnicity and class cemented in the same social formation. It was not just the exploitation and oppression of a few families and individuals. The entire tribal community was subjected to dehumanisation by the dikus. Even steps were taken by some leaders of various movements to discourage conversion of adivasis to Hinduism/Islam/Christianity. Several revivalistic movements emphasising the aboriginality of the tribals were undertaken during the 18th and 19th centuries.[14] However, in general, most of the tribal movements aimed at the uplift of the people drawing them away from the foreign yoke. The measures taken over a period of about one hundred years indicate such a 'mix' of issues

13. K.L. Sharma, op. cit., 1976; see also Ram Dayal Munda, 1988, 'The Jharkhand Movement: Retrospect and Prospect, *Social Change*, Vol. 18, No. 2.

14. K.S. Singh (ed.), 1982, *Tribal Movements in India*, 2 volumes, New Delhi, Manohar Publications, 1982. Specially see first seven articles in Volume 2. See also K.S. Singh (ed.), 1972, *Tribal Situation in India*, Shimla, Indian Institute of Advanced Study.

involved in these tribal movements. The following points may be noted:

1. Regulation XIII of 1833: the district of the Jungle Mahal was dissolved and a new district of Manbhum was formed.
2. Regulation XX of 1854: the division of Chhotanagpur was constituted under a Commissioner.
3. The Chhotanagpur Tenure Act, 1869.
4. Bengal Act 1, 1879.
5. Restoration of the khuntkattai system after the Birsa uprisings of 1895 and 1898–99.
6. Complete survey of land and compilation of record-of-rights.
7. Abolition of the bethbegari system.
8. General survey and settlement of Chhotanagpur.
9. Formation of Gumla sub-division in November 1920.
10. Formation of Khunti sub-division in December 1905.
11. Mundari Khuntkattai tenancies were established, and restriction was imposed on the sale and transfer of *raiyats* and other tenancies.
12. The Chhotanagpur Tenancy Act of 1908 was passed. This Act was an improvement over the Bengal Tenancy Act as it took local customs and other considerations into account.
13. Large-scale conversion to Christianity during the first two decades of the present century.[15]

Obviously movements prior to the Birsa uprisings highlighted the agrarian problems, need for awakening and politicisation among the tribals, antipathy to conversion to Christianity, and formation of organisations and institutions for the welfare of the people. Birsa, in particular, longed for a Munda Raj and projected himself as the Father of the World

15. K.L. Sharma, op. cit., 1976.

(*Dharti-Aba*). Even some of the 20th century revivalistic and reformative movements have emphasised eradication of social evils prevalent among the adivasis by emulating laudable habits and practices of other non-tribals. Several efforts were made to educate the adivasis for adopting a new pattern of life on the lines of those who were much ahead of them in Indian society.

IV

The two main objectives set out for the Adivasi Mahasabha, namely, (i) statehood for the Jharkhand region, and (ii) protection of the adivasis from the dikus, could be realised by vocalising them politically as envisaged by Jaipal Singh. These objectives were clearly indicative of the Jharkhand sub-nationality. Jaipal Singh, therefore, decided to form the Jharkhand Party in 1950 replacing the Adivasi Mahasabha. Singh had already unsuccessfully contested elections prior to this in 1946 for a seat in the Provincial Council. Jaipal Singh, though educated abroad, emerged as a leader—a sort of 'local' autochthon of the tribals of Bihar. He sought the cooperation of the non-tribals too, in his endeavour to fight for the tribal people. However. the Indian National Congress did not accept several of his demands and branded the Adivasi Mahasabha as a reactionary and Christian-dominated particularistic organisation.

After his defeat in 1946 at the hands of a Congress worker, Jaipal Singh vowed: "We shall take Jharkhand." He declared that it was the land of the adivasis, and the dikus (outsiders) had to leave this land. At this initial stage tribal identity was at its peal, emanating mainly from the hatred generated against the non-adivasis. Christian tribals in general and the Mundas in particular (Jaipal Singh was a Munda and so was Birsa) created a stir against the Congress party and the north Biharis labelling the latter as 'dikus'. The Christian missions were not only active instruments in such an upsurge but they also provided all the material help to accelerate the movement. The non-converts, while disagreeing with the Christian converts, preferred to maintain their aboriginal character, and some of them also leaned towards Hinduism—drifting towards the Tana Bhagat movement.

While analysing the background of the Jharkhand question Nirmal Sengupta deals with the concept of 'diku' at length implying 'outsider-exploiter' as the main cause of the Jharkhand movement in Bihar and the three neighbouring states of Bengal, Orissa and Madhya Pradesh.[16] The category of the outsider-exploiter comprises the non-tribal upper class bourgeoisie in the form of zamindars, moneylenders, top-level government officials, industrialists and businessmen. In particular, they are the people of north Bihar who have monopolised most of the lucrative and prestigious jobs and positions in the government and public sector. In view of such a situation, persisting ceaselessly for centuries, an identity of the exploited has emerged, particularly over the past one hundred years. It is a 'juxtaposed identity' as Sengupta rightly observes with respect to the concept of diku.[17]

Emergence of the self-identity seems to be a difficult task based on exploitation and oppression of the people in this region. However, most of the tribal movements have emphasised on the need for a regional sub-national self-identity of the adivasis of the region. The Birsa uprisings, Unnati Samaj, Adivasi Mahasabha and the Jharkhand Party have strived for achieving this cherished goal. In recent years, efforts have been made to bring together the adivasis and the Sadans by forging not only a strategic alliance between the two numerically most preponderant segments of the Jharkhand region but also to make them conscious of their similar existential conditions *vis-à-vis* the North Biharis, Panjabis and Marwaris. However,

16. Nirmal Sengupta, 1982, 'Background of the Jharkhand Question,' in *Fourth World Dynamics: Jharkhand*, Nirmal Sengupta (ed.), Delhi, Shankar Printing Service.

17. Ibid.

this kind of unity is only one of the several channels of bringing together the tribals and their non-tribal counterparts.

The phenomenon of identity is a complex one. It has not received due attention in scholarly writings. K.S. Singh, in his opening remarks, in *Tribal Movements in India*, observes: "The tribal societies in middle India, unlike those in the North-East, were closely integrated with the prevailing colonial system, its economy and administration."[18] Singh, in his writings on the Jharkhand movement, logically, therefore, derives that it is a 'separatist' movement in the sense that the tribals who have been integrated with the mainstream since the reign of the Raj are trying to detach themselves obviously for political gains. This is why he observes that alongside the agrarian struggles, Bhagat movement and sanskritisation process have been prominent features of the tribal society in middle India.[19]

Another observation rather an inference by K.S. Singh calls for a close scrutiny. He writes: "Studies of these (tribal) movements suggest that tribal unrest assumes an organised character only among the large homogeneous, landowning tribal communities who have a relatively strong economic base such as the Munda, Santhal, Bhil, Gond, etc."[20] Singh further mentions that literate and politically articulate tribals have taken up the issues concerning land and forestry. A new urban middle class from among the tribals is taking up the issues concerned with reservation of jobs, employment, exploitation, etc.

The leadership of the Jharkhand movement, despite ethnic divide, cultural barriers, political and factional cleavages and intrigues, has remained solely confined to the tribals. Birsa Munda, Jaipal Singh, N.E. Horo, Shibu Soren, Bagun Sumbrai, Justin Richard and several others could be mentioned as

18. See K.S. Singh, 1983, Vol. II, op. cit.
19. See K.S. Singh, 1972, op. cit., and 1985, *Tribal Society in India*, New Delhi, Manohar Publications.
20. K.S. Singh, op. cit., Vol. II, 1983.

well-known leaders of the adivasis of Bihar. Only during the past decade or so, with the emergence of the Jharkhand Mukti Morcha, Jharkhand Coordination Committee and All Jharkhand Students Union, and the people like B.P. Kesari, Santosh Rana, S.S. Besra, S.B. Mallick, M.I. Ansari and some others have joined the movement with a view to bring together the adivasis and Sadans to rejuvenate the movement with a broad-based secular ideology. However, still the core of the leadership of different political groups belongs to different tribes of the region.

This is not true of the non-tribal peasant movements. For example, AJGAR is a union of agricultural castes. On the contrary, the Bijolia movement in Rajasthan was led mainly by Brahmins and Banias with some Kshatriyas and Kayasthas. In various kisan movements in the Jat heartland of Rajasthan, leaders were from among several non-Jat communities.[21] Thus, to call the Jharkhand movement a 'separatist movement' in the past and now transforming itself into a 'regional movement' undermines its present-day reality, historicity and the concern for the oppressed of the region. Undue emphasis on the diffusionist perspective for analysing the tribal situation in Jharkhand tantamounts to the underestimation of the tribal pathology created by the colonisers both alien and indigenous.

Despite immigration and emigration in the Jharkhand region social differentiation and mobility, and influences of Hinduism, Islam and Christianity, *autochthons* are not only vividly visible and existent, they continue to suffer at the hands of the exploiters. The foremost among them are the tribal people. Existentially, their counterparts are the Sadans—people of those castes and communities, who are not 'scheduled' under the Constitution, but lead more or less a miserable social life comparable to that of the tribals of Bihar.[22]

21. K.L. Sharma, 1986, 'Feudalism and Peasant Movements in Rajasthan', *The Journal of Sociological Studies*, Vol. 5.

22. See Nirmal Sengupta, 1982, op. cit., and Myron Weiner, 1978, *Sons of the Soil*, Princeton, Princeton University Press.

It is increasingly realised that due to in-migration and out-migration, social mobility, education and electoral process, non-tribal communities and groups have come closer to the tribal people in regard to language, culture and occupation. However, the tribals are much closer to the Sadans than the upper castes, and through forging a unity between these strata a 'Jharkhandi identity' could be established. Active participation of the Sadan intellectuals and leaders with their tribal counterparts in the Jharkhand movement is considered as a step forward towards Jharkhandi identity. Efforts for evolving a common language and common cultural and social patterns by launching teaching and research at the university level are strong indicators of inter-tribal and tribal-Sadan identity in the region. Mahatos. Bhuinyas, Momins (Muslims) share the same existential conditions as are found in the case of Santhals, Mundas, Oraons and Hos. Some of these non-tribal communities have even demanded their inclusion in the scheduled lists of the SCs and the STs. Thus, today, Jharkhand, as Sengupta observes, is not merely a geographic region, it is a land of depressed people, it is a mass of destitutes. He further observes: "Jharkhand is developing; but not the Jharkhandis."[23] Thus, the identity is not to be seen in terms of its conventional meaning, namely, homogeneity of ethnicity, language, caste, religion, region, etc. In the Jharkhand region, now, the language spoken by the oppressed and the exploited is the basis of their identity formation.

Who are the 'sons of the soil'? Technically, those who have received education for one or two years, or whose parents have served in the state, could be considered as 'sons of the soil'. But those who are born and have lived for generations do not become 'sons of the soil' in the technical sense as they neither have the privilege of going to school or college nor their parents have been in employment of the government.

23. Nirmal Sengupta, 1982, op. cit.

Hence, they remain deprived of the privileged jobs and positions which in fact go to 40 per cent of those people who have settled in the Jharkhand region—the fortunate north Biharis. Precisely, due to this reason, bifurcating of the Santhal Parganas district into three districts was opposed by the adivasis as it would benefit only the non-adivasis. Similarly, opening of new developmental programmes and projects was resisted fearing that its dividends would be harvested by the dikus.

V

After the formation of the Jharkhand Party in 1950, the party delivered goods electorally and politically in the first three general elections of 1952, 1957 and 1962, and it remained as the main official opposition party in Bihar legislature under the stewardship of Jaipal Singh. The question of Jharkhand State was uppermost in the mind of the leadership during these 15 years following independence. The leadership was restricted with the Mundas and with some Oraons, and from among these communities some coverts to Christianity dominated the political leadership. Not only the leadership had close connections with the churches, they even received all the possible support and help from them. Even the offices of the party in some cases were housed in the Church premises. Thus, it was a period exclusively characterised by tribal leadership under solid command of Jaipal Singh.

Jaipal Singh, however, established contacts with Panjabis and influential Biharis, particularly with those who were not happy with the Congress rule in Bihar. Gopal Munjal, a Panjabi, was Secretary of the party at the time of its merger in 1963 with the Congress. Later on, one Juneja (Panjabi) and one Rajgarhia (Marwari) were associated with the party looking after its finances. The Raja of Ramgarh and Minoo Masani were not only involved in the affairs of the party prior to its merger with the Congress, they were even elected to Rajya Sabha as candidates of the Jharkhand Party. Jaipal Singh not only annoyed his associates in the party by seeking help from the capitalists, Panjabis, Marwaris, feudal elements, etc., but also distanced from the government of the day due to this 'unholy alliance'. Such an alliance with the influential non-tribal leaders and economic dominants did not help in the formation of the Jharkhandi identity. However, the movement remained confined mainly to the tribal leadership. Concretisation of the Jharkhandi identity and consciousness has become evident more with the upstaging of the JMM, JCC and AJSU. Intellectuals, youths and students in particular have contributed to the abridgement of the gap between the tribals and the non-tribals in the region.

6 Cultural and Ideological Dimensions of Jharkhand Movement in Bihar

I

This essay is limited in its scope as it seeks to understand mainly cultural and ideological roots and dimensions of the Jharkhand movement in Bihar. A sociology of knowledge perspective may help in identifying these aspects *vis-à-vis* the background of the individuals and groups involved in the Jharkhand movement. At the outset, a clarification may be offered. The Jharkhand movement in Bihar does not have a religious origin, nor religion has openly been used to speed up the pace and direction of the movement. However, religious underpinnings have at times been the source of contentions and mobilisations in the long and chequered history of the Jharkhand movement. Religion in the form of a *sui generis* phenomenon of social life (Durkheim), as a means of rationalisation of cultural and ideological moorings (Weber), and as an opiate of the masses could not entrench into the tribal social life (Marx).[1]

1. Karl Marx, Max Weber, and Emile Durkheim deal with religion as an opiate of the masses, institutional means of economic development, and a functional-integrative mechanism of social life, respectively. Religion in the context of Jharkhand movement has not been effective in any of these interpretations.

II

Three streams of religious consciousness, namely, tribal, Hindu and Christian, have co-existed with differing intents and at cross-purposes. Tribal consciousness seeks restoration of aboriginality and rectification of distortions in primitive religion and culture by revising some of the traditional institutions and practices. Exclusivity and distinctiveness are considered as salient features of tribal social life to fight against the onslaught of alien culture and domination. Hindu way of life is claimed as superior to the tribal and other non-Hindu cultures and practices. Such a notion of superiority of culture has allured many tribal groups towards the Hindu way of life. Acceptance of vegetarianism, teetotalism and Hindu rituals is evident among the tribal people in many parts of India. Tana Bhagat movement among adivasis in Bihar and Bhagatism among the Bhils of Rajasthan, Madhya Pradesh and Gujarat bring home the impact of Hinduism on the north Indian tribes.[2] Additionally, the tribals have also been brought under the influence of Hinduism by several organisations and groups to discourage them from conversion to Christianity in particular.[3]

Conversion to Christianity has created a distinct socio-cultural divide among the tribal people by splitting them into converts and non-converts. Christian missions shouldered

2. See, for example, K.L. Sharma, 1976, *Economic and Political Weekly*, Vol. XI, No. 1, pp. 37–43; S.L. Doshi, 1970, *Tribal Ethnicity, Class and Integration*, Jaipur, Rawat Publications; K.S. Singh, 1982, 'Transformation of Tribal Society: Integration vs Assimilation', *Economic and Political Weekly*, Vol. XVII, No. 33, pp. 1318–25; Sachchidananda, 1990, 'Patterns of Politico-Economic Change among Tribes in Middle India', in Francine R. Frankel and M.S.A. Rao (eds.), *Dominance and State Power in Modern India: Decline of a Social Order*, Delhi, Oxford University Press, pp. 278–320.
3. Academy of Indian Culture, an organisation sponsored and managed by the Birla industrial house, located at Ranchi, has been engaged in propagation of Hinduism and negation of Christianity among the tribes of Chhotanagpur. Several pamphlets and booklets to this effect have been published by the Academy.

the responsibility of converting adivasis to Christianity.[4] Inducements and allurements through churches were provided with a view to inculcate a new consciousness and ideology among adivasis. The beneficiaries of conversion to Christianity can be identified in terms of their better modern education, white collar employment, and improved standard of living, compared to the non-converts. The converts naturally had the support of Christian missions and churches in voicing the demand for the formation of the Jharkhand State. A number of leaders of this movement organised their political activities while remaining close to various missions and churches. Some of them even housed offices of their parties and organisations in the campuses of churches located at Ranchi and in some other towns.[5] Thus, cultural diversity is the hallmark of the loose configuration of Jharkhand region as reflected in the presence of the tribes such as Santhal, Ho, Munda, Oraon, Chero, etc. on one hand, and the non-tribal groups like north Biharis, Bengalis, Marwaris, Punjabis and Sadans on the other. Adivasis and Sadans are being put together as Jharkhandis in terms of their downtrodden existence and socio-cultural homogeneity.

III

The questions regarding the Jharkhandis are: Are they free and autonomous agents, able to create and control their own lives? Are there no alienation and dehumanisation? Is there no reified politico-administrative hegemony of the *dikus* (particularly of the north Biharis)? Without having freedom for determining their present and future state of affairs, the Jharkhandis cannot

4. See, K.N. Sahay, 1981, 'Indeginisation of Christianity', *Man in India*, January-March; L.P. Vidyarthi, 1974, 'Tribal Ethnography in India', *A Survey of Research in Sociology and Social Anthropology*, Vol. III, ICSSR, Popular Prakashan, Bombay, pp. 31–33.
5. For example, the office of the Jharkhand Party headed by N.E. Horo in the seventies was located in the huge campus of the G.E.L. Church at Ranchi.

create a 'community' of their own, and true wants and needs might not be crystallised and articulated. Why the Jharkhandis have not succeeded in elimination of such a sorry state of oppression and exploitation? The decisive thing is to establish the human conditions that will create a 'community' of the Jharkhandis in true sense as an alternative to the existing hegemonic, oppressive and exploitive situation.

A theory of practice reflecting the Jharkhandis as a 'homologous' entity, a cultural identity, and a fighting force, demanding total transformation of social life seems to be the only alternative to the age-old pathetic plight of the natives of the Jharkhand region. Logically speaking, control over the institutions and organisations by the natives in the Jharkhand region would regenerate and rechannelise the material wealth and bring about what is known as 'cultural' and 'symbolic' capital to the people in the form of knowledge, skills, cultural acquisitions, prestige and honour.[6] It would be a beginning of a new history 'deconstructing' the 'colonial history' which was transformed into the history of 'internal colonisation' by the north Bihari mandarins.

One reason for the non-realisation of the formation of a separate state of Jharkhand was lack of a clear vision of a new world for the Jharkhandis. In a political battle like this 'words' (ideology) are action; a new symbolism (character of power) substituting the existing one alone can stir the people emotionally in their actions and mobilisations. Slogans, programmes and commentaries are devised and used to construct and impose a particular vision of the social world.[7] In the case of the Jharkhand, it would be a diku-free socio-economic and political formation. People are mobilised to seek support for the practice of the new vision (programmes and

6. Bourdieu, Pierre, 1991, *Language and Symbolic Power*, see 'Editor's Introduction, by John B. Thompson. Cambridge, Polity Press, pp. 1–31.
7. Ibid., pp. 171–203.

policies). Formation of a political party is part of such a process, and the Jharkhand region is abundantly filled up with political parties and groups. In all, there were more than twenty political parties and groups claiming to work for the formation of the Jharkhand state. In the recent economic blockades as many as fourteen political parties were involved in the agitation as well as in the negotiations with the central government.[8]

A cursory look at the political situation in the Jharkhand region suggests that the politicians have been intensely competing with one another to such an extent that their relational status becomes a constraint and a serious handicap in the operationalisation of the cherished programmes and policies. The relation of the existing political milieu with the external groups and processes also becomes a constraint on political discourse and debate. New slogans, promises and pledges of support do not remain focused. Political parties get subscriptions and votes, and therefore, these parties and groups have diluted and marginalised the main issue. Hence, they are looked at with vulnerability of suspicion and scandal.[9]

The cultural and social exclusivity of the areas of Chhotanagpur and the Santhal Parganas has been accepted as a ground reality. Special Tenancy Acts for these areas were provided by the British. Districts like Manbhum and Singhbhum and sub-divisions like Gumla and Khunti were created keeping in view tribal cultural identity. The various movements, in which Chaurs, Bhumijs, Santhals, Kols, Hos,

8. See, for example, 'Pilot sets Jharkhand on fire', *Indian Express*, 21st August, 1994.; 'Jharkhand parties vow to unite', *Telegraph*, 27th April, 1995; 'Jharkhand or Jhaarkhand?', *Hindustan Times*, 13th September, 1995.; 'Bandh disrupts life in Jharkhand region', *Indian Express*, 16th March, 1996; 'Factionalism keeps Jharkhandis divided', *Indian Express*, 23rd September, 1996; *Times of India*, March 3, 20, 21, 26, April 19, 1993, and *Hindustan Times*, March 12, 15, 16, 18, 25, 26, 1993.

9. Bourdieu, Pierre, op. cit., pp. 194–202.

Mundas, etc. were involved during the 18th and 19th centuries, aimed at the formation of a distinct character and identity of adivasis. These movements were basically against the deconstruction of the adivasi culture and identity, which were being destroyed and deconstructed by the British in collusion with their collaborators like the Hindu zamindars and the Bengali moneylenders. Such a deconstruction of tribal/Jharkhandi identity and consciousness is still persisting as the Jharkhand region remains today under the politico-administrative grip of the north Biharis and under the material and cultural subordination of Marwaris and Punjabis.[10]

The movements between 1769 and 1900 (upto the Birsa uprisings) concentrated on the recognition of the distinct character of the adivasis and the region in which they lived by claiming their glorious past having administrative independence, cultural and ethnic exclusiveness, and autonomy of the region by calling it 'Kalkavan' and 'Khukhara', a land of forests.[11] Carving out a socio-cultural space in a plural society like ours may lead to such a state of atomism and boundary-maintenance in which certain anti-social, anti-national creatures may come to stay in the body politic. Politics of communitarianism communalism, regionalism in the form of a new social differentiation creating new power-wielders and parties and groups is the obvious logical product of such a situation. Reflections of identity formation or change of persisting identity imply socio-cultural outbursts and excessive

10. See, K.L. Sharma, 1990, 'Jharkhand Movement: The Questions of Identity and sub-nationality', *Social Action*, Oct.-Dec., pp. 371–381; Nirmal Sengupta, 1982, 'Background of the Jharkhand Question', in Nirmal Sengupta (ed.), *Fourth World Dynamics: Jharkhand*, Delhi, Authors Guild Publication; and 1980, 'Class and Tribe in Jharkhand', *Economic and Political Weekly*, Vol. XV, No. 4, pp. 664–71; Arun Sinha, 1978, 'Resurgent Adivasis', *EPW*, Vol. XIII, No.36, pp. 1544–46; 'Recurrent Pattern of Jharkhand Politics', *EPW*, Vol. XXII, No.45, pp. 1887–88.

11. Sharma, K.L., 1976, op. cit., see also K.L. Sharma, 1982, 'Folk-culture of Jharkhand Region in Bihar', in Buddhadeb Chaudhary (ed.), *Tribal Development in India: Problems and Prospects*, New Delhi, Inter-India Publications.

expression of collective consciousness. Rigidity of collective consciousness is followed by the creation of a new psyche and a renewed process of socialisation. A society is divided into categories distinguished by cultural characteristics and symbolic referents.[12] Two cultures and two histories are reflected in most encounters in the form of the establishing, affirming side, and the oppositional, polemical side.[13]

This may be termed as a conflict between the indigenous people and the outsiders, the poor and the rich, the exploited and the exploiter, the powerful and the weak, etc. Manifestation and expression of divergent cultures thus reflect the deep-seated structural realities of a given social formation. Such a situation cannot simply be characterised by having ethnocentrism, romanticism or indigenous complex. The question is: Who are the people who have not accepted such an ontological certitude, cognitive/ideological construction? The British rejected the exclusivity of the Chhotanagpur and the Santhal Parganas by framing new forest laws. The zamindars, with the connivance of the Raj, appropriated agricultural surplus and ultimately alienated the adivasis from their lands and forests. The moneylenders, by introducing usury, mortgaging, and unfair means, have destablised tribal economy and its institutional complex.[14]

IV

Twenty-eight districts of the Jharkhand region comprise of about 30 per cent of the total population of the area. However, adivasis, clubbed with Sadans, constitute about 85 per cent population of the Jharkhand region. Govind Kelkar and Dev Nathan write about the two communities as follows: "The symbolic relation between the adivasis and Sadans has resulted in the creation of a composite culture and a common world

12. Brass, Paul R., 1991, *Ethnicity and Nationalism: Theory and Comparison*, New Delhi, Sage Publications, p. 62.
13. Gouldner, A.W., 1975, *For Sociology*, Pelican Books, pp. 74–84.

outlook."[15] This composite culture and world outlook of Jharkhand, with its adivasi core, is somewhat different from the adjoining cultures of the plains. Kelkar and Nathan further observe that the Jharkhandi cosmology is different from the cosmology of caste society in the plains. Jharkhand has acquired a cultural identity of its own having the elements such as harmony with nature, equality in society, including that of gender, collective orientation in social and economic domains, etc. The colonial rulers, zamindars and moneylenders (all non-tribal) have created values supporting disharmony with nature, stratification, greater control over women, and individualism.[16]

The colonial state was alien to the Jharkhandi society. It created an administrative machinery over the area, and to manage the area and its people, the Raj sought the help of the non-tribal intermediaries, traders, landlords, moneylenders, administrators, clerks and policemen. The tribals never reconciled with their presence in the Jharkhand region. They treated them as the diku (exploiters). Thus, two conflicting cultures and styles of functioning emerged in the region due to the entrenchment of the British and its agents into Chhotanagpur and Santhal Pargans. The Chhotanagpur comprised of five districts until recently, and the Santhal Parganas was only a district. Now, the two divisions are constituted of eighteen districts. Thus, twelve more districts have been created in a period of two decades. Even 'development' is seen with suspicion and fraught by the Jharkhandis.

Javed Alam observes that it is a curious fact that the people of the region agitate against the construction of major

14. See, for example, K.L. Sharma, 1976, op. cit., Nirmal Sengupta, 1982, op. cit., and Boniface Minz, 1992, 'The Jharkhand Movement', in Walter Fernandes (ed.), *National Development and Tribal Deprivation*, New Delhi, Indian Social Institute, pp. 345–72.

15. Kelkar, Govind and Nathan, Dev, 1991, *Gender and Tribe, Women, Land and Forests in Jharkhand*, New Delhi, Kali for Women, pp. 21–32.

16. Ibid., p. 23.

irrigation projects or appose the setting up of big industries. For them, even the construction of a road means primarily opening the area to the dikus and the police, i.e., to exploitation and terror. Historically viewed, development activities have meant land alienation and pauperisation for the people of Jharkhand. Their opposition is not simply a misguided and misconstrued opposition of the primitive to the programmes of national development, as it is portrayed.[17]

In the early seventies the proposal to bifurcate the Santhal Parganas in two or three districts was vehemently opposed by the local adivasi leaders as they thought that it would help only the non-tribals in getting employment and administrative power over them. They categorically expressed the view that it would further fortify the north Bihari bastion in the Santhal Parganas. Thus even administrative expansion and realignment are taken as an onslaught on the Jharkhandi culture and identity. Jharkhand is not merely a region consisting of 18 districts of Bihar and 10 adjoining districts of West Bengal, Orissa, and Madhya Pradesh, it is a 'social space', which is being exploited by the north Biharis and other outsiders in the form of a 'colony', a 'field', and a 'market'. Thus, Jharkhand cannot be treated as a 'region' in geographical sense. Even as a boundaried territory it is more a social and cultural entity than an area constituted of 18 districts of Bihar and 10 districts from the other three neighbouring states.

The people of the region as a social category have opposed their subordination in the form of economic and cultural marginalisation. The movement for the formation of a separate state of Jharkhand is directed against the hegemonic conditions and practices created by colonialism, which were transformed into neocolonialism or internal colonialism after

17. Alam, Javed, 1989, 'The Category of Non-Historic Nations and Tribal Identity in Jharkhand', P.C. Chatterjee (ed.), *Self-Images, Identity and Nationality*, quoted from Govind Kelkar and Dev Nathan, 1991, op. cit., p. 27.

independence confirming control of the region in the hands of the dikus, namely, the north Biharis, in particular.

Susane Devalle examines the problems of Jharkhand mainly from a class point of view though not ignoring its socio-cultural dimension.[18] She writes: "Jharkhand's ethno-history reveals not the existence of tribes but rather a variegated development of its indigenous societies and processes of transition from lineage and community-based societies to a class-based society. A review of Jharkhandi ethnohistory makes visible the historical depth of its adivasi communities, socio-cultural styles and how social maintenance and the attachment to land and territory have acted as an axis for the reproduction of collective identities. These dynamics were present in the past, and they survive today."[19] According to Devalle, tribal groups are basically peasant societies inserted in a class society, portraying at the same time specific ethno-cultural styles.[20] Jharkhand is thus more than a geographical region and a class formation: it is a distinct socio-cultural and eco-region.[21]

V

Why Jharkhand movement? One of the reasons as mentioned by Boniface Minz is that because of the entry of outsiders into the Chhotanagpur region, the tribals lost their proprietary rights on land and control of the resources.[22] Land alienation

18. Devalle, Susane, 1992, *Discourses of Ethnicity, Culture and Protest in Jharkhand*, New Delhi, Sage Publications, p. 51.
19. Ibid., p. 52.
20. Ibid., p. 53.
21. Sharma, K.L., 1990, 'Jharkhand Movement: The Questions of Identity and Sub-Nationality', *Social Action*, October-December, pp. 368–81; See also K.L. Sharma, 'Case for Jharkhand', *The Hindustan Times*, December 14, 1989; 'Genesis and Resurgence: Jharkhand Movement', *The Hindustan Times*, April 27, 1988; and 'Jharkhand State is Inevitable', *The Hindustan Times*, September 11, 1992.
22. Minz, Boniface, 1992, op. cit., p. 345.

was the cause of many tribal uprisings in the past.[23] Another reason is that due to alien settlers in the reason the natives could not keep intact their own socio-economic system, cultures and values. There are no more the Khuntkatti land-tenure system and the system of Parha and Manki-Munka to have the original *hatu* (village) life.

By forming a state of their own in the region the natives can develop in their own way and assert their culture and identity, and reconstruct the destroyed cultural heritage.[24] Minz observes that the aspirations of the tribals have their roots in the values which they cherish as a community, and this they could realise by having self-determination and maintenance of their identity.[25] Age-old suppression and all forms of subjugation have to go. They suffer from the disadvantages of the development, planned and implemented by the central and the state governments. Development is essentially limitarian due to the constraints and pulls and pressures of political power.[26] Development has caused multifaceted alienation, namely, from land, forests and mineral resources on the one hand, and has also deprived the tribals and Sadans from its positive gains, on the other.[27]

The tribal societies in middle India (including the Jharkhand region) were closely integrated with the then prevailing colonial system, its economy and administration.[28]

23. Singh, K.S., 1966, *The Dust-Storm and the Hanging Mist: A Study of Birsa Munda and His Movement in Chhotanagpur (1874–1901)*, Calcutta, Firma, K.L. Mukhopadhyay; *Tribal Situation in India* (ed.), 1972, Shimla, Indian Institute of Advanced Study; *Tribal Movements in India* (ed.), Vol. 2, 1983, New Delhi, Manohar Publications; and *Tribal Society in India*, 1985, New Delhi, Manohar Publications.
24. Sarkar, Jagnath, 1988, 'Government to Blame for Jharkhand Demand', *The Times of India*, May 23; 'Jharkhand Problem in Perspective', *Mainstream*, Vol. 27, No.4, 1989, pp. 19–22. See also K.S. Singh, 1985, op. cit.
25. Minz, Boniface, 1992, op. cit., p. 349.
26. Sharma, K.L., 1992, 'Jharkhand State is Inevitable', op. cit.
27. Minz, Boniface, 1992, op. cit.
28. Singh, K.S., 1983, op. cit.

K.S. Singh states that large homogenous, landowning tribal communities with a strong economic base alone would be able to organise unrest.[29] The Jharkhand movement involves literate and politically articulate tribals, namely, a new urban middle class from among the tribals, voicing issues concerning land and forests. Hence, according to Singh, Jharkhand movement is 'separatist' and a 'regional' or a 'sub-regional' phenomenon, because it challenges the historically accomplished state of integration of the tribal people with the larger society, economy and polity. Such an observation by Singh calls for a serious scrutiny.[30] No 'anti-national' connotation can be attributed to the Jharkhand movement.

The Jharkhand movement is also viewed as a demand for bifurcation of Bihar and the creation of a new state of Jharkhand as the separate 'homeland' for the tribals.[31] The movement is being resisted by the central and the state governments and by Bihar's non-tribal population due to their strong vested interests in the region, which is rich in minerals and other resources.[32] However, some sweeping statements made by A.N. Das in this context are: India's indigenous peoples have not witnessed the mass extermination or brutal subjugation as elsewhere; the tribals have integrated with the non-tribal people; despite the integral role played by the tribal, they have been treated as 'alien', 'the other', 'the exotic' and 'the marginal'.[33] Near-total oppression, subjugation and exploitation of the tribals by the non-tribals are witnessed in history of tribal uprisings, revolts and movements. Again historical evidence is not lacking that outsiders have taken over the main sources of livelihood such as land and forests from the tribals;

29. Singh, K.S., 1985, op. cit.
30. Singh, K.S., 1972, op. cit.
31. Das, Arvind N., 1992, 'Jharkhand's Roots, *The Republic of Bihar*, Penguin Books, pp. 83–99.
32. Ibid.
33. Ibid., p. 82.

and the latter have been forced to leave the Jharkhand region to far off areas in Assam and Bengal for bare survival, to work as plantation workers and wage-earners.[34]

While heavily relying on the K.S. Singh's analysis of the Jharkhand movement, Das observes that the Jharkhand resurgence has been created in recent decades due to oppression, exploitation, ecological imbalance, commercial exploitation of forest resources, cultural humiliation, forced migration, land alienation and semi-enslavement of the adivasis by the outsiders. The emergence of a middle class among the adivasis has given a new complexion to the Jharkhand movement. Resistance to domination and exploitation, landlordism and usury has particularly been feared by the new middle class from among the Jharkhandis.

Further, Das opines that an overall radicalisation of the polity changed the character of the movement in the 1960s. The movement could be seen in terms of political 'extremism', agrarian radicalism, cultural revivalism of the subaltern groups, rise of urban and industrial pressure groups, etc. According to both Das and Singh, the movement was quite fragmented and factionalised during the 1960s. The movement has passed through several phases including the rise of the Jharkhand Party led by Jaipal Singh, followed by a lull and a hazy vision, emergence of militancy, and revivalism under the leadership of Shibu Soren, and incorporation of the non-tribal leaders and workers in the movement signifying Jharkhandi identity and consciousness despite persisting fragmentation of the Jharkhand movement.[35] Recent alleged acceptance of bribery by some Jharkhand leaders to vote in favour of the P.V. Narsimha Rao government has further demoralised the rank and file of the movement by inflicting a severe jolt on the demand for a separate state of Jharkhand. But as we know that despite all these decades old hindrances, political expediency of

34. Sengupta, Nirmal, 1980, op. cit.

35. Das, Arvind N., op. cit., pp. 82–92.

the present NDA government compelled it to create the State of Jharkhand along with two more states, namely, Uttaranchal and Chhatisgarh in the year 2000.

The Jharkhand movement was not a regional movement; it was not simply a tribal/ethnic protest movement. To call it a 'separatist' or 'anti-national' movement would tantamount to a ridicule of the sixty years old struggle for emancipation of the Jharkhandis from the dikus. Victor Das calls it a 'movement for political power'.[36] Power for whom? For the leaders or for the people? Fragmented and factionalised leaders of the movement evidently indicated empowerment of the leaders who used the movement as a handy instrument. But, the movement in the form of a voice against the dikus and the government spoke of its concern for the Jharkhandis. Das writes: "The term 'Jharkhandi' includes the tribals, the Sadans and other non-tribal people who are residing in Jharkhand with respect for the culture, tradition and religion of the tribals and support for their cause."[37] Reports after the formation of the movement are not quite encouraging. Clamouring for ministerial berths and high offices of power and prestige have often been reported in both national and local press. Jharkhand State is being seen as a replica of Bihar by the local people. The Bihar rut has to be curbed in the bud itself. Such observations have been articulated by the alert citizens.

The objective of the movement was to carve out a liberated social space for the Jharkhandis. It aimed to reconstruct its distorted past and to eliminate all social force and violence by the dikus. Thus, the aim of the Jharkhand

36. See, for example, K.S. Singh, 1985, op. cit.; Sachidananda, 1990, op. cit.; Ghanshyam Shah, 1979, 'Tribal Identity and Class Differentiations: A Case Study of the Chaudhari Tribe', *Economic and Political Weekly*, Vol. XIV, Nos. 7 & 8, pp. 459–69; 'Stratification among the Scheduled Tribes in the Bharuch and Panch Mahals Districts of Gujarat', in S.C. Malik (ed.), *Determinants of Social Status in India*, Delhi, Motilal Banarsi Das, pp. 149–83.

37. Singh, K.S., 1985, op. cit.

movement was to have a state of society in which the Jharkhandis were free, autonomous, able to create and control their own lives, where no alienation and subjugation persisted. Such a society would be a 'whole society'. Such a social transformation could take place through a political practice. However, this aim could be realised if the leaders and champions of all shades and hues joined hands in a community that shared a common language. Only through the instrumentality of a community formation they could uproot and demystify the established ideology and consciousness created by the Raj and perpetrated by the central and the state governments and the ruling parties. A coherent ideology emanating from such a community could produce an emancipated society. Vested interests had been detrimental to the formation of such a community in the past.

There is a long history of the 'breakdown' of the community formation in the Jharkhand region. Political parties, electoral politics, and the hold of a select group on institutionalised power have come as a stumbling stone in the construction of the community of the Jharkhandis. The political leadership is distancing itself from the masses creating independent source of their power and influence. This may be termed as 'political fetishism'. Instead of fighting for the cause of the Jharkhand state, the leaders of this movement were indulging in the creation of 'political capital', namely, votes and money for themselves. No doubt, they had produced new slogans, promises and pledges to the people, but without a convincing appeal. They had become vulnerable to suspicion and corruption. Each one was engaged actively in the construction of a 'political field' for himself.

VI

The Birsa uprisings (1895–1900) aimed at the economic liberation and an overall emancipation of the tribals from the hegemonic control of the Raj, zamindars, and moneylenders.

Not much difference could be seen in today's Jharkhand movement as it was directed against the dikus. Most of the uprisings, including the Birsa movement, focused on the immediate problems of the people and agrarian issues, but very effectively they also created social awakening, politicisation and disenchantment with outside interference among the tribal people. The Jharkhand movement can be treated therefore as a carrying forward of the Birsa uprisings and the movements prior to it. Another offshoot of the Birsa uprisings was a sort of realisation that to wage an effective and successful war against the north Bihari mandarins a lot more upgradation in socio-cultural field was required. The formation of the Unnati Samaj in 1915 was a direct positive consequence of such a realisation.

Despite the ruthless repression of the Birsa uprisings and a subsequent lull for about fifteen years, as early as in 1902, the Bhagat movement was launched by the Oraons.[38] The Oraon Bhagat (prophets) not only promised their followers safety and security from the capricious and blood thirsty tribal spirits, but also assured them of relief from the oppressive and unjust revenue system and exploitation by the landlords, usurers, and government officials.[39] Both Oraons and Mundas glorified their past as a Golden Age. The Bhakti movement and Christianity had a great impact on the Bhagats. Jatra Bhagat, Shibu Bhagat, and Tana Bhagat in particular inspired the tribals for emulating 'superior' traits of culture, and emphasised on vegetarianism and teetotalism with a view to restore the Oraon Golden Age. A sort of renaissance wave engulfed the people for emulative and revivalistic socio-cultural transformation.[40]

The young educated tribals were moved by the unbearable plight of their community, hence they realised an urgent need for a united organisation of tribals. The prominent

38. Das, Arvind N., 1992, op. cit., p. 91.

39. See, K.S. Singh, 1985, op. cit., Arvind N. Das, op. cit., and K.L. Sharma. 1976, op. cit.

40. Das, Victor, op. cit., p. 202.

leaders who joined this organisation known as the Unnati Samaj were Bandi Ram Oraon, Alfos Kujur, Elias Topno, Bir Singh Munda, Joel Lakra, and Anand Mashi.[41] As a social and cultural organisation it adopted a liberal democratic style of functioning much different from the organisations which had launched several movements and uprisings in the past. The two main objectives of the Unnati Samaj were: (i) to uplift Chhotanagpur from its backward state of affairs; and (ii) to improve the social, political and economic conditions of the adivasis.[42]

It is interesting to note that these objectives were propagated through a magazine called *Adivasi*, published in four languages, namely, English, Hindi, Kurukh, and Mundari. The Unnati Samaj contributed to inter-tribal unity and harmony, and gave the slogan: "If we want to hold on our own in India we must hang together or we shall be hanged separately."[43] The formation of Kisan Sabha and Chhotanagpur Catholic Sabha fragmented the tribal consciousness to some extent, hence the Unnati Samaj could not remain as a strong instrument of renaissance. The Kisan Sabha was constituted of mainly the non-convert tribals, whereas the Catholic Sabha comprised of the tribals converted to Christianity.[44]

The Unnati Samaj, being a socio-cultural forum, concentrated on the creation of ethnocentrism and tribal brotherhood. The Adivasi Mahasabha, which replaced it in 1938 under the leadership of Jaipal Singh, was more of a political organisation as it enlisted members from both tribals and non-tribals, and clearly outlined its main objectives as (i) statehood for the Jharkhand region, and (ii) protection of the adivasis from the dikus.[45] The shift from socio-cultural

41. Ibid., p. 203.
42. Sharma, K.L., 1976, op. cit.
43. Ibid., pp. 200–3.
44. Fuchs, Stephen, 1992, *The Aboriginal Tribes of India*, New Delhi, Inter-India Publications.
45. See K.L. Sharma, 1976, op. cit.

upliftment to power-politics was clearly visible in Jaipal Singh's efforts to have close relations with the Indian National Congress. The Adibasi Mahasabha demanded its representation in Bihar Pradesh Congress Committee and its Working Committee. The Congress party did not accede to this demand, and this was ensued by a series of clashes between the workers of the Mahasabha and the Congress. Jaipal Singh even lost an election in 1946 for the Provincial Council against a Congress candidate.

Role of Christian missions in the Adibasi Mahasabha in particular was resented by many newspapers and political leaders. A clear strategic change in 1945–46 was effected by Jaipal Singh as he roared: "We shall take Jharkhand"; "Jharkhand was the land of the adivasis"; "The intruders had to quit the Jharkhand". He even preached violence to oust the outsiders to achieve the goal of a separate state of Jharkhand.[46] All this attracted the educated adivasi youths towards Jaipal Singh, and also surcharged the atmosphere with tribal ethnocentrism and primordialism. A clear transformation of the Adibasi Mahasabha into a political apparatus was realised with the formation of the Jharkhand Party in 1950.

The chequered history of the Jharkhand movement has some bright spots too showing its graph moving upward between 1952 and 1962 under the leadership of Jaipal Singh. During this period the Jharkhand Party made its presence felt in the Bihar Legislative Assembly in the form of the largest opposition party. The party proved its worth and relevance despite the rejection of the demand for the formation of a separate Jharkhand State by the State's Reorganisation Commission in 1955.

The merger of the Jharkhand Party in the Indian National Congress in 1963 brought a severe jolt to the

46. This is based on the author's interview in the summer of 1973 with the late Joel Lakra, the only then surviving founder member of the Unnati Samaj, Lakra was honoured with Padma Shree and was a Member of the Bihar Legislative Council.

movement and created a lull and confusion among the rank and file like the one after the suppression of the Birsa uprisings at the end of the last century. Factions and cleavages surfaced claiming support of the people for the cause of the movement. N.E. Horo's efforts to rejuvenate the Jharkhand Party resulted into partial restoration of the lost prestige after the merger. Birsa Seva Dal (BSD), Jharkhand Morcha, Jharkhand Mukti Andolan, Hul Jharkhand Party, All India Jharkhand Party, etc. were the main political parties and groups espousing the cause of the Jharkhand movement between 1964 and 1977.

The late 1970s witnessed the emergence of some new parties and organisations with revitalised and re-energised strategies and action plans. Shibu Soren emerged as the most popular leader heading the newly formed party—Jharkhand Mukti Morcha (JMM). His Marxist leanings helped him in focusing on the problems of the poor and downtrodden Jharkhandis. Other political parties and groups became weak *vis-à-vis* JMM. JMM's success as a political party could be seen in its performance in General Elections of 1990 when it was able to capture 19 seats for Bihar Legislative Assembly, and six seats for Lok Sabha in 1991 elections. However, its dismissal performance in 1996 elections and the alleged involvement of the leaders of the movement, including Shibu Soren, in a bribery case have practically paralysed the movement, at least for a foreseeable future.

Another important organisation was the Jharkhand Coordination Committee (JCC). The main purpose of this organisation was to bring together various factions and groups under the umbrella of JCC, and also to elicit support of the non-tribals. Popularisation of the Jharkhandi identity and consciousness by bringing together sadans and adivasis was taken up seriously by the JCC.

The formation of the JMM and the JCC certainly created a new stir and awakening taking out the people from the slumber and desperation cast by the merger of the Jharkhand Party with the Congress in 1963. Two other organisations, namely, the All Jharkhand Students Union (AJSU), and the Jharkhand People's Party (JPP) have also contributed immensely to the movement. Both the organisations were formed by students, teachers, and intellectuals. The details of these political parties and organisations along with their leaders, support base (vote-banks) and mobilisation strategies could be discussed separately.

Let us reiterate once again that the Jharkhand movement cannot simply be termed as a 'mobility' or 'religious' or 'agrarian' movement. It cannot be narrowed down just to a struggle against the dikus. In fact, it is an all-inclusive, a composite movement aiming at the deconstruction of the imposed alien structures of relations and normative patterns on the one hand, and reconstruction of the positive features of the Jharkhandi social formation, on the other. The domination of the Jharkhand by the north Bihar has also created notions of fear, false pedagogy, and a sense of self-depreciation.[47] In a way, a Jharkhandi is a colonised man and a north Bihari is a settler in his homestead. The north Bihari mandarins have written the history of the Jharkhand, from their point of view, being in control of the administration and political machinery. Deconstruction of such a situation calls for an all-out attack on the 'colonising institutions' and on the people who derive power and privilege from such a system.

VII

Listed in this section are expressions and articulations (collected during my fieldwork in 1973) in the form of slogans by various Jharkhand parties and groups. These are as follows:

1. We shall take Jharkhand.

47. See K.L. Sharma, 1976, 'Jharkhand Movement in Bihar since 1947' (mimeographed).

2. Jharkhand was the land of the Adivasis, and the non-tribals had exploited them economically and politically.
3. Dikus quit Jharkhand.

There were also slogans against the Jharkhand Party headed by Jailal Singh. Those were:

1. Jharkhand Party is a means for raising money and acquiring power in the hands of the self-appointed leaders of the Adivasis.
2. The Jharkhand Party is an association of Christians.
3. Jharkhand State is an impossibility; and it is exclusively a demand of the Christians.
4. The common people including the tribals are not with the Jharkhand Party and its movement, hence it is a demand of few powerful reactionaries.
5. The government must crush such a separatist movement with a heavy hand.

Such slogans are not heard currently because of broadening of the support base of the movement and incorporation of the non-tribal influentials in the leadership of the movement.

In the 1970s the following statements were made in the magazine *Jai Jharkhand*.[48]

1. Colonialism implanted by North Bihar in the Chhotanagpur division and the Santhal Parganas must be mitigated by adopting the revolutionary method.
2. Loot and exploitation cannot continue in the region.
3. The government at the Centre and in Bihar do not give us anything except atrocities, exploitation and suppression.
4. Injustice cannot be tolerated any longer.

48. See, for example, a local magazine called *Jai-Jharkhand*, August 15, 1972. However, local newspapers, periodicals and magazines such as Ranchi Express, The New Republic, Abua Jharkhand, Adibasi, Jai Jharkhand, Chhotanagpur Sandesh, Ranchi Times, etc., provide very useful information. Some of these publications are however, no more in existence.

5. People will rest only if they get justice and progress towards a better society.
6. The people of north Bihar cannot understand the problems of Chhotanagpur.
7. We need justice, peace and equality.

The Jharkhand Party and the BSD gave the following slogans during the 1970s:

1. The government is a dacoit.
2. Jharkhand is ours.
3. The movement for liberation of Jharkhand will not stop.
4. The middlemanship of the Bihar Congress Party is murderous for Jharkhand.
5. Now we will not be afraid of the Biharis.
6. Abolish colonialism.
7. Push out the Biharis.
8. Flattery, dishonesty and black-marketing by the Biharis will not be tolerated any longer.
9. We want salvation through struggle.
10. Outdated practices and hollow slogans would take us away from the realities of life.
11. Life is given to you once only, love for the first cause of the world.
12. Liberation of mankind is our motto.
13. Long live Birsa Seva Dal.
14. Join thoughtful BSD for liberation.
15. No revolution, no liberation.
16. Don't run, transform the society.
17. Discard reactionary and dogmatic ideas.
18. Accept the new and progressive thinking.
19. The Great Birsa long live.

20. Become progressive and save yourself from ruin.
21. The Biharis do not have courage to destroy the Jharkhandis. They live on our mercy, and not us on theirs.
22. You Biharis, quit Chhotanagpur and Santhal Parganas.
23. You exploiters leave Jharkhand.
24. Stop exploitation.
25. Now Jharkhand movement will not stop.
26. Remove Bihar administration.
27. Jharkhandis must get united and leave suspicion and power.

Two slogans, which were in vogue by the end of the 1970s, were also uttered even upto November 15, 2000. These are: (1) *Bihar Se Hamko Mukti Do, Jharkhand Rajya Banane Do* (Emancipate us from Bihar, let us have Jharkhand); and (2) *Adivasi Aur Sadan, Apas Men Hain Bhai Saman* (Adivasi and Sadan are like brothers).

Efforts for the Jharkhandi identity and consciousness began genuinely around this time. Since the demand for the formation of a separate state for the adivasis alone was realised as antithetical to the interests of other sections and communities living in the Jharkhand region, the widening of the support base of the movement by forging Jharkhandi identity and consciousness claiming similarity of the existential conditions of the adivasis and the Sadans on one hand, and incorporation of the non-adivasis to lead the movement on the other significantly marked the events in the 1980s and the 1990s. The committee coordinating the movement comprising 14 political parties and groups incorporated several non-tribal leaders. Though the non-tribal leaders had been associated with the movement right from 1950, yet they had generally been an object of suspicion and distrust in the minds of the adivasi leadership.

VIII

The Jharkhand movement was a multifaceted phenomenon as

it aimed at the construction of a new social formation in the Jharkhand region by way of establishing a new identity and consciousness among its people. This could be achieved by implementing a twofold plan of action: (i) destruction of the institutions and mechanisms by which the dikus had been able to dominate and subjugate the Jharkhandis; and (ii) the creation of a separate state as a an instrument of empowering the Jharkhandis.

We have enlisted the cultural and ideological factors and their role in the process of the Jharkhand movement. The Jharkhand is not simply a geographical entity, a territory, and a land of adivasis. It is a socio-cultural region and an ecosystem. In support of this hypothesis we have examined the viability of the Jharkhand identity and consciousness as an ideological weapon for emancipation of the downtrodden.

7 Social Stratification among Tribes in India

I

For a long time tribal people were seen as an undifferentiated lot. However, they have gradations based on age-sets, sex and kinship which did not form the basis for social stratification as found among the non-tribal people in terms of property, wealth, power and authority. Several studies of social stratification, ranking systems and class formation among the tribes all over the world have reported absence of social differentiation in tribal societies. Social stratification as an existential phenomenon among the tribes is, however, different from that of the advanced agricultural and industrial societies. It is not unique as it is generally considered. The principles of social stratification such as ethnicity, class and power are the same everywhere. The difference lies in the operationalisation and actual functioning of these principles due to structural differences in various tribal societies in regard to their history, level of economic development, nature of colonial impact, and exposure to modern forces of social transformation. Thus, to the extent the tribal people are different in terms of these criteria, social stratification and class formation are also different among them in comparison to non-tribal societies.

It has been debated by the academia and policymakers

whether tribals should be allowed to retain their cultural identity or they should be assimilated with the rest of Indian people. This culturological perspective is not specifically articulated for the study of social stratification as such among the tribal people, but rich data have been generated regarding intra-tribal and inter-tribal status distinctions.[1] More specifically, the ethnic and class perspectives have been in currency for the study of tribal social stratification.[2] Emphasis in the ethnic perspective is laid on inter-tribal distinctions in terms of historicity, land relations, colonial impact, contact with non-tribal people, economic development and socio-political awakening, etc. However, the class perspective emphasises on formation of class relations among tribes keeping in view their economy, patterns of exploitation, alienation and backwardness. In a couple of studies convergence between the ethnic and the class perspectives has been greatly emphasised.[3]

Finally, we may identify the major tribal ethnic structures in terms of their internal differentiations and inter-ethnic differences and ties to ascertain ramifications of social stratification and class formation. Class formation as a structural process is based on increasing differentiation among the tribal people in terms of property, wealth, landownership, exploitation, pauperisation, education, political power, social movements, migration and social mobility. We may relate

1. Vidyarthi, L.P., 1974, 'Tribal Ethnography in India', *A Survey of Research in Sociology and Social Anthropology*, Vol. III, ICSSR, Bombay, Popular Prakashan, pp. 31–33.
2. See, for example, Sachchidananda, 1990, 'Patterns of Politico-Economic Change among Tribals in Middle India', in Francine R. Frankel and M.S.A. Rao (eds.), *Dominance and State Power in Modern India: Decline of a Social Order*, Vol. II, Delhi, Oxford University Press, pp. 278–320; Badgaiyan, S.D., 1986, 'Class and Ethnicity: Chhotanagpur in the 19th Century', in K.L. Sharma (ed.), *Social Stratification in India*, Delhi, Manohar Publications, pp. 293–308; Doshi, S.L., 1990, *Tribal Ethnicity, Class and Integration*, Jaipur, Rawat Publications; and Singh, K.S., 1985, *Tribal Society in India: An Anthropo-Historical Perspective*, Delhi: Manohar Publications, pp. 3–18.
3. See Badgaiyan, 1986, op. cit., and Doshi, 1990, op. cit.

these aspects of class formation with the ethnic structures to find out the nature of correspondence/non-congruence between ethnicity and class.

II

'Tribe' may be distinguished from 'caste', but it is not that 'tribe' is a homogenous entity and 'caste' is characterised by complexity and heterogeneity. There are distinctions within a given tribe and between different tribes. Certainly tribes are considerably distinct from the non-tribes. But then the question is: What is so distinctive about 'tribe' that makes it distinct from other entities such as caste, class, race. Some tribes are quite large in size and are also spread over several states of India. Certainly tribes are not 'organically' related to each other as castes are under a common principle. But tribes are also not exclusive systems as they are not small in size and bear a great deal of heterogeneity. Historically, a 'tribal society' has not been static, and yet it has retained its exclusivity from a 'caste society'. There are 427 tribes in India and they can be classified on the basis of language, religion, degree of their isolation, the pattern of livelihood.[4] Some of these attributes of tribes often resemble with the non-tribal people in a given region than the tribal people of another region.[5] The tribals are hunters, fishers, shifting cultivators, settled agriculturists, plantation workers and industrial wage-earners, hence some of them resemble with the non-tribal people. The large tribes such as Bhils, Gonds, Santhals, Oraons and Mundas are not only settled agriculturists, some of them are found in modern occupations in which members of caste Hindus are also found.

The tribal economy is also largely like the village peasant economy. Division of labour based on gender, work

4. Béteille, André, 1974, *Six Essays in Comparative Sociology*, Delhi, Oxford University Press, pp. 63–64.

5. Ibid., p. 63.

specialisation, tenurial differentiation and class distinctions are found among the tribal people like any non-tribal peasant community. Despite these similarities tribes remain distinct from castes because of their geographical isolation, language or dialect and religion.[6] Even these criteria are not a rigid basis of distinguishing tribes from castes. For example, Meenas in Rajasthan are listed as a scheduled tribe, but they have always lived in multi-caste villages as a part of the village system. Meenas were also one of the functionary castes, under the *jajmani* system, and in fact, they are/were always referred as a caste. Certainly, tribes have been large and small both, but never without internal social differentiation. Béteille argues that a substantial number of tribal people are peasants today,[7] hence tribes are in transition.[8] There is class and social stratification (implying stratified peasantry) among tribes in India. In no way, tribes can today be treated as 'primitive'. Besides differentiation of peasantry, there is also a middle class among the tribal people. Migration, education, mobility, social and political awakening have contributed to the emergence of a small middle class. State-sponsored measures including the constitutional provisions and special programmes for their development have set in a new process of differentiation and stratification which would mean consideration of more or less same criteria of status determination which are normally applied to the non-tribal people.

There is more or less unanimity among the students of tribal social life in India regarding the presence of social stratification. However, B.K. Roy Burman cautions that social

6. Ibid., pp. 72–73.
7. Ibid., p. 70.
8. Majumdar, D.N., 1937, *A Tribe in Transition: A Study in Culture Pattern*, Longmans, quoted from André Beteille, 1974, op. cit., Sinha, Surajit, 1965, 'Tribe-Caste and Tribe-Peasant Continua in Central India', *Man in India*, Vol. 45, No. 1, p. 62; Oraons, Martin, 1969, 'A Tribal People in an Industrial Setting', in A.R. Desai (ed.), *Rural Sociology in India*, Bombay, Popular Prakashan, pp. 232–41.

stratification by itself is not enough to mobilise the people to actively resist alienation from their land.[9] More important is the nature of social stratification. Roy Burman cites a few examples in support of this observation. The Gonds were a highly stratified community, but there was no significant revolt by them till the 1940s. "The presence of a state structure and the shifting nature of political contacts with the outside world led to both stratification and segmentation of Gond society."[10] Among the tribal people, "the upper strata emerged as a multi-focal aristocracy". A new elite emerged among the Gonds, and the British rulers transformed them into new zamindars. Thus, the Gonds synthesised the old and the new, the tribal and the peasant cultures. A tribal movement gets a start generally when it has support of a combination of factors including inequitous relations, middle class interests, philanthropism and ethnic/ community identity. But the point is that tribal people are like other people, engaged in similar pursuits in the same area(s), and they are also different from them, and it is this difference/ dissimilarity that makes social stratification in tribal society somewhat different from the non-tribal people.

Let us analyse a 'functional' formulation of 'tribe'. Tribes are not castes or caste-like entities, though some of them have followed the path of sanskritisation and conversion to Christianity and Islam. Tribes are a highly differentiated lot both ethnically and culturally. Some adhere to 'tribalism', others have converted to Christianity by rejecting tribal pantheon, and some have taken up Hinduism by adopting vegetarianism, teetotalism and other Brahmanic ideals and practice. Tribes are also differentiated based on landholdings, rural-urban background, education, occupation, income and political power. Tribes have been granted special treatment under the Constitution of India. They have also many

9. Roy Burman, B.K., 1984, 'Challenges and Responses in Tribal India', in M.S.A. Rao (ed.), *Social Movements in India*, Delhi, Manohar Publications, pp. 319–40.

10. Ibid., p. 325.

attributes, practices and 'styles of life' that distinguish them from the non-tribal people. It may be seen how their 'distinct' and 'general' characteristics get reconciled in their social life. What keeps them partly different from others, and what impinges upon their life to bring them closer to non-tribal people? The tribal situation is complex in the sense that the tribals depend upon forest-based sources of livelihood, they are engaged in settled agriculture, and are working in factories and industries, some of them are educated and are employed as professionals, civil servants and white-collar workers, and some are active politicians and social workers. Ethnic and cultural differentiation can be seen in terms of tribal identities and religious pursuits. Thus, the nature of social stratification is also quite complex corresponding with the heterogeneity of their socio-cultural and economic structure. Therefore, it would be unwise to consider tribes as the people dependent mainly on what the rest of the people (non-tribals) produce, on simple agriculture, and living far off from modern civilisation. They are a people who have a lot of attributes in common with the non-tribal population, and at the same have their own 'tribal identity'. Social stratification among the tribal people is, therefore, neither simply based on criteria like age, sex and kinship, nor it can be characterised by property, education, occupation, income and power. A semblance of two sets of criteria, one for the tribals and the other for the non-tribals, may distinguish the two from each other.

III

Sachchidananda reports that social stratification in West Bengal, Bihar, Madhya Pradesh and Orissa in the pre-colonial period could be observed through the ranks such as the *khut-kattidars*—the village headmen and the masses. Later on some artisan castes such as blacksmiths, potters and weavers further differentiated the tribal society. From class point of view the village society was divided into the khut-kattidars and the *praja horoko* (masses).[11] The latter depended on the goodwill of the former and were rated as second-class citizens. The khut-kattidars were the real owners of the village land. Sachchidananda writes: "The khut-kattidari system was thus an arrangement for the management of the resources relating to land on a communal basis. The headman managed the affairs of the village with the help of some influential village leaders. He dispensed justice, fixed the dates of village deities and collected dues from landholders for payment as *chanda* (contribution) to the tribal chief."[12] Under such a situation lineage or clan was the basis of socio-economic differentiation. The khut-katti system was mainly confined to the Munda tribe. Thapar and Siddiqi also find the khut-katti system as the basis of the Munda society. The Mundas, Pahans and Mahtos were heads of their clans. Besides these heads of the clans/lineages, the khut-kattidars were powerful as they collected a tribute from the *praja* living in the villages.[13] Thapar and Siddiqi, after tracing the history of social structure and its difference in ancient period, write: "Thus, the tendency towards social stratification which had already begun with the khut-katti system was not only intensified and accelerated under the state, but was also made more complex with the interpolation of various levels of intermediaries."[14] The tribal mode of production broke down and gave a way to the emergence of a new correlation of social status with landholding and power. The lineage rights over land became weak, and a feudal state on tribal society was superimposed. Tribal identity was also weakened by commodity production.

Individual ownership of land was found among other tribes. The headmanship was not confined to a member of a clan or lineage as it was in the case of the Munda tribe having

11. Sachchidananda, 1990, op. cit., pp. 280–83.
12. Ibid., p. 280.
13. Thapar, Romila and Siddiqi, Majid Hayat, 1991, 'Tribals in History: The Case of Chhota Nagpur', in Dipankar Gupta (ed.), *Social Stratification*, Delhi, Oxford University Press, pp. 419–30.
14. Ibid., p. 425.

the khut-katti system. But all the tribes had the institution of headman, and he acted as a patriarch. The khut-kattidars were not completely autonomous as the king was the supreme authority in his state. Sachchidananda observes that such a system did not persist for long as feudal superstructure was set in place not only in Chhotanagpur but also among the Gonds in Madhya Pradesh. He writes: "Scions of the Raja's family carved out feudatory estates and principalities, the most famous of which was the kingdom of Chanda. The emergence of the feudal system marked the beginning of the breakdown of the tribal polity characterised by communal ownership of land."[15] At this stage, a clearly visible system of social stratification could be seen among the tribal people. A sort of economic explanation of this is provided by Sachchidananda though without using clearly relevant concepts and categories. He writes: "Social stratification based on differential command over economic resources began to emerge. The development of trade and commerce facilitated the growth of small urban centres. A variety of castes, ranging from Brahmins and Rautias to many artisan communities, flocked to these centres."[16]

Sachchidananda mentions about the grant of *jagirs* by the Raja of Chhotanagpur in early 17th century. As a result of this a new class of merchants, moneylenders and Brahmin priests emerged. The emergence of this new class proved antithetical to the principle of communal and egalitarian character of the tribal society. Since the new grantees of lands in the tribal areas enjoyed more or less permanent and usufructuary rights, they soon began to exploit the tribal people uninhibitedly with the help of village officers such as the Munda and the Pahan. The *khut-katti* system also began to crumble down along with the *parha* system. Thus, a new basis of power and social status emerged and replaced the traditional arrangement. Land did not remain any more a communally

15. Sachchidananda, 1990, op. cit., p. 281.
16. Ibid.

owned and controlled phenomenon. However, the village officers like the Munda, the Manki and the Majhi were given police powers by the British in their own interests to establish their rule over the masses by granting a small minority such benefits which made them to fight for the Raj and to suppress their own people.

It can safely be deduced from the available literature that isolation of the tribal people has been decreasing, and this has benefited some sections of the tribal society, and at the same time new forms of social stratification among tribes in India have been variously characterised in terms of peasantisation, detribalisation, Hinduisation, conversion to Christianity, etc. Some caste-Hindus, because of pre-eminence of tribal society in a given region, have adopted some tribal attributes, and such a process has been called as 'tribalisation'. Despite these changes tribal society can be distinguished from the Hindu, Muslim, Christian and other non-tribal communities. However, this does not imply that tribes in India have remained or continue to remain isolated, homogeneous, small in size, and unique compared to the non-tribal people.

The British affected the tribal people in several ways. The intrusion of the British in the management of forests depossessed the tribals from their age-old control and use of forests. Besides the British officers, a lot of other sections like suppliers, traders, clerks and workers started living in the tribal areas. In course of time some tribals were also benefited by the British encroachment, and they became a distinct class of the privileged few. Education was one way by which a select group of tribals became superior to the masses. Conversion to Christianity also helped the converts in education, employment, and in fact, in acclaiming a higher status for them.

K.S. Singh highlights some dysfunctional consequences of the British colonialism.[17] The agency system

17. Singh, K.S., 1978, 'Colonial Transformation of Tribal Society in Middle India', *EPW*, Vol. XIII, No. 30, pp. 1221–32.

established by the British was used for ruthless suppression of the tribal uprisings. The colonial system also strengthened the feudal elements in tribal society as it encouraged the chiefs and landlords to extract surplus from the tribals as much as possible for the well-being of the Raj in India. The moneylenders had their heyday as no one was there to check the usurious activities perpetrated by them.

From various accounts it is evident that during the British period class-based distinctions were replacing the traditional status system among the tribes of India. It could be seen in the alienation of land, control of forest economy by the state, emergence of moneylenders and traders, close but exploitative contacts by the non-tribals with the tribal people, etc. All these sections of society including the British officers, zamindars, moneylenders and traders and non-tribal agriculturists were superior in skills and resources even before they landed on the tribal soil. This implanted a hiatus between them and the tribals, and the policy of the government created status-cleavages among the tribals. This is why, some non-tribals are regarded as 'dikus' (exploiters). The tribals, in general, faced acute pauperisation and were forced to migrate in search of employment to far off places in Bengal, Assam, Maharashtra, etc. The tribals are found divided even today due to the process of acculturation started by the Christian missions and Hindu organisations. Conversion to Christianity and Hinduisation brought about at least three orders, namely, Christian convert tribals, Hinduised tribals, and non-converts. All these tribals were also stratified internally based on their economic standing and ethnic status.

Inter-ethnic relations between different groups with varying degrees of structural distance have been highlighted by S.D. Badgaiyan.[18] Ethnicity and class as the two main principles of social differentiation have provided multiple ways to the

18. Badgaiyan, S.D., 1986, op. cit., pp. 293–94.

people for organising their social relations. Within the same ethnic group there are wide-ranging class differences, and the hostile ethnic groups may be found in the same class. The searching questions posed by Badgaiyan[19] are: (1) How people resolve the contradictory claims on their sentiments and impulses to act? (2) Do they allow their ethnic sentiments to ride over class interests or do they permit class interests to prevail over their ethnic obligations? (3) Is it the context that decides as to which affiliation will prevail over the other? (4) Do all ethnic groups behave the same way? (5) Are ethnic groups swayed more by primordial sentiments than by contextual logic? These questions are explicated in the context of the historical development of Munda society. The four phases noted by Badgaiyan are: (1) The traditional Munda society before the emergence of kingship among them; (2) Munda society under kingship but before the imposition of British colonialism; (3) Munda society under British colonialism; and (4) Munda society in independent India.[20] The account provided by Badgaiyan about the pre-British period resembles with those given by Sachchidananda and Thapar and Siddiqi.

Rent-collectors in Chhotanagpur were recognised as 'jagirdars' (owners of land) after the British had taken over the Dewani of Bengal in 1765. The jagirdars accelerated the process of expropriation of native owners of land. Ejection became an easy affair, and some proprietary cultivators were forced to become tenants and agricultural labourers. By the middle of the 19th century the number of jagirdars had gone upto 600. In addition to rent, they imposed new taxes and levies.[21] Badgaiyan writes: "Practorian obligations of service, gifts and presentation now became necessary for holding the land. Forced labour came to be extracted more and more. The

19. Ibid., p. 294.
20. Ibid., p. 295.
21. Ibid., pp. 300–1.

jagirdars introduced the *thekedars* to collect revenue. These *thekedars* used all their means and power to extract as much as they could from the tenants."[22] Thus, three new classes, namely, jagirdars, thekedars and tenants emerged replacing the rent-collectors and cultivators. With the intervention of the British the moneylenders and the merchants also entered into socio-economic fabric of tribal life. Another dimension to social stratification among the tribes of middle India was added by the coming of Christianity as it brought about differentiation initially on religious basis and later on the basis of education, occupation and income. By the end of the 19th century the divide between the non-tribal elite and the tribal masses had become so wide that the Birsa movement emerged as a strong wave against the Hindus, Christians, jagirdars, thekedars and colonial rulers.

Badgaiyan observes that by the end of the 19th century the tribal situation had become quite complex. For example, the Mundas had to deal with a number of other tribal groups like Oraons, Hos and Cheros; they had also to deal with the non-tribal groups like the Hindus, the Muslims, the Sikhs and with the Christian and the Birsaite sections among themselves. These ethnic distinctions reflected to some extent status distinctions as well. The tribals who converted to Christianity were able to improve their socio-economic position by having modern education and white-collar employment, hence were generally considered superior than those who adhered to their traditional pattern of social life. All these developments accentuated the role of class in patterning of social relations. What Badgaiyan observes is that "the objective reality was thus characterised by a multiplicity of social groupings based on ethnicity and class, religion and language. But the Munda consciousness visualised this diversity falling into a trichotomy: tribals, *dikus* and non-tribals but non-*dikus*."[23]

22. Ibid.
23. Ibid., p. 305.

Around this time the word 'diku' became quite expressive signifying non-tribal exploiters such as jagirdars, merchants and moneylenders. The character of the dikus has changed considerably after independence as the north Biharis employed in government departments are treated as dikus because they deprived the tribal people aspiring for white-collar jobs. In any case the word 'diku' is used for the non-tribal exploiter of the tribal people. Thus, from the point of view of class, there are the classes of the exploiters and the exploited. However, both the classes are internally highly differentiated, hence no uniform pattern of exploitation. These outsiders also became local administrators and this too helped them in the oppression of the tribal people. But K.S. Singh takes a different view as he observes that most of the tribal population in India was integrated within the administration of the provinces of British India or within that of the Indian states. He calls it the "mode of protective administration, established *chatties* along highways to supply the army which brought in merchants, traders and peddlars, and set up cantonments and centres of administration and trade. The colonial system ended the relative isolation of the tribal society; brought it into the mainstream of the new administrative set-up, policy and programmes; put an end to the political dominance of the tribes in the region; and roped the tribal communities which had been spared from the strain of the surplus generation by their states into a new system of production relations."[24] Singh's observations thus do not synchronise with that of Sachchidananda and Badgaiyan. However, Singh makes a reference, though a passing one, about the dual policy followed by the Raj as it strengthened the feudal crust on one hand and the forces of market cutting the very roots of tribal economy and polity on the other. All these changes were reflected in social stratification. Let us now discuss the situation in the post-independence period.

24. Singh, K.S., 1985, *Tribal Society in India: An Anthropo-Historical Perspective*, Delhi, Manohar Publications, pp. 3–18.

IV

K.S. Singh observes that the economic and political processes of tribal transformation get reflected in social stratification.[25] Social stratification among tribes has always existed in various forms such as social and physical distance, notion of purity and pollution, prestige and status, habits and customs. The system of social stratification in the form of the feudatory chief zamindars at the top, the well-to-do headmen in the middle, and the general mass at the bottom has changed since independence. A class of insider diku and professional tribal moneylender, as a result of the anti-land alienation laws, has emerged in the post-independence period. A small section of the tribes has gone up in socio-economic hierarchy, and some members of this upwardly mobile group are engaged in land transactions and moneylending.

In another context Singh provides a four-fold classification of social movements with special reference to middle India. These movements are: (1) movements for political autonomy; (2) agrarian and forest-based movements; (3) sanskritisation processes; and (4) cultural movements based on script and language.[26] All these movements could be understood as efforts on the part of the tribal society to find for itself a place of honour and status at least equal to other sections of Indian society. In other words, the tribal people expressed anger against their political and economic suppression and also desired to move up in socio-cultural hierarchy as reflected in the efforts to convert and, or adopt, Christianity and Hindu way of life.

There are not many studies available on the social stratification among the tribes in India. The Indian State has provisions in its Constitution with regard to uplift of the tribal people living in different parts of India by reducing age-old socio-economic inequality. In the field of education, socio-economic and political awakening and employment, part

25. Ibid., p. 7.
26. Ibid., p. 18.

success has been achieved as a result of the policy of reservation of jobs, seats in educational institutions and earmarking of constituencies for the scheduled tribes and the scheduled castes. The anticipated consequence of these provisions could be seen in new forms of socio-economic and political inequality between different tribal communities.

Sachchidananda seems to be apparently, though unintentionally, inclined towards an economic analysis of social stratification among the tribals of middle India. He writes: "Since the advent of colonial rule and the unrestricted movement of plainsmen into the tribal areas, the tribal population has been subjected to unemiting economic exploitation. Massive alienation of tribal lands to moneylenders and superior cultivating castes left the majority of agriculturists steeped in poverty and debt."[27] Such a situation characterised by isolation, economic backwardness, lack of education, social fragmentation, and distinctive ethnic, religious and linguistic affiliations forced upon the state to declare the tribal people as a 'scheduled' category, providing them protective discriminatory treatment leading to their integration with the wider society in India. Sachchidananda's description of the tribal situation lacks requisite rigour as it neither makes use of the categories like class, class consciousness, class antagonism, change, relations of production and role of state, etc., nor it examines the role of ethnicity, isolation, assimilation, kinship, etc., as the main tools of his analysis. However, studies by P.K. Bose[28], Jaganath Pathy[29] and Ghanshyam Shah[30] examine the tribal situation

27. Sachchidananda, 1990, op. cit., p. 278.
28. Bose, P.K., 1981, 'Stratification among Tribals in Gujarat', *EPW*, Vol. XVI, No. 6, pp. 191–96.
29. Pathy, Jaganath, 1984, *Tribal Peasantry: Dynamics of Development*, New Delhi, Inter-India Publications.
30. Shah, Ghanshyam, 1979, 'Tribal Identity and Class Differentiations: A Case Study of the Chaudhari Tribe', *EPW*, Vol. XIV, Nos. 7 & 8, pp. 459–69; and see also Ghanshyam Shah, 1986, 'Stratification among the Scheduled Tribes in the Bharuch and Panch Mahals Districts of Gujarat', in S.C. Malik (ed.), *Determinants of Social Status in India*, Delhi, Moti Lal Banarsidas, pp. 149–83.

from the class perspective about which we would make a brief reference later on.

Sachchidananda reports that the weak impact of the measures taken by the Indian state for the welfare of the scheduled tribes has resulted into the continued dominance of the new outsiders as the colonial rulers have been replaced by the indigenous elites.[31] The illegal transfer of land from tribals to non-tribals has become an established fact of life. Surplus land has not been distributed to the poor and deserving tribals. Even the land distributed is, in fact, so meagre and qualitatively so poor that it has not proved to be a viable source of livelihood. Industrialisation has displaced the tribals as their lands have been taken over by the state. A large number of 'outsiders' have again come to the tribal areas due to industrialisation further widening the gap between the tribals and the non-tribals (dikus). Contractors, petty businessmen and government officials have taken strong roots in tribal society though still they look to be anachronisms and unwelcome elements. Even infrastructural facilities like roads, electricity and means of communication have been made available in the tribal areas keeping in view the needs of the 'outsiders' rather than the tribal autochthons. Education, employment and representation in legislative bodies from village panchayat to parliament through the policy of 'protective discrimination' have created an elite section among the tribals rather than bringing about social mobility among the tribal masses.

Sachchidananda observes that "a significant impact of politico-economic change in independent India is the accentuation of social inequalities in tribal society".[32] Sachchidananda's argument is that most tribal societies in middle India were egalitarian. Social stratification emerged among them in the pre-colonial and colonial periods in the form of semi-feudalism

31. Sachchidananda, 1990, op. cit., pp. 297–98.
32. Ibid., p. 305.

and exploitation by dividing the tribal society into the upper class and the commoners. The outside moneylenders were a third notable class which has been replaced by the inside dikus after independence.[33] Social stratification is a relational and relative phenomenon, and therefore, it can be observed only in terms of relations between individuals, between individuals and groups and between groups over a period of time based on a certain value frame. It has been reported earlier that social stratification has always existed among the tribes of India though its value frame has changed from time to time. Social stratification existed not only between tribals and non-tribals, but it was also found between tribes, clans and lineages based on kinship status, age, sex, hereditary office, possessions, etc. After independence, education, employment and political power, though these are in a certain way interrelated phenomena, have become the main bases of social stratification among the tribal people. Since these bases did not exist earlier, their emergence after independence, in a particular way, cannot be taken as an accentuation of inequality. A small section of tribals has come directly close to the non-tribals through these new bases of social status, and some of the tribals have even gone higher than the non-tribal people based on these criteria. Other tribals have been beneficiaries at the secondary and tertiary levels. A large number of tribals still remain unbenefited from these scare resources like education, white-collar jobs and positions and offices of power. Class distinctions have crystallised among the tribals like that of the non-tribal people in terms of upper, middle and lower classes, because all the people have not been benefited in equal measure, and it is hard to believe that a majority of the tribals have been harmed by the development process in the post-independence period. The high level of socio-political awakening among the Mundas, Oraons, Santhals, Hos, Bhils, Raj-Gonds, Chaudharis, etc. is self-explanatory of their betterment

33. Ibid., p. 306.

compared to their own past during the British period.

The most important bases of social stratification among the tribes of middle India are ethnicity and class. Despite being interrelated aspects, these are not found in the same proportions of interconnections and efficacy in all tribal societies. The tribal people who have been exposed more to the influences like Christianity, modern education, developmental programmes and industrialisation would have more of class and power as the bases of status determination rather than ethnicity in the form of stratified lineages or clans. Let us have a look at these criteria in the context of the present-day tribal society.

V

Ethnicity becomes distinctly observable if a community is viewed in terms of its independent existence rather than as an interdependent entity. The creation of scheduled areas, provisions for special measures for the development of tribal blocks, reservation for representation in parliament, state legislatures and local bodies and for admissions in schools and colleges/ universities and for jobs have further strengthened the ethnic identities of the tribes of India.

Thus, in any given region, we may find ethnic differentiation within a given tribe in terms of the non-converts and the converts. The benefits accruing from adhering to one's own religion or from conversion to Hinduism, Christianity and Islam would determine to a large extent social status of the tribal people. However, conversion is not being perceived as a desirable path of development. We are just reporting the ethnic differentiation within and between tribes in India.

Fuchs is, however, right in his observation that most tribes are divided in two sections—a Hinduised upper section, and a lower tribal section. He cites examples of the Gond (Raj-Gond and Jungli-Gond), Kokru (Muasi and

Paharia), Bhilala (Bara Bhilala and Barela), Raj-Banshi and others.[34] Hinduised tribes have been relegated to the status of outcastes and untouchables. Only some tribes living in Chhotanagpur have developed some degree of consciousness and they also assert themselves almost equal to the non-tribal people. Fuchs shows his serious concern about adoption of the Hindu way of life by the tribes in Central India, but his silence regarding conversion to Christianity speaks volumes of his approval. He also deplores the absence of a strong tribal solidarity among the aboriginals of Central India. They do not have organisational support base nor are economically and socially well-placed.

Romila Thapar and M.H. Siddiqi ask the question as to how tribal identity survived.[35] Though they do not provide a complete answer, but observe that the preservation of tribal identity was in part due to the nature of land relations. The expansion of tribal identity was to some extent watered down by the cultural legitimation of the tribal elite in terms of a wider Indian context (sanskritic courtly culture). With the emergence of a well-established agricultural base and a network of trade connections not only further elaborated the system of social stratification but also weakened the exclusivity of tribal/ethnic identity. Thus, going by Thapar and Siddiqi's view, we may infer that the tribal identity was always coloured by economic differentiation and power hierarchy.

Class and ethnicity were inextricably intermixed in Chhotanagpur in the 19th century.[36] In the context of the Mundas of Chhotanagpur, Badgaiyan mentions about khut-katti clan Mundas, non-khut-katti clan Mundas, non-Munda tribals and Hindu caste functionaries in the period before the

34. Fuchs, Stephen, 1977, 'Central Indian Tribes', in Romesh Thapar (ed.) *Tribe, Caste and Religion*, Delhi, The Macmillan Co. of India, pp. 47–53.
35. Thapar, Romila and Siddiqi, M.H., 1991, op. cit., pp. 425–26.
36. Badgaiyan, S.D., 1986, op. cit.

emergence of kingship among them.[37] The Munda and the Manki were not only heads of their clans and villages, respectively, but were also khut-kattidars. Later on, the khut-katti system was destroyed and it was replaced by *bhuinhari*, *rajhas* and *manjhihas* tenures. There were non-tribal jagirdars in large numbers when the Munda society was under the system of kingship. Hinduism made inroads into the tribal heartland, and it was strengthened by the recruitment of Hindu militia and administrative staff. Brahmin priests and other functionaries found a convenient place for themselves with the patronage of the king as lower level feudatories; Hindu and Muslim merchants also found opportunities for trade and barter in the region.

In the first phase new ethnic groups entered into the Munda society as a subordinate class—the producers of surplus; but in the second phase the class that entered was the subordinate class—the appropriator of surplus. "Entry of this new class radically changed the production relations. In order to justify and support the new production relations new concepts of ownership and authority as well as new ideology came to be imposed on the Munda society and polity."[38] "The Mundas themselves became greatly differentiated on class lines."[39] Thus, a new complexity arose between class and ethnicity. In fact, Badgaiyan also analyses the patterns of dominance along with ethnicity and class. He refers to the subordination of all non-Munda ethnic groups in the early period followed by the subordination of the Mundas by a dominant section of the immigrant ethnic groups. The ethnic divide gets further blurred by sharing of class positions by the Mundas with the non-Mundas. There were Munda zamindars and non-Munda zamindars; and there were similarly Munda tenants and non-Munda tenants. Perhaps ethnicity has an edge over class

37. Ibid., pp. 295–97.
38. Ibid., p. 299.
39. Ibid.

because "relations between non-Munda jagirdars and Munda tenants were reported to be far more strained and antagonistic than those obtaining between Munda jagirdars and Munda tenants."[40] However, Badgaiyan infers a somewhat different conclusion from such a situation. He writes: "This leads one to hypothesise that agrarian relations are more strained when class stratification is compounded with ethnic differentiation."[41] However, we may make two observations. Firstly, the Munda jagirdars had a legitimacy of their rule much before the non-Mundas encroached upon the tribal areas as jagirdars, hence they were not acceptable to the Mundas as their masters. Secondly, the strained relations between the Munda tenants and the non-Munda jagirdars symbolised the non-acceptance of the alien rulers on the Munda land.

The ethnic structure of the Mundas became further weak due to the British takeover of Bengal in 1765 (Bihar was part of Bengal) and entrenchment of Christianity. Rack-renting and ejection from the rajhas and manjhihas land became frequent reducing the Mundas to the status of tenants and agricultural labourers. Forced labour was almost a routine activity. Thekedars as collectors of revenue were a new institution in the system of exploitation.[42] Thus, with jagirdars, thekedars, British administrators, moneylenders and merchants the authority of Mundas and Mankis deteriorated further. Earlier Hinduism and later on Christianity proved to be an attack on the ethnically monolithic character of the Mundas as a community. The Birsa movement was a direct reaction to the onslaught committed on the Mundas by the British administration and Christianity.

Ethnic situation had become quite complex as the tribal groups came closer to each other and they also dealt with the non-tribal groups like the Hindus, Muslims, Sikhs, Christians.

40. Ibid., p. 300.
41. Ibid.
42. Ibid.

Besides this, the Mundas had Hindu, Christian and Birsaite sections among themselves. Badgaiyan observes that it was not that everything was seen in terms of ethnicity and class.[43] Mundas and Hindus both had jagirdars and tenants. Ethnicity was thus not coterminous with class. Objectively, there were several groupings based on ethnicity and class, religion and language. The Mundas perceived, according to Badgaiyan, three main groups: tribals, dikus and non-tribals but non-dikus. Ethnicity and class coexist among the Mundas. Badgaiyan writes: "In the light of the behaviour of the Munda tenants and agricultural proletariats with regard to Munda and Hindu jagirdars it can be said that the ethnic solidarity is diluted by class differentiation."[44] Class solidarity is eroded by ethnic differentiation. Identity of both class and ethnicity has resulted in greater solidarity among the Mundas. Today the question is: Whether ethnicity represents a bundle of primordial sentiments and ties or is it an identity which is contextually manipulated? In many a time ethnicity is articulated and twisted according to the compulsions of given situations. Badgaiyan writes: "Ethnicity is not just having a set of external attributes. It is essentially a question of subjective perception. It is this subjective perception that gives people a sense of belonging to an ethnic group."[45] Members of one ethnic group could belong to more than one class, and members of one class could belong to more than one identity at a given point of time, and they may not be in mutual harmony.

Ethnicity in the context of wider socio-political and economic development has acquired a great deal of instrumental significance. Measures like the constitutional provisions and reservations and special schemes for development have strengthened rather than weakened the ethnic and primordial solidarities among the scheduled tribes. It is felt by the

43. Ibid., pp. 304–5.
44. Ibid., p. 306.
45. Ibid., p. 307.

articulate section of the tribal people that they could persist with the existing benefits and also demand more and better amenities for their development by asserting their ethnic unity and solidarity as expressly as possible. In this way 'ethnicity' among tribes and 'caste' among Hindus have become convenient means of political mobilisation. Sachchidananda does not find any real contradiction between elaboration of stratification and hardening of ethnicity.[46] Though apparently the two seem to be antithetical to each other, but in real life they are found in specific contexts without being antagonistic. Diversification and development impinge upon the monolithic character of the tribal society, hence weakening of ethnic solidarity becomes a logical and natural consequence, but 'ethnicisation' is brought in by making best possible efforts to ensure availability of maximum benefits from the processes of development.

Expression of ethnic identity depends upon the contexts and the issues at a particular point of time. Lack of inter-tribal solidarity has always been one of the serious obstacles in achieving the most urgent common ends. Different tribes have not come together to share the same platform mainly because of the perception of exclusivity of one's tribe and a sense of pride of being superior or at least not inferior compared to any other tribe. Mobilisation even against the non-tribal people has suffered from such perceptions regarding inter-tribal and intra-tribal relations and notions of superiority and inferiority. However, ethnic identity has found its place in different spheres of life such as language, education, politics and culture. Students have formed from time to time associations and unions comprising adivasis (tribals) alone.

A detailed treatment of the 'tribal question' in Chhotanagpur is provided by Myron Weiner in *Sons of the Soil: Migration and Ethnic Conflict in India.*[47] One gets the impression

46. Sachchidananda, 1990, op. cit., p. 309.

47. Weiner, Myron, 1978, *Sons of the Soil, Migration and Ethnic Conflict in India*, Princeton, Princeton University Press, pp. 145–216.

from Weiner's study that the main cause of the backwardness among the adivasis is economic as he emphasises on the problems of land alienation, exploitation by dikus (earlier moneylenders and zamindars and now white-collar workers, politicians and traders and businessmen), unemployment, etc. This explanation is based on the perceptions of the tribals about their own problems. Their perceptions about the outsiders and their impact on the politics in the region have been considered by Weiner as the basis of his argument in regard to what he calls 'tribal encounters' for analysing relationship between tribals and migrants. The economic problem forced the tribals to emigrate in large numbers to work as plantation labourers in Assam and Bengal. Ethnicity is reflected in some of the statements made by the respondents.[48] All dikus were Bihari Hindus and that they (tribals) were exploited by the Bihari landlords. The tribals lost their lands to non-tribals. Here Weiner observes that some well-to-do tribals who have acquired land, and some of them who are themselves substantial moneylenders are not hated by the tribal folk.[49] In fact, some tribals feel proud of their wealthy tribals, whereas they express antagonism against the wealthy non-tribals. Thus, Weiner clearly advocates an ethnicist perspective rather than a structural view for analysing relations between tribals and non-tribals. He writes: "Given a choice, people prefer to hate others because of their religion, or race, caste or tribe, rather than because of their wealth. The wealthy in one's own community are a source of vicarious pride. The status (and accomplishment) of members of one's own community provides self-esteem to all members of the community. For this reason it is not easy to create cleavages and parties based on class in a multi-ethnic society except where class and ethnic cleavages coincide. Class antagonisms then become veiled expressions of ethnic hostility. This is probably why

48. Ibid., p. 169.
49. Ibid., p. 173.

ideological parties of the left based upon class appeal have not done very well in India, and this is why peasant revolts against landlords are more likely to occur when the peasants and landlords belong to different religions or castes, or one is tribal and the other is not."[50]

Migration of the tribals from their native places has certainly weakened ethnic bondage because class differentiation forces them to treat themselves also as unskilled workers, mechanics, clerks, teachers, rural, semi-rural and urban inhabitants, etc. Some tribals have become professionals like university teachers, doctors, engineers, lawyers, social workers and politicians. Professionals from among the tribals identify themselves more with the non-tribal middle class people rather than with the rest of the tribal people. Weiner overemphasises the ethnic perspective undermining the role of class and power in weakening the ethnic character of the tribals on one hand and socio-political differentiation among the tribes on the other. All the queries made by Weiner refer to the ethnic question. Some of the queries are as follows:

(1) Why have the tribals remained 'backward'?

(2) Why are they looked down upon by the non-tribals?

(3) Why have they not moved into skilled jobs in industry, or into managerial posts?

(4) Why have they not successfully competed against the migrants who have moved into Chhotanagpur?

(5) What can be done to change the situation?[51]

Certainly, ethnicity holds its strong ground among the tribes of India, but it is also a fact that as a result of some reforms, administrative measures and implementation of given policies, ethnicity has become visibly weak and class differentiation has surfaced significantly. Therefore, a simple formulation referring to tribals versus non-tribals or local

50. Ibid.

51. Ibid.

people versus outsiders in the context of jobs and opportunities forecloses the analysis of the role of class and power in the context of social change since independence. Without any conscious effort, class differentiation itself brings about de-tribalisation among the tribes of India. Conversions to Christianity and Islam and impact of Hinduism and other cultural forces have already shown a great deal of de-tribalisation. The Christian tribals are superior to the non-converts in socio-structural terms. The Hinduised tribes consider themselves culturally superior to the non-converts as they have adopted vegetarianism and have discarded drinking of alcohol.

Despite conversion to Christianity the ethnic dimension remains intact though in a somewhat new and changed form. Conversion to Christianity has brought about 'double allegiance' among the tribals as they are unable to forget their past and simultaneously they are made to be a part of a new world-view, namely, Christianity. This double identity, though broadens economic and socio-cultural base of the converts, but they are not able to get out of the ethnic bondage in larger sense of the term. Most of the educated tribals converted to Christianity have/had their training in theology and have remained attached to one or other church. Missionary schools, colleges and other organisations have invited strong reactions in which some of these convert educated tribals are employed.

VI

Economic and political processes accompanied by urbanisation, industrialisation and political awakening have brought about visible differentiation among tribal people on class lines. K.S. Singh observes: "The major thrust of change has been from tribes into peasants. By the end of the 18th century communities of peasantised tribals had emerged in Assam,

Rajasthan, middle India, etc."[52] A hierarchy of land tenures in the form of tribal chiefs and occupancy tenants emerged with the coming of the British administration. Taking over of the forests from the control of the tribals made them to work as manual workers. With the emergence of industrialisation in the post-independence period tribal people have also become unskilled, semi-skilled and skilled workers in industries. A class of well-off non-tribal people co-existed with the tribals in the form of moneylenders, shopkeepers and white-collar workers. These non-tribals are now expressly considered as 'outside exploiters'. Class differentiation is a double-edged phenomenon because there has been a differential impact of the factors and forces of social change due to the uneven nature of intra-tribal and inter-tribal situations. As a result of this we can find today hunting and food-gathering tribal people on the one end of the continuum and highly educated people engaged in government jobs and other lucrative pursuits on the other. Thus, there is no uniform principle of hierarchisation among the tribes of middle India. The differentiation between various tribes and between the families of a tribe in a given context indicate clearly that different segments of tribes and specific families have carved out particular 'social spaces' or placements for themselves. In many ways, they resemble with each other and also with the non-tribals though in varying degrees. Neither all tribal people have been equally involved in class and power struggles against their oppressors nor they have been benefited uniformly from the positive consequences of these collective or semi-collective mobilisations. But all tribals were not oppressed or deprived of in the same manner, hence their involvement in the emancipatory efforts has also varied. Some of these points have remained unattended in most of the studies of class and power among the tribes of middle India.

52. Singh, K.S., 1985, op. cit., p. 5.

Observations made by Thapar and Siddiqi seem to be quite convincing about the connection between socio-cultural and politico-economic dimensions among the Mundas in ancient period.[53] They write: "The more fundamental changes were, however, related to rights over land. The axis shifted from clan to territory: tenurial rights based on kinship were encroached upon by those based on professional services. The raja granted lands and villages on perpetual tenures of military, administrative and personal services—the services required by the infrastructure of a state. The grantees were appointed to appropriate the maximum rights."[54] Certainly, a distinction existed between the lineage lands or bhuinhari and the rajhas lands. Thapar and Siddiqi report presence of *manjhas* (grantee), *rajhas* (crown) and *kanwars, thakurs* and *lallas* (who were given maintenance grants), and retainers. Thus, alongwith ethnic (clan, lineage) stratification, a quite elaborate class stratification existed. They write: "Thus, the tendency towards social stratification which had already begun with the khut-katti system was not only intensified and accelerated under the state, but was also made more complex with the interpolation of various levels of intermediaries."[55] Now from lineage economic and political functions passed into the hands of professionals outside the lineage. A new nexus emerged between social status, landholding and power, though lineage still did not become defunct. It is evident from this account that feudalism had taken over the tribal society and the classes mentioned above also existed in the princely states till India achieved her independence.

The hypothesis put forward by Thapar and Siddiqi regarding decline of ethnicity and emergence of class relations also finds substantiation in S.D. Badgaiyan's systematic historical analysis of 'class and ethnicity' among the Mundas of

53. Thapar, Romila and Siddiqi, M.H., 1991, op. cit., p. 425.
54. Ibid.
55. Ibid.

Chhotanagpur. Badgaiyan provides a detailed account of the simultaneous emergence of feudalism and complex class structure among the Mundas, and observes that "social relations were defined not entirely by *ethnic membership*. They were influenced also by the class structure."[56] However, the two were not coterminous nor they were reducible to each other. Another important point in Badgaiyan's analysis is regarding what he calls "objective reality and subjective dispositions", particularly in the context of dikus (exploiters) in Chhotanagpur. The Mundas consider all the non-tribal exploiters, despite their ethnic and class differences, as dikus. "The definition of an objective situation is subjective."[57] The tribal exploiters today and earlier the tribal jagirdars have/had not been perceived as dikus. Thus, the objective reality and its subjective perception do not necessarily coincide, and therefore, class and ethnicity coexist in certain respects and cut across each other in some contexts. When class and ethnicity are perceived in consonance, there is greater solidarity among the tribal people. Leaders of various tribal movements generally strive to emphasise on such an accord between ethnicity and class.

A large number of researchers observe that in the pre-British period with the encroachment of feudalism on tribal life the process of emergence of a new class structure set in replacing the tribal patriarchal clanish system rooted into the khut-katti system of land tenure. Thus, feudal classes such as rajhas, jagirdars, grantees, bhumihars, retainers, tenants on the one hand, and priests, merchants, moneylenders and masses emerged on the other. Such a change affected significantly the tribal polity too. Sachchidananda observes that the political authority of the head of the *parha* (confederation of villages) disappeared, and many Mundas migrated to other parts of tribal Bihar where they could retain their traditional institutions.[58] In Madhya Pradesh and Orissa too, individual

56. Badgaiyan, S.D., 1996, op. cit.

57. Ibid., p. 305.

58. Sachchidananda, 1990, op. cit., p. 283.

ownership of land had become a fact of life. The British used some traditional/hereditary village officers for collecting revenue by granting them powers of a police force. In Bihar, Munda, Manki and Majhi thus became once again powerful under the British patronage. But the market forces further more rapidly accentuated in the British period along with new administrative system. Land alienation, usurious practices by moneylenders, heterogeneity brought-in by the influx of non-tribal communities and new categories of people like traders, contractors and petite administrative officials not only proved a serious blow to the pre-colonial tribal system, but also accentuated a two-pronged class-based stratification between the tribals and the non-tribals and among the tribals themselves. Now one could easily find among the tribals proprietary tenants, tenants-at-will, sharecroppers and landless agricultural and manual workers. Classes other than these were formed by non-tribals to a large extent. These included government employees and officers, professionals like doctors, lawyers and professors, and merchants and traders. The post-independence period has witnessed strengthening of this class structure, and side by side some new communities and social categories too have acquired a united access to some scarce and much desired positions and offices. The new political system has certainly created a class of tribal power elite. This new class is largely a transformation of the class of educated tribals of the pre-independence period who were engaged in various reform and other movements and also employed as professionals and administrative workers.

Socially and culturally, the tribals have not assimilated to a considerable extent even today with the non-tribals. Conversions and adoptions of other religions and practices have created somewhat limited cleavages among the tribals rather than restructuring the tribal society. But this is not true in the same way about economic and political relations among the tribals and of the tribals with the non-tribals. Class structure and relations among the tribals resemble with the non-tribals, and so are power relations. The hiatus between the socio-cultural and politico-economic structures and relations could be attributed to the differential impact of macro-structural forces and factors which was perhaps intended by the colonial rulers and it is persisting even today because of the policies pursed by the Indian state since independence. Ethnicity has thus remained a force to reckon with for mobilising the adivasis against the atrocious class structure which was superimposed upon them by the pre-colonial and the colonial rulers and continues to be there to a great extent even after independence.

Recent studies of social stratification among tribal people highlight on class hierarchy and its socio-cultural consequences. A study of the Chaudhari tribe in Surat district of Gujarat by Ghanshyam Shah shows the presence of four economic strata on the basis of occupation and ownership of land.[59] These strata are: (1) agricultural labourers and poor cultivators; (2) middle cultivators; (3) rich cultivators; and (4) white-collar employees. The first three strata constitute more than 92 per cent of the total working population of the Chaudharis, while in the fourth category there are less than 3 per cent people. Shah writes: "Labourers and poor cultivators are at the bottom of the occupational hierarchy. It is the single largest stratum, constituting 61 per cent of cultivators, of which 24 per cent are almost landless and 37 per cent have land between 1 and 5 acres. Their main source of livelihood is manual labour."[60] Shah provides other details about economic life of this largest segment of the Chaudharis of Gujarat. Of the middle cultivators 33 per cent own land between 5 and 15 acres. These are a better off section as 20 per cent of them have wells for irrigation and half of them have diesel or electric pumpsets. They use chemical fertilizers, and about 70 per cent of them

59. Shah, Ghanshyam, 1979, op. cit., pp. 459–69.

60. Ibid., p. 290.

have a pair of bullocks. Rich cultivators are about 5 per cent and each one of them own more than 16 acres of land. They are better off than the middle and poor cultivators. They have electric or diesel pumpsets, use chemical fertilizers, hire wage labourers, produce for market, and their womenfolk and children are educated and do not do manual work even on their own farms. These all the three classes are related to agriculture though unevenly and enjoy different social statuses. The white-collar workers who are about 3 per cent of the population are engaged in non-agricultural white-collar jobs particularly in lower level school teaching. Besides teachers, there are also clerks, postmen, *talatis*, *gramsevaks*, extension officers, etc. Some are employed in cooperative societies in various capacities. "Middle and rich cultivators dominate the stratum of educated white-collar employees."[61]

In another study of stratification among the scheduled tribes in the Bharuch and Panch Mahals districts of Gujarat, Ghanshyam Shah observes that status distinction based on achievement in such respects as wealth, property, income, occupation, education and power is emerging, and it is similar considerably with the pattern in the wider Indian society.[62] Status-determination based on ethnicity is being slowly replaced by the new criteria such as wealth, income, occupation, education and power. Economic and educational aspects and the style of life are today the bases of newly emerging stratification. Differences in these aspects between the tribals and the non-tribals and within the tribals would provide an objective assessment of social stratification. The categories and groups in these two districts are more or less the same as Shah has found in Surat district. Different tribes are divided on the basis of interests. Besides land as the principal basis, there are differences of status based on education and lifestyle. Stratification is reflected in almost all aspects of social

61. Ibid., p. 292.
62. Shah, Ghanshyam, 1986, op. cit., pp. 149–83.

life of the tribal people. Contradictory changes have also been noted. Some have become quite rich and better off, and others have slided down in class hierarchy. However, change in social stratification has not been uniform in Bharuch and Panch Mahals district. Shah observes as follows: "There is sharper stratification in Bharuch than in Panch Mahals. The number of landless labourers is larger in the former area than in the latter district. The rich and the middle peasants of Bharuch purchased more land than their counterparts in Panch Mahals. So is the case with government benefits. The differences in lifestyle between the rich and the middle peasants are more widespread and sharper in Bharuch. These differences are perhaps because of uneven development in the two districts. Because the one which is more developed grows faster and develops sharper stratification, inequality increases and becomes sharp with development."[63]

From both these studies of three districts of Gujarat, namely, Surat, Bharuch and Panch Mahals, Shah concludes that there is nothing like an all-India tribal culture and world-view. Tribals are also not isolated from the non-tribal people. It is a fact that they have become highly differentiated socially and economically and in certain respects the persisting socio-economic distinctions between them and the non-tribals have also accentuated mainly due to uneven consequences of lopsided development policies and their faulty execution. Despite this the tribal people are being 'integrated' with the wider society, though not in an uniform manner. The better-off tribals, namely, the middle class Chaudharis of Surat, have developed a certain commonness, cutting across tribal boundaries, with their counterparts of other tribes, in social and cultural matters and in lifestyles. In fact, middle and rich cultivators as well as the middle class (white-collar workers) do not have a clash of interests, hence commonality of attitudes and aspirations for further betterment of their status.

63. Ibid., p. 179.

Pradip Kumar Bose also identifies four main classes among tribes in Gujarat, though mainly based on landholdings.[64] These are: rich peasants, middle peasants, poor peasants, and agricultural labourers, and these have also been found by several researchers among the non-tribals as well. A given tribe is generally distributed among all the four classes. However, all the tribes are not the same as some are better-off than others, and accordingly the proportions of different classes would also be different. Bose reports that the tribes in Gujarat today are equally affected by the processes of planned and unplanned changes and by the continuous structural and institutional shifts in rural India. He writes: "They are stratified in terms of control over resources", hence, these four classes. This class hierarchy is reflected in all aspects of tribal life including education and political power. But Bose does not highlight the emerging patterns of social mobility among tribals brought about by developmental programmes and education as we find it in the two studies of three districts of Gujarat by Ghanshyam Shah. Jaganath Pathy's study of five tribal villages in Gujarat is similar in terms of its framework and methodology. The five economic categories in the Pathy's study are: landlords, rich peasants, middle peasants, small peasants and farm workers. The distribution and characteristic features of these classes are the same as we find in the study conducted by Shah and Bose. It seems that in a broad sense, the studies of class stratification among the tribes of Gujarat reinforce each other. While referring to an earlier study by Pathy, *Political Economy of Kandhaland*, Shah observes that "there is a case for closer examination in the tribal communities."[65] Further, Shah finds that the rich have become richer, and the poor, poorer, because of 'free competition' among the unequal competitors.

B.K. Roy Burman[66] emphasises on both class and ethnicity perspectives, but he does not spell out the nexus

64. Bose, P.K., 1981, op. cit., pp. 191–96.
65. Shah, Ghanshyam, 1986, op. cit., p. 179. See also Jagnath Pathy, 1984, op. cit.
66. Roy Burman, B.K., 1989, op. cit., pp. 693–97.

between class and ethnicity and status and class. The notion of status is inherently present in the ethnic identity and kinship system of the tribal society. In an edited volume Bhadra and Mondal also emphasise the role of class and ethnicity as the main bases of social stratification in North-East India.[67] There are also tribes like Meenas of Rajasthan which have hardly any tribal characteristic features in terms of ethnicity and class, yet they are scheduled as tribes. The Tharus of Bihar have all the prerequisites for being scheduled as a tribe, but they are not scheduled as such.

K.S. Singh though admits the emergence of social stratification as a historical reality created by the colonial administration and the processes of sanskritisation and conversion to Christianity, but observes that "there are also contrary pulls in the opposition direction. The bonds of ethnicity and the appreciation of the political advantages of the tribe as an ethnic minority are still strong."[68] This view is also shared by Sachchidananda. While commenting on the class approach of Pathy, he writes: "These economic categories may be considered classes only in a limited sense; ethnic consciousness dominates over class consciousness. Similarly, production relations cannot be clearly characterised as feudal or capitalist. Primordial forms of slavery, revolving indebtedness of small peasants and agricultural labourers for consumption loans, the lack of a free labour market, forced labour, labour exchange, institutional credit and some commodity production confuse the total picture."[69] But, the question is: Do these four or five classes not exist among the tribes of Gujarat, Bihar or Rajasthan? Are they simply 'constructions', not really identifiable groups of people? Kulkarni observes that the question of

67. Bhadra, R.K. and Mondal, S.R. (eds), 1991, *Stratification, Hierarchy and Ethnicity in North-East India*, Delhi, Daya Publishing House.

68. Singh, K.S., 1985, op. cit., p. 8.

69. Sachchidananda, 1990, op. cit., p. 307.

class in the tribal society is more pervasive than the caste-tribal approach.[70] Class interests do not obey caste or tribal boundaries.[71] Land-alienation is a class question. The demand for the formation of Jharkhand state was a class question. The 'tribal question', the 'forest question' are all questions of 'class interests'. The forest policy in India in its present form serves the capitalists rather than the poor.[72] 'Tribal unrest' is a class question. Both positive and negative consequences of the role performed by law and the state refer to the question of class in terms of gainers and loosers, more gainers and less gainers, more loosers and less loosers, and so on. Thus, there are three viewpoints regarding ethnicity and class as the bases of social stratification: mainly ethnicity, mainly class and both class and ethnicity.

VII

Social stratification among the tribes of India is different compared to the non-tribes to the extent the tribal people are dissimilar in terms of their history, level of economic development and impact of modern forces of social change. Several studies of social stratification bring out the convergence of ethnicity and class as the main basis of status distinctions within and between different tribes. However, emphasis on ethnicity and class as exclusive bases of social stratification remains central to some scholars who look at the tribal social stratification either in terms of ethnic reality or as an economic phenomenon—a part of global class formation.

The Raj created new structures and institutions and thereby provided a new system of social stratification. Landlords,

70. Kulkarni, S.D., 1979, 'Class and Caste in Tribal Movement', *EPW*, Vol. XIV, Nos. 7 & 8, pp. 465–68.

71. Sengupta, Nirmal, 1980, 'Class and Tribe in Jharkhand', *EPW*, Vol. XV, No. 4, pp. 664–71.

72. Guha, Ramchandra, 1983, 'Forestry in British and Post-British India: A Historical Analysis', *EPW*, Vol. XVIII, Nos. 44, 45 & 46.

contractors and moneylenders were alien to the tribal society before the advent of the British. Differentiation of the peasantry in terms of tenure-holders, tenants-at-will and jagirdars was also created by the British. A class of outside exploiters in terms of zamindars and moneylenders was not known to the tribals till the British took over the forests. Since independence ethnicity is being viewed in a changed form as a means of mobilising the tribal people with a view to have access to economic and political opportunities. Inter-tribal and tribal-non-tribal distinctions on one hand and processes of conversion and initiation on the other are being highlighted by the tribals as the basis for demanding special treatment by the government. However, the tribals are not an exclusive component in India's fast changing social situation. A new middle class is emerging among them like the one we find among the non-tribals.

Ethnicity is on decline on one hand, and it is being reviewed in myriad ways on the other. De-tribalisation and ethnicisation co-exist today both as a reality and as a strategy for change. Uniformity is not found in regard to convergence between ethnicity and class. Processes of socio-cultural and structural transformation are also not uniform in different parts of India. At the same time, now the 'forest question' and the 'tribal question' are being considered more as class questions. The phenomenon of power and dominance is increasingly dependent upon the questions of ethnicity and class.

8 Education and the Scheduled Tribes in India: A Sociological Analysis

I

It is needless to mention that education is an instrument of social change. But the kind of education and conditions in which it generates and strengthens the process of modernisation in a society are very important considerations. Despite the positive role of education in social change the question is: Can education lead to social change? Controversies regarding the role of education have not deterred massive expansion of education all over the world. Education has been perceived largely as a resource, both material and cognitive. As resource education becomes power, a means of control and domination in the hands of those who are highly educated over those who are less educated and illiterate. Education is also a means of socialisation and a basis of formation of status-personality. As such education implies social mobility. Education creates in essence contest/competition for mobility. The essence of achievement is intrinsic to education. Since education is highly structured and inegalitarian, role of ascription and sponsorship cannot be ruled out in attainment of higher education in particular. Parentage, cultural heritage and networks provide ascriptive basis for attainment of higher education and employment.

Education is a paradoxical phenomenon because it implies both equality and inequality. Educated individuals become equal or near-equal among themselves and they become unequal to those who have remained uneducated despite such a paradoxical nature of education. Inculcation of a value system is inherent in it. Inducement for change through education, a message of change, training of minds, equality of opportunity, etc. are cardinal points of education in all societies and at all levels.

Theoretically speaking, all over the world, education and equality of opportunity co-exist. Education can benefit all those who have ability and desire to be educated. It can permit development of a scientific and objective outlook. And it can create a social environment free from caste, class, linguistic, regional and religious barriers. It can minimise gendered social relations because education is also an instrument of understandable communication.

II

The role of the state in providing education particularly to weaker sections of society and women is acknowledged all over the world. Even in advanced countries, particularly in western Europe, education is mainly supported and funded by the state. In this context the idea of Marxist Educational Praxis (MEP) advocated by Lenin and others is essentially a theory of practice to bring about change and modernisation.[1] The main components of the MEP are:

1. There should be free public education, compulsory and uniform for all children, assuring the abolition of cultural or knowledge monopolies and of privileged forms of schooling. The purpose of this theory was to weaken the role of the family in social reproduction, to bring up

1. Bottomore, Tom, et. al. (eds), 1985, *A Dictionary of Marxist Thought*, Oxford, Basil Blackwell, pp. 144–45.

children under less unequal conditions, to utilise the socialising force of the community. As such hierarchy of schools would vanish, and the role of family and parentage remain checked. Such a theory can ensure coexistence of education and equality. Mahatma Gandhi campaigned for compulsory education for all which incorporated elements of basic education which would facilitate employment to the educated.

2. The MEP emphasises on the contribution of education with material production (the combination of instruction, gymnastics and productive work). The aim is to close the gap between manual and mental work, between conception and education, by assuring to all full understanding of the productive process.
3. Education has to assure an all-round development of the personality. The aim is to activate the individual in all spheres of social life including consumption, leisure, creation and enjoyment of culture, participation in social life, interaction with others and self-fulfilment (auto-creation). The realisation of this objective requires the transformation of the social division of labour. Various tribal and feminist movements in India have focused on this particular aspect in relation to education. Tribals in particular need education which can touch upon the totality of their social life. Formal education alone would not do justice to them.
4. The community is assigned a new and vast role in the education process. This changes the in-group relations in the school which implies more open relations between school and society, and a dialogical relation between teacher and taught. This can be possible only if school is treated as a community rather than a formal bureaucratic organisation.

From a different perspective the well-known French sociologist Emile Durkheim considers education as an eminently social thing in its origins and in its functions.[2] He

2. Durkheim, Emile, n.d., "On the Learning of Discipline," from Talcott Parsons, et. al. (eds.), *Theories of Society*, New York, Free Press, pp. 860–65.

conceives education as intimately related to a society's structure. Thus, for Durkheim, education reflects and maintains the society and it can only partially change it. However, in the MEP, education is considered a very strong vehicle of social change. It is not a system of reinforcing persisting collective practices, social ideologies and cultural values. Education for Durkheim was not a means to bring about equality for all men and women or to mitigate social- cultural differences and distinctions in society. However, Durkheim considered education as an ever-changing social process and not a static phenomenon. He considered transformation in education always as a result and as a symptom of social transformation.

Open schools, community education, adult education, literacy mission, ashram schools, etc., have to be understood in terms of the nature of Indian state *vis-à-vis* Indian society. Education is to be considered necessarily as a positive phenomenon to bring about development and change. Education and the process of social control and power system and the preservation of culture are interrelated phenomena. A tribal society which has remained deprived of education and development for centuries would consider education as an emancipatory phenomenon rather than a force of the status quo.

School is a social system, it inculcates a culture, a pattern of socialisation, and social interaction. School provides definitions of various social positions in society and community. School makes people aware about leadership roles and power relations. It creates a feeling of community living.[3] Theories of isolation and assimilation/integration in relation to tribal people of India have become obsolete as they imply extreme solutions to understand their problems.[4] It is more

3. Entwistle, Harold, 1979, *Gramsci Antonio, Conservative Schooling for Radical Politics*, London, Routledge & Kegan Paul.
4. The two well-known views are: (1) tribes of India may not be disturbed and may be allowed to pursue their culture-specific way of life; and (2) they cannot be allowed to remain isolated from the mainstream of Indian society. The first view emphasises on their uniqueness and the other on their development alongwith other components of Indian society.

important to bring about change in such a way that neither it affects culture of the tribal people adversely nor eliminates them from the mainstream. Education without distorting and disintegrating cultural system can significantly transform tribal society. It is necessary that tribals know the language of the dominant groups and at the same time the latter should understand the cultural intricacies of tribal people. A certain level of clear communicability between the two alone can bring about required transformation among the tribal people. Tribes in India are highly diversified. At the one end are totally isolated vanishing Negrito tribes of Andaman islands belonging to the hunting and food gathering stone age, and at the other end are the highly advanced Mongoloid tribes of the north-east who have a very high level of literacy, employment, and contacts with the outside world. Hence, educational problems of scheduled tribes are diversified corresponding to diversity of the tribal people.

III

In the early 1970s the Indian Council for Social Science Research (ICSSR) launched a nation-wide study of the educational problems of Scheduled Castes and Scheduled Tribes, focusing particularly on students of these two weaker sections of society. The main objective of this study was to assess the status of SC and ST students in institutions of learning, and to compare them with non SC and non-ST students. Another objective of this study was to identify the kind of discrimination and difficulties and obstacles students of the weaker sections encountered in schools and colleges.[5] In general, the academic life of the students could be studied with reference to the type of courses, study habits, carrier and performance in studies, participation in extra-curricular activities, patterns of

5. The ICSSR conducted a nation-wide study of the educational problems of the SCs and the STs. The mega project was directed by the late I.P. Desai and Suma Chitnis. Some of the authors were also published subsequently based on data relating to different status.

life, aspirational levels and nature of encouragement and support received from their families and communities. But such a frame of reference is unrealistic so far as SC and ST students are concerned as they are lagging far behind their counterparts from upper and upper-middle castes and classes. Even factors like the role of mass media, politicisation and migration would not make much difference in their case as they have not yet begun their journey of having equal status with students of the general category. Even awareness about constitutional and other provisions has not reached to a large number of the rural ST and SC students and their families. Several studies conducted on behalf of the ICSSR revealed pronounced differences between the students of these weaker sections and other students. Most of the problems faced by the ST and the SC students are due to deprivation they suffer in relation to higher status groups. They also receive differential treatment from the power elite who come from both the general category and from among themselves. One can say that ST students today encounter disparities at three levels:

1. Between STs and general population.
2. Between the various STs.
3. Among the STs in a particular region/district.[6]

As such the rate of drop-outs among SC/ST students increases from primary school to middle and from middle to secondary level. It goes further down at the college and university levels. Over the years, the ratio-of unfulfilled seats is more in highly professional and science programmes of study. The quantum of available educational facilities for attaining higher education is not a clear indicator of actual achievements. The reports of the SC and ST Commission have shown invariably that advantages of reservation in education and employment have been cornered by a small number of castes

6. Sharma, K.L., 1994, *Social Stratification and Mobility*, Jaipur, Rawat Publications, Chapter 8, pp. 164–195.

and tribes in various states.[7] The advantaged groups after independence have turned as interest groups. Their differential background, social networks, status and power determine their level of education considerably in a different manner than their fellow members. In fact, correspondence is found between an increase in the educational facilities and the lessening of the gaps between the caste Hindus and the STs, and also between different STs. It is the privileged sections of the STs who have been recently designated as 'creamy layer'. Creamy layer is now being deprived from the benefit of reservation.[8]

In terms of sheer placement of students one can find significant differences. For example, differences can be discerned based on rural/urban background, and caste and class positions of the students. Besides differences with regard to their socio-cultural background, and caste and class positions of the students and economic standing, differences also exist in their schooling and higher education in terms of quality, performance and extra-curricular activities. Within each category several sub-categories can also be found on the basis of some other relevant criteria.

IV

Several studies have clearly shown that the tribes which have taken up education have moved up socially, culturally and economically. Without referring to the controversy regarding conversion of tribal people to Christianity or Islam, it can be said that Christian missions established, in some parts of the country, a chain of schools and colleges. The tribes such as

7. Some of the reports of the SC and the ST Commission of India, particularly authored by B.D. Sharma have focused on the unequal access to various provisions and facilities by the SCs and the STs. New forms of inequalities have thus occurred among the deprived groups.
8. The 'creamy layer' refers to a stratum of the SCs, STs and the OBCs which has been benefited considerably from the reservation policy. Such beneficiaries are denied further benefits after the implementation of the recommendations of the B.P. Mandal Commission.

Mundas, Oraons, Hos and Santhals in Bihar, who converted to Christianity, are better off educationally and better employed, more awakened socially and politically than their counterparts who did not convert to Christianity. However, this does not imply that socio-cultural and educational advancement is possible only through conversion to one or other religion. The tribes in north-east India are highly educated; the Necobari tribe in Andaman Islands, due to conversion to Christianity, has gone ahead of the rest of the tribes. The tribes like Jarawas and Synteneles are not only illiterate but they are still in the hunting and fishing stage of food-gathering. Not knowing anything about the outside world, they are rapidly vanishing mainly due to hunger, mal-nutrition and lack of health care.

V

B.K. Roy Burman has shown that there is a great urge for education among tribes. However, he fears that ecology, culture, history, political economy and social demography of the specific tribal communities may be endangered due to faulty approach to education. The formal literacy and education must be related to the life-line of the tribal people such as forests, agriculture, nature and health care. The reading materials must be prepared in such a way that the tribal culture and tribal history get reflected properly and positively. Indigenous character of the people and formal literacy and education must be found in harmony.[9]

Education is conducive to the creation of equality, but it can bring out social stratification and inequality as well within the tribal communities if access to education is selective and scarce. However, in the long run education creates conscientisation about the state, bureaucracy, moneylenders, contractors, outside exploiters, etc. As education provides

9. Roy Burman, B.K., 1989, "Problems and Prospects of Tribal Development in North-East India," *Economic and Political Weekly*, Vol. XXIV, No. 13, pp. 693–97.

ability to communicate with others, it makes a difference in dispelling the persisting distortions and misrepresentations. Hence, education is indispensable as a first step towards empowerment of the tribal people. Education is, in fact, cultural, social and political empowerment of the weaker sections. Education implies learning and sharing language with others. Command on language implies control and share over meaning systems, and therefore, learning of language is cultural empowerment. If a large number of members of a society share the same language, it implies greater equalitarian sharing and distribution of resources. This is possible if access to and control of resources are available to a large majority of the members in a given society. In a normal situation in a given society people compete with each other to have access to different forms of resources, but persisting rigid inequalities become a stumbling stone in this exercise. Hence, sponsored education for the weaker sections becomes an instrument of emancipation. Emphasis must be laid on the communicative action, communicative process and competence for all. Only through new meanings and patterns of action, cultural consciousness can be redefined, and a cultural mediation can be achieved having education as an alternative to the existing modes of cognition and behaviour.

With regard to tribal people it is necessary to transform them into 'cultural objects' with new communicative skills. Time and space as 'boundary conditions' have to go. The everyday life in which the tribal circumscribes his life has to be changed through education. If there could be a division of work in the non-tribal society, a tribal could also become a farmer, a manual worker, a teacher, a trader or a professional. The nature of tribal society would determine the degree of educational attainability for its members. Socialisation of the individual determines his aspirations, and education can bring about a new pattern of socialisation, not by destroying necessarily the persisting one. The whole way of life of a tribal society through education can be transformed.

Culture provides a conception of consciousness and conscious existence, and this is possible through education alone.

Culture has also two sides. One is affirmative, as an instrument in the hands of the rich and resourceful; and the other, culture becomes a commodity. Both the conceptions of culture are inadequate to explain the tribal situation in India. French sociologist Pierre Bourdieu writes: "To change the world one has to change the ways of working the world, i.e., the vision of the world and the practical operations by which groups are produced and reproduced."[10] This is how we have to understand and change our tribal people.

The way the British shaped the tribal people has not been undone by the rulers of free India. The British rulers imagined India for their prosperity and then initiated symbolic and cognitive discourse to change the country at the ground level as Ronald Inden observes. Thus, a vision of social division, of gendered relations and meaning systems have to be shaped and reshaped in view of the present situation. The power of imposition of the rulers on the tribal people has to be withdrawn. The power to accept or not to accept in view of the ground reality of the people is to be acknowledged. A new educational practice is required with a new political philosophy regarding the following:

Continuity between the culture of the school and that of the daily life,
language and literacy in education,
role of the State in the provision of education,
the cultivation of elites and the role of intellectuals,
the relative function of authority and spontaneity in education; and
the role of all the cognitive systems, ideologies, behavioural patterns.

10. Bourdieu, Pierre, 1991, *Language and Symbolic Power*, Oxford, Polity Press, Chapter 11, pp. 229-251.

Gramsci though talks of the politics of education, but at the same time he also refers to counter-hegemonic educational activity (education of the working class). He considers school as a political hegemony. Gramsci is for radical form of schools especially having curriculum and pedagogical processes. Education implies not only learning of language but also command over new practices and creation of a field or habitus as it provides a set of new dispositions, meanings, and hence power.[11] *Pedagogy of the Oppressed* by Paulo Freire is comparable with the counter-hegemonic educational activity of Gramsci. Paulo Freire is against the educational system which maintains the 'culture of silence', domination, and which submerges the oppressed destroying their existence.[12] A need for unity of theory and practice is central to some of these explanations. A rediscovery of the humanising vocation of the intellectual, and the power of his thought can help the oppressed, namely, the tribes of India.

Man's ontological vocation through education can equip him to encounter with the oppressor. A peasant, a worker, a tribal should know his right to say about his own world, he should have capacity to name the world as education must give him a new awareness of self, a sense of dignity, a new hope. His self-realisation means to know contradictions in his life, hence education is not simply literacy, but it is critical consciousness. It emancipates from colonised mentality, supremacy of the rich, of the moneylender, and the landlord. Education with a dialogue, freedom and humanising pedagogy alone can salvage the tribal people.

The futility of the schooling thesis given by Evan Illich applies to the western modern post-industrial societies where school encapsulates the young minds more or less mechanically. For the poor in India the school has not become

11. See Entwistle, Harold, 1979, op. cit.
12. Freire, Paulo, 1972, *Pedagogy of the Oppressed*, Penguin Books.

a 'sacred cow' so far. Hence, it is not a central myth-making system for the SCs, STs, OBCs, women and others. The 'deschooling society' thesis does not apply to the Indian situation as there are no schools for the poor to de-establish them from their cultural roots. There is no ritualisation of schooling particularly in case of those who have not yet seen the school.[13]

Education as an agent of modernisation must correspond with welfare, social mobility, and socio-cultural awakening. These three postulates constitute the policy of 'protective discrimination'. If these ideals are properly and faithfully translated into practice, the scheduled tribes and other weaker sections can get equipped to overcome their low status, exploitation and oppression. Many studies have revealed that so far the modern education among the STs and other weaker sections has created a new elite and a new middle class, who have cornered most of the benefits made available by the Indian State.

Corruption has made a definite space for itself in educational field. Education as a scarce resource and opportunity is being exploited by a selected few in terms of control over educational institutions. Brahminic hegemony on education, hegemony of the English educated, mushrooming of public schools, and emergence of private professional institutions have distorted the very purpose of education after independence. Education is under siege. The question then is: What is education? Education does not mean 200 odd universities, five IITs, 300 engineering colleges, several hundred polytechnics, more than one hundred medical colleges, and thousands and lakhs of schools at various levels. Even today, we do not have compulsory and free education for the children upto 14 years of age. Education is iniquitous. SCs, STs, OBCs, women, rural poor, slum-dwellers are far behind in the field of education compared to the rest of the people. Questions are

13. Illich, Ivan, 1971, *Deschooling Society*, Penguin Books.

therefore being raised about access, quality, relevance, vocationalisation, curriculum, management of education, dominance of English language, etc. Many traditional institutions of higher learning have degenerated into educational ghettos, and many new educational shops have surfaced. The hierarchy of educational system is so complex and so intense that it has become impossible to compare schools, colleges and universities in India. How one can help educating the tribal people in such a situation? Certainly, the present system cannot salvage the tribal and other weaker sections. A more relevant down to earth approach and practice are required to educate the tribals and other weaker sections without destroying their ecology, culture and everyday life.

9 Social Consequences of Economic Development in Chhotanagpur in Jharkhand

I

Despite change and development in Indian society since independence, tribal economy has remained distinct from the Indian economy in general. Transition in tribal economy is seen generally from hoe to settled agriculture. In some recent studies the role of market and traders has been analysed with a view to highlight the exploitation of the tribal people. Socio-cultural changes can be attributed to two sources: (i) caste and Hinduism, and (ii) conversion to Christianity. This essay highlights the problems of tribal development, impact of industrialisation, role of market, alienation of land, etc. Tribals are relatively isolated, homogeneous and are economically more backward than the rest of the population. It should be made clear that tribal people are also different socially, culturally and economically. Differential impact of conversion to various religions, development programmes, industrialisation, education, etc., has created status distinctions and cleavages among tribes across the country.

M.K. Sharma, lecturer in sociology, Government College, Beawar (Rajasthan) provided useful inputs in preparation of this essay. I am grateful to him for this act of generosity.

II

In the pre-British period, tribal economy and the ecosystem were closely interrelated. Production and distribution were governed by bonds of kinship operative through families, clans and kindred. Technology was at a very rudimentary level and production was mainly for consumption. Family was the unit of production without any division of labour except the one based on age and sex. British period witnessed land reforms, in-migration and out-migration, superior agricultural technology, commodity production, and increase in markets. The British made inroads into the tribal heartland by imposing land revenue and control of forests. A new class of intermediaries was created by the British in the form of Hindu zamindars. Moneylenders also migrated to tribal areas from various non-tribal parts of the country. Since independence the situation has taken a new turn. Industrialisation took place in tribal areas mainly because of the availability of mineral resources and raw materials. This has caused exploitation of forests and other natural resources. In-migration has suddenly accelerated. Out-migration of tribals has decreased. Alienation of tribals from their land due to industrialisation has acquired the magnitude of a serious problem.

III

About 7 per cent of India's total population comprises tribal people. In Bihar, the tribal population is concentrated mainly in the areas of Chhotanagpur, south Bihar and Santhal Parganas, which comprise of the state of Jharkhand since November 15, 2000. Within these areas the districts of Ranchi, Palamau, Singhbhum and Santhal Parganas have more tribal people. In these areas, about one-third of the total population consists of the tribal people like Hos, Oraons, Mundas and Santhals. Besides these four main communities, there are 26 other tribal groups.[1]

Tribals differ considerably in terms of their socio-economic development. Some of them are still engaged in traditional mode of hunting and food-gathering, and some are dependent upon shifting cultivation. However, about 95 per cent of Chhotanagpur's tribal people are settled agriculturists living in the plains. Some of the tribals dispose of their cash crops in weekly markets in the vicinity. A few educated and literate tribals are employed in various government departments. Many have also migrated to Assam and Bengal for seeking employment in tea gardens, jute mills and brick klins.[2]

Since independence industrialisation has taken place in some parts of tribal Bihar in a big way. Agricultural land of the tribal people has been taken over by the government for establishing industries at Bokaro, Hatia, Jharia and Sindhri. In the corporate sector, Tatas, Birlas and several other industrialists have started industries further adding to the problem of land alienation. Along with out-migration and industrialisation several programmes for the development of the tribal people have been initiated by the government. Voluntary agencies, including Christian missions and some Hindu organisations, though for different reasons, have also undertaken some welfare activities, mainly in the field of education and health.

The tribal people have not been benefited from industrialisation to a considerable extent. They are mainly engaged in those unskilled and manual jobs in industries which are normally not taken up by north Biharis, Marwaris and Punjabis. For a long time, no facilities were made available to train tribal people for various jobs in the industries at places such as Hatia and Bokaro. There are several reasons responsible

1. Roy Burman, B.K., 1971, "Tribal Demography: A Preliminary Appraisal", in K.S. Singh (ed.), *Tribal Situation in India*, Delhi, Banarsidas and Shimla, Indian Institute of Advanced Study.
2. Singh, K.S. (ed.), 1982, *Economics of the Tribals and Their Transformation*, New Delhi, Concept Publishing Company.

for the backwardness of tribal regions and its people in Bihar (now Chhotanagpur).

IV

Dietmar Rothermund's[3] analysis of coalfields as an 'enclave' in a backward region brings out the role of feudalism and colonialism in the economic development of tribal people. The local people established a kind of marginal symbiosis with the enclave (coalfield). "Whosoever was in need of some additional income would put in a few days of work as temporary unskilled labourer in the enclave rather than spend his time and energy in converting upland into rice terraces in his village."[4] Rothermund observes that the enclave reduced incentives for land reclamation by offering opportunities for casual and temporary labour. It resulted into a 'persistent dualism'.

However, a permanent miner was given a higher wage, and often in the form of an advance by his contractor. "Once the enclave was safely established in this way its demand for labour would not lead to a size of wages in agriculture in its vicinity nor would the wages of permanent enclave labour ever approximate to the low wages of local agriculture labour."[5] The rural hinterland of the coalfield remained as backward as ever. The segmental process of boom, stagnation, and depression of the enclave isolated it from its hinterlands in the formative years. However, today the enclave has become a part of life in the region and in the national economy.

Before the size of the enclave there were no major centers in Manbhum district. Rajas of Jharia and Katras profited from the coal bases and built large palaces. Quasi-urban settlements also emerged due to colonisation for mine workers. Jharia emerged as a sizeable market town with traders

3. Rothermund, Dietmar and Wadhwa, D.C., 1978, *Zamindars, Mines and Peasants*, Manohar, Chapter I.
4. Ibid.
5. Ibid.

and entrepreneurs of all hues. The town of Dhanbad also owes its importance to the enclave. Railways have had a heyday in the region due to trade in coal. Most of miners for a long time lived alone leaving their families at their native villages. Marwaris working in Assam, Bengal and Bihar too left behind their families for a long time in their native states of Rajasthan and Haryana.

V

Rothermund mentions 'three types of captivity' as the determinants of the enclave economy. These are: agrarian system of Chhotanagpur, British managing agency system, and colonial system of labour recruitment. "All three determinants are characterised by the common feature of captivity as contrasted with freedom."[6] The agrarian system regulated the control of land in the hinterland of the coalfield. Prevailing feudal structure precluded an adequate response to the challenge of new economic activity and placed severe constraints on development of the region. "The agrarian system is based on the captivity of the peasant who owes his lord rent and service."[7] The British managing system was geared to a restricted market and to the making of huge profits with minimum of capital investment. It operates in a captive market where there is no fairplay between supply and demand. The third determinant is the colonial system of labour recruitment which was shaped by the demand for Indian labour abroad and in tea plantations of Assam, adversely affecting recruitment of labour for the coal mining enclave.

Thus, it depends on the captive worker, who is bound by contract, indenture and advances which curtail his free mobility. Most labourers were not free and masters of their own fate. "They fled from rural poverty and captivity only in

6. Ibid.
7. Ibid.

order to submit to a new servitude under tough 'raising contractors' who made their profit by exploiting their labour force as much as possible."[8] Three types of captivity form an interdependent pattern as sub-systems of the colonial system.

Rothermund concludes his book, *Zamindars, Mines and Peasants* by stating that in the rural sector, a quasi-feudal system of the control of land and labour acted as an impediment to agricultural productivity. British colonial rule, zamindars and moneylenders reduced the peasantry to the status of a tenantry. The coalfield enclave, stagnated agriculture, drifted cultivators towards coal mines. Urbanisation resulting from the coalfield enclave mainly benefited entrepreneurs from outside the region. Rothermund provides quite dismal a picture of the situation, and concludes: "It is a perspective of an economic backwardness which remains a liability and cannot be turned into an asset, because there is no response of an adopting system as a whole, but only isolated impositions and fragmented responses which do not contribute to economic development."[9]

VI

Of the several factors for the formation of a separate state of Jharkhand, one was the exploitation of tribal people, and mineral, material and forest resources by *dikus* (outsiders) even in the post-independence period. In fact, this factor was nothing but a transformed continuity of the role of feudalism and colonialism in persisting economic backwardness of the region in the pre-independence era. The tribals responded to their outside rulers and exploiters by launching several movements, reform organisations and political parties. These responses attracted the rulers resulting in several legislative steps related to tenancy reforms, administrative measures and welfare programmes. But all these steps remained largely incon-

8. Ibid.
9. Ibid.

sequential and helped only a small segment of the tribal population. Voices such as Jharkhand sub-nationality and 'sons of the soil' were surfacing due to continued oppression and exploitation of the tribal people.

Tribal areas comprised 46 per cent of total area of Bihar, which are now in the state of Jharkhand, but the tribal population was just one-fourth of the total population of the state. However, in Jharkhand, scheduled castes and scheduled tribes are about 42 per cent of total population of the state. Mahatos, Bhuiyans, Momins and some other non-SCs and non-STs are no better economically and socially than the tribals like Santhals and Mundas.

Nirmal Sengupta observed that the concept of Jharkhand was not merely a geographic region.[10] Jharkhand implied 'a mass of destitutes', and the 'development of Jharkhand' must imply the eradication of contradictions of conditions which had resulted into the emergence of destitution. Of the total mining sector in India, more than one-fourth is in the Jharkhand state alone. Of the total industrial investments in the country one-fifth is invested in Jharkhand. TISCO and TELCO and several large, medium and small industrial enterprises are located in the region.

An aluminium factory at Muri, copper plant at Ghatshila, lead smelter at Thudoo, uranium mining at Jadugoda and mica industry at Giridih and several cement, bricks and tiles and glass and glassware industries are located in the region. We have already mentioned about steel plants, irrigation schemes, heavy engineering units, fertilizer complexes which have contributed to the growth of the region and a number of towns. But who benefits from this development? This is the question which is being asked time and again. The formation of the state of Jharkhand has not relegated such questions to the background. Data regarding

10. Sengupta, Nirmal (ed.), 1982, *Fourth World Dynamics: Jharkhand*, New Delhi, Authors Guild Publication.

immigration reveals that in-migration has constantly increased in the region, of which at least 60 per cent is from outside the state. Most of these immigrants have sought employment in the industrial sector depriving adivasis and other poor sections of society. Thus, the local population has been deprived of the benefit of development.

Most of the Jharkhandis find employment in household and cottage industries, and as unskilled workers in large and medium sized industries. Even in these jobs, they do not have more than 50 per cent of workers. Those who have received education at least for one year are considered as 'sons of the soil' for the purpose of getting a job. Such a norm takes away even the arduous jobs from the adivasis. The traditional modes of livelihood have collapsed, and those who do not find alternate avenues for survival are forced to migrate to other parts of the country in search of work.

VII

The main highlight of this essay is to analyse the problems of development in the Chhotanagpur region of Jharkhand, which is dominated by adivasis such as Hos, Oraons, Mundas and Santhals. It is evident that prior to independence, British rulers, zamindars and moneylenders harvested the fruits of local mineral and material resources. Since independence, outside exploiters have been benefited to a large extent. This is evident from data regarding immigration and employment in the public and private sectors. Dietmar Rothermund and Nirmal Sengupta alongwith several other scholars observe that the region has developed but this development has not benefited the people who are the 'sons of the soil' in the real sense of the term.

Index